Levels of Incompetence

For Moses & Dinah
& all the Gliddens.

Bob Davis

Sun Lakes, AZ
11/10/14

Levels of Incompetence:

An Academic Life

Robert Murray Davis

LAMAR UNIVERSITY press

ISBN: 978-0-9911074-3-8
Library of Congress Control Number: 2014932380
Manufactured in the United States of America

Book Design: Carol V. Weishampel

Lamar University Press
Beaumont, Texas

In Memory
of
Elizabeth Murray Davis

who got it started

Other Books from Lamar University Press

Jean Andrews, *High Tides, Low Tides: the Story of Leroy Colombo*
Alan Berecka, *With Our Baggage*
David Bowles, *Flower, Song, Dance: Aztec and Mayan Poetry*
Jerry Bradley, *Crownfeathers and Effigies*
Jeffrey DeLotto, *Voices Writ in Sand*
Gerald Duff, *Memphis Mojo*
Mimi Ferebee, *Wildfires and Atmospheric Memories*
Ken Hada, *Margaritas and Redfish*
Michelle Hartman, *Disenchanted and Disgruntled*
Gretchen Johnson, *The Joy of Deception and Other Stories*
Gretchen Johnson, *A Trip Through Downer, Minnesota*
Lynn Hoggard, *Motherland, Stories and Poems from Louisiana*
Dominique Inge, *A Garden on the Brazos*
Christopher Linforth, *When You Find Us We Will be Gone*
Tom Mack and Andrew Geyer, eds, *A Shared Voice*
Janet McCann, *The Crone at the Casino*
Erin Murphy, *Ancilla*
Dave Oliphant, *The Pilgrimage, Selected Poems: 1962-2012*
Harold Raley, *Louisiana Rogue*
Carol Coffee Reposa, *Underground Musicians*
Jan Seale, *Appearances*
Jan Seale, *The Parkinson Poems*
Carol Smallwood, *Water, Earth, Air, Fire, and Picket Fences*

www.LamarUniversityPress.Org

Other Books by Robert Davis

Born-Again Skeptic & other Valedictions
Interchanges
Live White Male and Other Poems
Mid Life Mojo: A Guide for the Newly Single Male
A Lower-Middle-Class Education
Midlands: A Family Album
Outside the Lines
The Literature of Post-Communist Slovenia, Slovakia, Hungary and Romania
Mischief in the Sun: the Making and Unmaking of The Loved One
Playing Cowboys: Low Culture and High Art in the Western
Brideshead Revisited: The Past Redeemed
Evelyn Waugh and the Forms of His Time
Evelyn Waugh, Writer
Critical Essays on Evelyn Waugh
A Bibliography of Evelyn Waugh
*A Catalogue of the Evelyn Waugh Collection at the Humanities Research
    Center, The University of Texas at Austin*
Evelyn Waugh: A Checklist of Primary and Secondary Material

Acknowledgments

In order to give what I hope is a plausible account of the profession since 1955, I have drawn upon printed sources and upon the memories of colleagues. But I have relied more heavily on what seems to me fairly representative experiences in classrooms, libraries, and professional, departmental, and committee meetings over four decades. Therefore, I cannot list the names of all those who are ultimately responsible for contributing material which went into this book for whom each draft has to make distressingly more frequent use of the past tense. Special mention is due to David McPherson and Keith Odom, who helped me remember; Jeannette Harris, who read and made suggestions for improving a second final draft; the libraries at the University of Oklahoma, Yavapai Community College, and the Yavapai County Public Library; and Moses Glidden and Dinah Owens, who provided a congenial place to work and rest.

Preface

I began writing this book under the illusion that it would tell readers outside the academy what it was like to be a professor of English. After several revisions and some belated introspection, I realize that my account is rapidly entering the realm of the purely historical.

The realization came late because no individual is prepared to think of himself—I use the masculine consciously—as transitional until the transition has become inescapably obvious. Nor does anyone trained in the graduate programs of the late 1950s and early 1960s hear the words "historically important" without a shudder because that was the code for terminally dull writers whom one had to read because they would probably appear on the preliminary or general examinations for the Ph.D. Of course, a number of even duller writers didn't merit even that label, and most of us would, in frank moments, be willing to settle for any kind of importance that anyone is willing to accord us.

Most of the time we don't like to be reminded of that. Not long ago a younger colleague, recognized more for his industry than his sensitivity, remarked that when I and my contemporaries retired, his cohorts would be able to remake the whole department, presumably in their image. "But by that time," I replied, "you will be the old guys." He didn't have a response, perhaps because he has not yet learned to think of himself as transitional. There was no point in assaulting him, verbally or otherwise, because he wouldn't have understood any more than I would have at his age.

But he's a member of the Boomer generation, one that has trouble believing in its own transience because many of its members seemed to believe that all human progress pointed toward them. My generation, called Silent and born roughly between 1925 and the end of World War II, has been acutely aware of our transitional state since the late 1960s, when supposedly anyone over thirty, as we were or were rapidly becoming, couldn't be trusted. Or, as William Strauss and Neil Howe put it in *Generations*, we came to "realize that [we] are the generational stuffings of a sandwich between the get-it-done G.I. and the self-absorbed Boom." In our darker moments, we might even acknowledge the truth of Strauss and Howe's generalization that "Today's 50- and 60-year-olds have been less successful in forging a sense of national or personal direction than any generation in living memory."

This is particularly true of my contemporaries who became English professors. When we arrived in graduate school, the battles between the New Critics and the literary historians had subsided into occasional grumbling and had resulted in a tacit agreement to divide territory. Undergraduate courses drew heavily upon formalist methods of close reading promulgated in Cleanth Brooks' and Robert Penn Warren's popular *Understanding Poetry, Understanding Fiction*, and *Understanding Drama*. Graduate courses were more or less historical, though without any passion or apparent conviction on the part of older professors and with considerable infusion of formalist analysis on the part of the younger who felt no obligation to choose either camp.

If this was a dull period, it was far from uncomfortable. Many of our parents would not have even considered going to college, let alone to graduate school. When we emerged, the influx of Boomers meant jobs for everyone, and we were tenured before the academic job market collapsed—and by 1960s standards stayed collapsed—in 1969. Looking back, some of us can see how lucky we were.

My late friend Charles Linck reviewed the events that led to a career unheard of by his family in these terms:

> It was the WWII experience that made it happen, the GI Bill made it happen, the faith of Earle Davis of Kansas State, the need of KU for slave labor manning freshmen/sophomore classes during the 50s, the demands for re-treading of Texas junior college teachers in the 60s and 70s that made it happen. Good Lord! Professor Emeritus! What is this world coming to?

Charles was my senior by a decade, but our careers followed a similar path and were shaped by forces, in my generation merciful, that we understood dimly if at all.

Levels of Incompetence concludes the narrative begun in *Mid-Lands: A Family Album* and continued in *A Lower-Middle-Class Education*. The current label for this kind of book is "creative nonfiction," but that seems far too general to describe my intention, and "memoir" seems far too restrictive. I have obviously used my experience in all three, but I become more and more aware of the ways in which my experience was anticipated, shared, and followed by others.

In fact, in *Mid-Lands* I used "we" at least as often as "I" because the book begins as a recreation of a particular place, Boonville, Missouri, at a particular time, the half-decade after World War II. As the book progressed and I began to define myself in terms of and in opposition to the people and institutions that surrounded me, it grew more personal, but the book is really about a world encapsulated by highly selective, somewhat sentimental memory unleavened by scholarly investigation.

The second volume, *A Lower-Middle-Class Education*, is like a negative image of the first. Because Kansas City and Rockhurst College were new and unfamiliar worlds, the book begins with the self and traces the struggle to find ways that were comfortable or even possible for me to come to terms with these worlds and with the intellectual and cultural climate in early 1950s America, some of which I remembered, a good deal of which I had to recover, or discover, in magazine and newspaper files. The sentiment of *Mid-Lands* necessarily gives way to irony directed at institutions and even more at myself.

Although *Levels of Incompetence* deals with a longer period (1955 to the present) than the first two volumes, it has a narrower focus: in the first half, with the training and professional conduct of my generation of professors of English; in the second, with an apologia for the kind of scholarship and criticism which we were taught and practiced. Like the first two volumes, it focuses on my experience and moves to broader social and historical considerations. As seems appropriate, it draws more heavily than the first two volumes on research, including highly selective use of others' observations about the present and future of the profession. But after an early trip to the library produced all seven of the books I was seeking, I realized that drawing from them might alienate more readers than it would attract. No one had checked out any of the books; no one had stolen them; no one had even taken them off the shelves and misfiled them. Those who rely on open-stack university libraries know that a 100% retrieval rate is highly unlikely. The reason may be that the only thing duller than being a graduate student or a professor is reading solemn discussions of their activities.

In recent years several noted scholars have published more personal accounts of their careers. Paul Fussell is older than I, having served in World War II, but his *Doing Battle: The Making of a Skeptic* (1996) indicates that he and I have more in common than we do with the younger Frank Lentricchia (*The Edge of Night*, 1994) and Jane Tompkins (*A Life in School: What the Teacher Learned*, 1996). Fussell is more interesting about war than he is about his academic life, which he seems to regard as special rather than typical. Lentricchia and Tompkins, former colleagues at Duke, also tend to see themselves as unique, but they seem to be writing through mid-life crises, in large part occasioned by loss of faith in or nerve about the activities that brought them academic fame, that Fussell and I have survived.

Levels of Incompetence, like the two previous volumes, is an attempt to see my life and career in historical context. A reader of an earlier draft complained that, in effect, the manuscript had no climax. Like most of us, he prefers drama to sober fact, and the fact is that most academics live fairly placid and comfortable lives even through the romantic and economic vicissitudes that beset most of us. Another, friendlier reader gave me the normally superfluous advice that I should be angrier, especially about the fact that recent generations of theorists dismiss or ignore the kind of scholarly and critical work I've done. As Tompkins says, "holding controversial views was professionally sexy and would get me further than sounding nice." But I can remember the tolerance, sometimes strained, of the people whom I supplanted, and anger is inappropriate to a sober and I hope disinterested account of what happened in and to the profession.

I think that narrative worth recording and analyzing, in part because everyone who goes to college has had, regardless of major, to deal with English teachers. Knowing more about who they are, how they are trained, and what they think they are doing may help present and former students understand how we got to be that way. And understanding what happened to change the Fifties conception of the ivory tower into the expansionist hubris of the Sixties and then, beginning in 1969, to the image of the bread line or casting call ("Next!") may help those who think of entering the profession to examine their motives and make their desires more realistic. And perhaps to understand and value scholarship and the criticism on which it is based even in an age when "theory" has all but overwhelmed the approaches that we inherited and developed.

Contents

"In the study of humane letters and the languages a definite period of time for their completion cannot be established, because of the differences in abilities and knowledge of those who attend the lectures, and because of many other reasons which permit no prescription of time which the prudent consideration of the rector or chancellor will dictate for each student."

The Constitutions of the Society of Jesus

Rock Chalk, Jayhawk

I

In May, 1955, at the age of twenty, I acquired one of the few existing Bachelor of Science degrees in English (no Latin, no BA) at Rockhurst, an all-male Jesuit liberal arts college in Kansas City, Missouri. Besides twenty-seven hours in religion and an updated and simplified version of medieval scholastic philosophy, I had taken the usual surveys of English and American literature, Shakespeare and Milton, and a few period courses in literature after 1800 and had written some research papers that were as limited by the materials of Kansas City's libraries as by my ability to deal with them. I had taken four semesters of Spanish, the minimum amount of what was reportedly the easiest language. I could parrot arguments for the Catholic doctrinal positions then taught and attempt to demolish the opposition by using Jesuitical tactics, and I had acquired what I thought was a prose style, though I dimly realized that the subject matter and tone of my writing would not translate to what has come to be called the real world.

In any case, I had to figure out what to do with the rest of my life. I had come out of high school with the desire to be a reporter, and nothing in my training had changed my mind. I had acquired some hands-on experience in back shops and had served as editor of my college newspaper. So I applied for that kind of work. It took less than three months as general news and sports reporter-photographer for the Great Bend, Kansas, *Daily Tribune* to realize that I was not cut out for small-town journalism, and I could see no prospects of doing any better.

A few months before my graduation, Professor Robert Knickerbocker, who was working on a Ph.D. at the University of Kansas, some forty miles to the west of Kansas City, encouraged my friend Jim Scott and

1

me to apply to KU for admission to the graduate program in English and for teaching assistantships. Jim's grades were considerably better than mine, and he was admitted and offered an assistantship before we graduated. I had almost forgotten my application when, late in the summer, a letter arrived in Great Bend notifying me that I had been accepted to the graduate program and given a half-time, or one-course, assistantship.

I had no idea what a graduate program involved or what a teaching assistant did, and even after living on a beginning reporter's salary of $55 a week, I realized that I could not survive on the T.A. stipend. But my mother valued education and maintained that, since I had only cost the family eleven years of primary and secondary school, I should go back on the payroll. My father, perhaps smarting from years of an older brother's claims to intellectual superiority, may have been pleased that I was the first male in the extended family to graduate from college in living memory and may have thought that having a son who taught in college would rest the case for his branch. (I say "may" because my father was a man of strong feelings that he seldom expressed.)

Having received the support and encouragement of the family, I gave notice at the *Tribune*, turning down the offer of a small raise with thanks, packed my few belongings into the 1951 Chevrolet sport coupe I had bought from my father, and drove to Lawrence to find the apartment that Jim had rented. My mother picked up the car for my father to re-sell. It was the first I had owned after years of longing for one, and I began to realize that I was voluntarily committing myself to a life of asceticism.

I had never seriously thought of becoming a priest, even a Jesuit, because the vows of poverty, chastity, and obedience seemed too onerous. It didn't take me long to realize that graduate school imposed even stricter, if less formal, limits than the vows would have. Parish priests had cars, and even the Jesuits at Rockhurst could use the college's cars whenever they needed transportation. Every kind of priest seemed to eat regularly, and though I had never been inside a cloister, I had an image of the rooms as bare, clean, and stern.

Jim's and my apartment had none of the cloister's imagined qualities. He had never lived away from home, and the one he chose without my seeing it showed his inexperience. It had one room with the only Murphy bed I had ever seen except in silent movies, a minuscule kitchen with a drainpipe that disgorged squads of large cockroaches every time we ran the water, and a bathroom in the hall, under the stairs, that must have been far worse, since it has been erased from my normally excellent memory. Before too long, largely because he was tired of hearing me complain, we rented the top floor of a house that was cleaner and larger and had an extra refrigerator which Jim used as a laundry hamper.

The food was not much better than the lodging. We hoped to save money by eating at home, but Jim knew even less about cooking than I did, and I thought that you set Jell-O by putting it in the freezer. We got better with practice, the food at the Union cafeteria was edible, and when we went to Kansas City for weekends—almost always in his case and frequently in mine—his mother tried to make up in two days for what we had missed the other five. We never reached the level of the graduate student in history who scrounged parsley from others' plates to avoid scurvy.

As for chastity, it turned out to be far less of a problem than it had been at Rockhurst, where I had been celibate if not chaste. I had almost always had a girl friend, and when one departed, another seemed to show up. In fact, I had consciously rejected the most suitable because I had the vague but very strong sense that marriage, which seemed the inevitable next step, would prevent me from doing whatever it was I thought I wanted to do.

Nevertheless, I liked the fact as well as the idea of having a woman somewhere in my life, if not at the center, and I assumed that I would find someone at KU. That never happened. For one thing, Jim had a girl friend in Kansas City, and often I went with him and double-dated with whichever of his girl's friends was not otherwise occupied. For another, as a graduate student, I didn't have access to the informal dating service provided by dormitory culture and by mixers. In those days, the proportion of women graduate students in English—and I never came in contact with any others—was far lower than it is now, and in any case, four years at an all-male school had not prepared me to consider classmates as romantic objects, even if I had been attracted to any of them. Undergraduate women seemed off limits either because they were intellectually too naive or socially too sophisticated. As a result, in two years at Lawrence I kissed only one girl, in the summer of my second and final year, and left Lawrence purer, in fact if not desire, than I had arrived.

Other senses seemed equally deprived. Lawrence had a population of 23,000 to Kansas City's 456,000, but it didn't have public transportation even if there had been anywhere interesting to go or diverse neighborhoods to explore, so I felt more hemmed in than I had in Kansas City. And to someone not involved in undergraduate parties—and it took a while to be included in graduate student parties and even longer to find the nerve and resources to give our own—Lawrence seemed much duller than Kansas City, which was a stop on the big-band circuit and had a thriving jazz scene of its own in dozens of little clubs. I could sometimes hear Jay McShann at one of these a few blocks from my Rockhurst dorm. The only live music I heard in two years at KU was the Dave Brubeck quartet playing in a theater where Brubeck shushed the audience for making noise. This seemed to me not just narrow but a constipated rejection of what jazz was all about, though it did seem to suit the general atmosphere of Lawrence. Even my AM radio was duller, for the stations on which I had listened to jazz and rhythm and blues in Kansas City did not reach Lawrence.

The local Catholic church was also disappointing. My home town parish had a literate pastor with a sense of humor, and some of the Jesuits at Rockhurst were subtle and eloquent enough to justify their order's reputation. The priest at Lawrence was not only uninspiring but sentimental. Once, at the end of my confession, he asked if I wrote to my mother. More often than she writes to me, I said. Thereafter, my religious exercises were limited to the required observances.

I got even less physical exercise. As an undergraduate, I had smoked two packs of cigarettes a day, but I had played basketball regularly in intramurals and pick-up games during the school year and city-league softball in Boonville during the summer. At KU, the only exercise I got was walking up and down Mount Oread, the hill on which the University stands, and the stairs of Fraser Hall, where the English department was located. (Not the current Fraser Hall on the same site, which is not at all Gothic and houses Sociology.) This was good for the calf muscles but not very aerobic.

But the climb had aesthetic value, for the tower of Fraser Hall provided an impressive view, and on the crest of Mount Oread, a tree-lined street lined with large and impressive brick buildings curled around the bowl from which the football stadium rose. Unlike Rockhurst, KU looked like a college campus was supposed to look. It was the first school I'd attended to have a football team, however mediocre. And Wilt Chamberlain arrived at KU when I did.

But at first I didn't have time to wander dreamily about the campus or think about spectator sports or pity myself about being poor and chaste and limited and flabby because I was too busy trying to adjust to the idea of a university. If Lawrence was smaller than Kansas City, the University of Kansas, with an enrollment of almost 10,000, seemed unimaginably large, more than six times the size of Rockhurst. It had more faculty members than Rockhurst had full-time students, though the jump from 537 in the 1956 *Americana* to 684 the following year strains credulity and can probably be explained by the administration's decision to re-label graduate assistants as "assistant instructors," to the inexpressible advancement of human knowledge. More intimidating still, I was attending a secular school for the first time since kindergarten, and though I had more immediate things to worry about, years of being warned by priests and nuns about the depravity inherent in secular institutions left vestigial marks. And there was the possibility that I would encounter not just Protestants—I was related to a number of those—but exotic and intellectually superior types like Jews and even easterners.

While there wasn't enough depravity to suit me, there was a sometimes daunting, sometimes welcome sense that I was going to have to get serious, and I gradually began to formulate a different view of discipline—another and to me a much better way of saying obedience. I had always had trouble with the parochial school definition of that term, and years of listening to sermons enabled me to tune out exhortations. At Rockhurst, orientation had been designed to convince us to be serious about developing our intellectual and spiritual powers, but it didn't take some of us long to realize that one could get by on a very modest level of seriousness.

KU was obviously different. The graduate program in English seemed to a sometimes lazy, sometimes distracted student like a cross between monastery and boot camp. Instead of lectures about educating the whole man or adjusting to the fact that more and harder work would be expected, the new graduate students were given a diagnostic test which involved facts, dates, and perhaps identifications but no essay responses. In other words, there was no way for me to fake my way around the gaps in my education. Jim Wortham, the chairman, looked at my exam and remarked that I didn't seem to know much about the eighteenth century. I replied that, since I had never had a course in the period, I could have told him that before I took the test. A Renaissance specialist who later spoke feelingly of *sprezzatura* or casual elegance, Wortham did not seem to resent this casual attitude but merely advised me to take a course in the period. That and some orientation for people teaching for the first time—in my case, students no more than three years younger than I and in some disconcerting cases older—was the only orientation we had. Either the expectations were so obvious as to be unworthy of mention or the ability to figure them out was part of our job.

Although I prefer to figure things out for myself, I was rather intimidated by this attitude. And I discovered that learning by experience takes longer than learning by rote—in my case at least ten years.

As I had done as a college freshmen, I looked to see what standards my contemporaries seemed to follow. That did not take long, for it was a small group, perhaps because the normal entering cadre had been born around 1933, the period of the lowest birthrate in the country's history. Many of us, including the older graduate students, were from a socio-economic class that would not, twenty years earlier, even have thought of going to college, let alone to graduate school. Therefore, the social adjustment was not difficult. I already knew Jim Scott well enough to count on him as a whetstone or foil to my temperament and abilities. The other new graduate students did not seem overwhelmingly daunting. Dick Gustafson, from Gonzaga, another Jesuit university, was clearly bright, but had a familiar vocabulary and frame of reference. Unlike most of us, John Hill was married. He clearly intended to get through graduate work as efficiently as possible; later he became an administrator. John Lewis came with an M.A. from Kansas State, an encyclopedic knowledge of jazz recordings, a stint in the Army, and an off-center knowledge of English literature—not Henry Fielding's *Tom Jones*, for example, but the novels of his sister Sarah.

One man did not stay past the first semester, but I was grateful for his presence because he showed that the department was willing to reach farther down than me. He had supposedly majored in education or something equally beyond the pale, but he was alert enough to notice that other graduate assistants kept books on their office desks. In an attempt to look normal, he brought a copy of The *Search for Bridey Murphy*, a pre-Shirley MacLaine attempt to provide evidence of reincarnation. This did not raise his status, and though we did not shun him, we couldn't figure out what to say to him.

There were several women who, after my years at Rockhurst, seemed alien to the educational process. Two were literally alien. A young American woman married, got pregnant, and dropped out of the program. There may have been one other in our group and others slightly ahead of us. But none of these gave any sign they wanted to be included in the male group which formed around the Jesuit-educated contingent. In our second year, a woman new to the program began to hang out with us, and while she was not unwelcome—two men were clearly attracted to her, and one of them married her—her presence required some adjustment because, as a conversation I'll discuss later will show, we knew very little about women and not much about men.

For now we were concentrating on books. Except for the Bridey Murphy man, my contemporaries were serious and hard-working, so I never had the temptation, as I had in my freshman year, to fall among evil companions. It was just as well, for it was clear in the first class I attended that we were not going to be coddled. Not only was it Old English, but it was taught by Professor Holger Nygard, a name that, with its harsh Nordic trochees, was daunting all by itself. Worse was to come: Nygard did not attend the first class. In his place appeared an older graduate student, impeccably dressed, speaking with a New York accent. He gave us the first assignment (from Matthew's Gospel, I think) in Bright's *Anglo-Saxon Reader* and left before we could ask him any questions. We sweated over the unfamiliar words and characters, and when we discovered belatedly the sound values of the eth and the thorn, we cursed Nygard's substitute for leaving us on our own.

Most of the other advanced graduate students were less reserved, but they were intimidating enough. For one thing, they were alarmingly old. Many were veterans of the Second World War. Quite a few were married. Some were, as I had feared, Easterners, even Jews, and seemed alarmingly sophisticated. And all of them knew more about literature, the profession, and the system than we did. Some did very little to dispel the impression of superiority. One man, from Philadelphia, condescended to talk to me about *Heart of Darkness* until I quoted, in my native accent, Kurtz's dying speech, "The horror. The horror." His neck swelled as he shouted, "No! The harrar! The harrar!"

It must have been about this time that I read Grantland Rice's autobiography. Most people have probably never heard of Grantland Rice, which shows that there is some progress. He was the founder of modern sportswriting and its most famous practitioner well into the 1950s. He wrote his book from the pinnacle of success in a mood of complete self-satisfaction. And as I read the book, I could think only, "What an awful way to spend your life." So when a former colleague from Great Bend called to ask me to apply for the job of sports editor of a morning newspaper in Joplin, Missouri, I thanked him and told him that I had decided to stick it out as a graduate student.

I realize now that the the older graduate students were conducting a kind of initiation parallel to the one I had undergone at Rockhurst. But this one, which did not involve wearing beanies or appearing before kangaroo courts, was more painful, more subtle, and more useful, because it gave me some indication of how far I had to go.

Still more useful was the horrible example of the man who failed his Ph.D. general examinations the month his twin daughters graduated from college. This showed what could happen to me if I was not very diligent or very lucky.

Still, even though I felt deprived and intimidated, I stuck it out. This was partly because I didn't know what else to do and partly because I was beginning to see the pleasure, if not always the point, in graduate work. For example, I had read the first two books of *Gulliver's Travels* as a child after my aunt presented them to me in a lightly expurgated edition. Now, assigned the fourth book in the eighteenth century course, I read it, then the third book, and then, well into the early hours of the morning, all four books from beginning to end. As an undergraduate, I had been used to staying up all night, but that was mostly under the influence of hormones or alcohol. But now the work kept us going. One night either Jim or I was reading, without being assigned, a Yeats poem from an anthology and was puzzled enough to ask for help in understanding it. We had not encountered Yeats in our undergraduate poetry class, but he seemed odd and intriguing. We worked through the poem until we thought we could see what Yeats was all about. Then we looked at the next poem and found that our system did not work. This was stimulating rather than discouraging because clearly there was a great deal to find out.

Besides, on the social level the senior graduate students turned out not to be as remote and superior as they at first seemed. They were not analogous to the upperclassmen I had seen at Rockhurst. Those men had seemed to me already formed, fully developed physically and intellectually, not models to emulate or even think much about. The older graduate students, though they were far ahead of me, were recognizably involved in the same process, and they and my contemporaries were colleagues rather than, as the Rockhurst freshmen had been, mere companions. In fact, they turned out to be far more amusing and instructive than all but the best of my contemporaries at Rockhurst.

It took a while to discover this, partly because the new graduate assistants were put in an office at the top of the south tower of Fraser Hall until it was condemned as unfit even for graduate student occupation. But gradually the older students allowed us to see that they could play human if esoteric games like round-robin poems passed from desk to desk, a line added at each stop until inspiration or interest flagged. These efforts were held to be the output of the Vacuous School of Poetry—literary history was still more important than New Criticism at KU—and distinctions were made between the three-minute vacuous poem and the five-minute vacuous poem.

We were not that ingenious, but one day, while an office-mate struggled with a Milton paper and called plaintively for a transition, we pooled our ideas and came up with a set of transitions that could be used for any topic, of which I remember only the one into the final paragraph: "Thus we have seen" whatever it was that had been evident from the start. In my second year I was allowed to join in a frenzy of limerick-writing, rhyming on the names of other graduate students performing a series of improbable activities. That same year, my circle entered a bowling team in the intramurals and, thanks to the handicapping system, won a trophy.

Sometimes the younger graduate students tried to be serious. In one of the few moments when I thought that I might be a writer as well as a scholar (on my own time, since if KU had a creative writing program, I was either not aware of it or had decided that writing like T. S. Eliot was just too hard), I transcribed a three-way conversation involving a man who later published a book on D. H. Lawrence, another who became a poet, and me as straight man. It began with the poet saying, "Love is sense of freedom, a buoyancy" and referring to the mystics. It slid off into Thomistic discussion of substance and accidents, Lawrencian distinctions between unity and fusion in love and sex, and a lot of other embarrassing stuff that shows we had not shed our undergraduate seriousness about life and love. It was the last conversation of this kind I can remember having at KU, and it would have been unthinkable in the Ph.D. program at Wisconsin.

More important, we talked about our work and how to do it. I can't remember any details except for the recurring debate about whether it was better to take notes on 5x7 cards (more room) or 4x6 cards (more manageable)—this was before computers or even Xerox—that was as inconclusive as the great taste/less filling arguments in the lite beer commercials. There were arguments about literature—what it meant, was it worth it, whose chosen writer was better, and why, than someone else's. Even the course work—pretty much straight literary history with only a little New Criticism and no Freudianism or Marxism—was a source of discussion, as it had seldom been at Rockhurst. Some material was more or less interesting, but almost all of it was new to me.

Occasionally there were some moderately raucous parties, at one of which the Lawrence expert capered faunishly over the furniture to a recording of *The Rite of Spring* after a quasi-frightened pseudo-nymph. But mostly we were too poor and too preoccupied for revelry.

Some graduate students had cultural as well as professional interests. Keith Denniston and his wife painted and wrote, and when the Lawrencian and I sub-leased their married-student apartment for the summer, I first heard Stravinsky, Ravel, Bix Beiderbecke, and Lester Young and lived for the first time in rooms with original art on the walls. In many ways, this was a better indication of the real quality of academic life than even the best courses. But if professors lived like that, I at least did not know it.

II

As I realize from the reminiscences of an older graduate student who only later became a friend, I did not stay at KU enough to know the professors very well or to be aware of the aura of juicy gossip that surrounded some of them or even to see them as human. Some I avoided because of their reputations or because their subjects did not appeal to me. But those I did encounter seemed very different from my teachers at Rockhurst, though it is hard to say how. They were not priests, of course, but in an odd way they seemed more like the Jesuits than they did the laymen who had taught me at Rockhurst. Perhaps this was due to my sense that having the Ph.D. set the KU professors apart from ordinary people as the chrism of ordination set priests apart from the laity and that, while neither priest nor professor was unconcerned with my welfare, neither regarded my mundane pursuits as interesting or relevant to their vocations. Moreover, I had a sense that both performed their rituals, lecture or Mass, not for the physical audience of which I was part but for an invisible and exalted host. I can only say in my defense that I was barely twenty-one and a lot more credulous than I was able to admit or recognize.

Graduate students knew that some of the professors had published books—another obvious contrast with my teachers at Rockhurst—but I at least was vague about what and when. Recently I checked a national OCLC data-base and was surprised to discover how young my professors were and that two of my favorites never published a book. Others had, but some did so belatedly enough that today they could have presented very weak cases for tenure.

Not all of the professors were superior to the priests as teachers or intellectuals. Fr. McCallin, my dormitory counselor, confessor, and history teacher leaned toward the darker and more poetic philosophy of St. Augustine rather than the more logical and schematic views of St. Thomas Aquinas that the Jesuits officially preferred. He seemed more intellectually alert, wilier in dialectic, and more ironic about human behavior than Frank Nelick, who was Thomist by way of the Anglican Thomas Hooker. And Fr. McCallin would never have repeated, as Nelick once did, a story about a professor who began the semester by saying, "You probably won't learn much this semester, because I'm not first-rate. But then if I were first-rate, I wouldn't be here." However, I realized that I could never be like Father Mac, even if I had had a similar vocation, and becoming something like Nelick seemed at least possible. And his class was so reassuringly familiar to products of the Jesuit system that a young woman visiting from the University of Colorado, caught in the cross-fire of a four-way Thomistic debate about Stephen Dedalus's Aristotelian aesthetics in *A Portrait of the Artist as a Young Man*, put her hands over her ears and said, "Please stop!" Besides, Nelick gave me B's, confirming my view of his perceptiveness.

In most comparisons, though, the advantage fell to the professors. For example, one Jesuit taught a number of required courses in a consistently flamboyant manner, regardless of the topic or situation, whirling, pointing, raising his voice, and in general putting on a performance and relying as much on profile as strength of intellect to deal with problems which he regarded as already solved beyond doubt. His nearest counterpart at KU was William D. Paden, who taught late Eighteenth Century through Victorian literature and into modern poetry. He gave the most dramatic classroom performances I have ever seen. One day he read aloud, with great feeling, the description of the heroine's death from *Clarissa*, his voice rising and falling, breaking and recovering. When he finished, he rushed to the side of the room, leaned his head against the wall as if overcome by emotion, and laughed boisterously. Probably, I realize only on writing this, he was adapting Oscar Wilde's view of the proper response to Dickens's treatment of the death of Little Nell. But he was making a point about sentimentality, not just dramatizing himself.

Paden's Keats seminar was the reverse of histrionic. He had us read most of Keats' work, but he concentrated on secondary sources in a way that I had never seen. My English teachers at Rockhurst had barely mentioned biographical and critical materials, and none of the libraries to which we had access in Kansas City had significant, or perhaps any, holdings of scholarly journals. Paden not only taught us that such things existed but that some of their contents were simple-minded or idiotic, that scholars could contradict each other without any of them getting things right enough to satisfy him, and that by studying others' mistakes we could develop our own skills. Still more impressive was the fact that he contributed to knowledge as well as transmitted it. Older graduate students spoke of his book *Tennyson in Egypt*, and I at least thought that it had been published recently. In fact, I discovered from the data base, it had appeared thirteen years before I encountered him. Now I know that, for my professors at KU, it was recent. But even had I been aware of the date of publication, I would still have been awed in the presence of a man who had actually written a book.

I was also impressed by the rumor that he had recently recovered from a nervous breakdown. This too seemed a sign of greater sensitivity than normal because no one else in my experience, especially teachers, had seemed to have any nerves.

He obviously did, or at least sensibilities, for he seemed genuinely to care not only about critical dialogue but about the tone and texture of literature in ways that seemed new and exciting. So did Jim Wortham, who scheduled extra sessions of his Renaissance literature course in which we took turns reading aloud the first two books of *The Faerie Queen*. As far as I could tell, he wasn't trying to teach us anything or develop our minds in the usual ways; he just liked to hear the language. If we learned to hear it too, so much the better.

It was even possible to benefit from professors who were less stimulating. KU required a course in bibliography and methods of research, taught by a man whom I thought the dullest teacher of anything besides philosophy I'd ever seen. Years later, trying to pound those techniques into graduate students myself, I realized that the material was partly at fault, but he had none of Paden's panache or Nelick's penchant for impromptu speculation. One day, explaining to us the terminology used for physical description of books, he said, "And on the title page, we have...uh...the title."

However, he did push us through the 148 pages, fifteen to twenty items per page, of Arthur Kennedy's 1954 edition of *A Concise Bibliography for Students of English,* practically line by line, section by section. (The 1972 edition is 267 pages. That was the last edition; perhaps Kennedy's successors realized that it was no longer possible to be concise about the field.) Almost every line showed me something I hadn't realized I had always wanted to know. I have forgotten all of the bibliographical exercises I was assigned, but I remember vividly the visits to the dim, narrow stacks of the library because I had never seen anything remotely like them. The library at Rockhurst occupied about half of one floor of a not very large building, and even the main branch of the Kansas City Public Library, far more impressive than the one in Boonville, Missouri, differed from it in degree rather than kind. The KU library had more square footage than all of Rockhurst's classrooms and labs and administrative space and probably the dormitories. It was even more different qualitatively.

I had always been comfortable in libraries because I liked to read (not, I have since discovered, a self-evident requirement for graduate school), but I had read more or less for escape or distraction or self-aggrandizement. But on one of my first trips to the KU stacks, I noticed a large, dusty dictionary of the Cheyenne language. I didn't want to learn Cheyenne—German was already defeating me—but it seemed to me marvelous that such a book should exist. And there were hundreds of thousands of other books and topics that offered not an escape but a recognition of my mental boundaries and the means by which to expand them.

Still, the more advanced library research and the classes I took had some resemblance to my undergraduate program. Teaching freshman English was completely different from anything I had ever done. Fortunately, the man in charge of the composition program was Albert R. Kitzhaber, the first man I ever knew and for years one of the very few who wanted to specialize in composition. Judging from my subsequent experience at four other universities, his training program for new graduate assistants was unusual, at least before the 1980s. He taught two one-hour courses for beginning graduate assistants that sometimes functioned as workshops for assignments and sometimes as forums for our written work.

One of our first assignments was to write an essay about why we wanted to teach. I can remember the title of mine—"Convert to the Classroom"—and something of what I said about moving from journalism to teaching, inflating the minimal experience I had as a college newspaper editor and baseball coach and avoiding the real reason, which was that I didn't know what else to do with my life. Fortunately, I cannot remember the way in which I said any of this. The assignment itself called for rhetoric, not sincerity, and though I had tried to ignore official Jesuit training, I had learned to disguise ignorance with verbal dexterity. Another assignment called for us to write short discussions of grammatical rules—mine was "such" and "so" as intensifiers—partly because Kitzhaber was putting together a grammar handbook. My paper wasn't much use to him because I tried to introduce humor and drama. Later he gave each of us a freshman textbook to review. I was not impressed with the pastel cover or the contents, but I was stunned that he could bring himself to give away a book.

Kitzhaber was doing a considerable amount of research and publication in composition studies, in which he was a pioneer and ultimately a nationally visible figure. Most of us weren't aware of that, but we did appreciate the equanimity with which he regarded the assistants and their vagaries. More than forty years later, I can remember some of his very useful dicta: "Remember that your first obligation is to your own program"; "If you oversleep, come and confess before the students turn you in"; "A perfunctory assemblage of commonplace ideas is not a C paper"; "When in doubt, give the lower grade." Or, in a conference after he visited my class, "THE-ater; not the-ay-ter. Now you try it." I was abashed but grateful.

Grading standards were a major concern as a matter of fairness rather than grade inflation. That wasn't an issue for me: in seven classes spread over two years, I gave no more than 4 A's. And I don't think that I was far off line, partly because Kitzhaber scheduled periodic grading sessions to promote more consistent if not uniform standards. All of the graduate assistants, senior as well as junior, would be given copies of selected papers and told to assign grades and be prepared to defend them. The sessions were always lively, for, besides the inevitable disagreements, one or more of the senior assistants (usually Kitzhaber's brother-in-law) would give an obviously outrageous grade and defend it heatedly against massive opposition—probably, we suspected, on Kitzhaber's orders.

Grading standards were important not only for academic integrity but for public relations. Responses to written work are thought to be notoriously subjective, and it is important that the judged, and their parents and state representatives, be convinced that justice is done. Moreover, like many other schools at the time and later, KU required that all candidates for graduation pass a written proficiency examination, given in the junior year so that students could have at least four attempts to pass it. (Like many other attempts, such as dormitory rules, to enforce standards, this kind of exam tended to disappear in the early 1970s.)

Kitzhaber left as little as possible to chance in a very slippery enterprise. I still have my copy of his syllabus for required English courses. It offers guidance not only on syllabi but on every possible topic related to the conduct of a class. Some beginning teachers resent this kind of structure, but I was grateful for any help I could get. I was assigned to teach a section reserved for engineering students, though the syllabus and textbooks—Perrin and Smith handbook, an anthology of essays, and a novel as consolation for the instructor—were identical. The engineering dean had once complained to Kitzhaber about the inclusion of something so frivolous as a novel, but after Kitzhaber obligingly included *Moby Dick* in the syllabus on the grounds that Melville uses all kinds of technical details about whaling, he made no further trouble.

My first class did not begin well and almost did not begin at all. That semester IBM cards were used for the first time at registration, and the system failed so completely that clerks had to go back and do everything by hand, delaying classes for a week. When I finally entered my classroom, a week after my twenty-first birthday, the first student I saw was bald and obviously some years my senior. Fortunately, he was a retired petty officer, and like the younger, quieter veteran in the class, experienced in handling green superiors. The other memorable student ("That kid with the Okie accent," Kitzhaber called him after he visited the class) was a young Texan who invented a rat-milking machine to help check the effects of radiation on lactating rats.

Several others stick in my mind for reasons that have nothing to do with competence. One boy was from a family who owned a restaurant that my parents had patronized in their home town; I think he was the one who informed me that he hadn't turned in his paper because he wanted to do a good job decorating his fraternity house's Christmas tree. Another wrote a paper about making out with a girl at a party and was almost immediately killed in a car wreck—going, I was almost certain, straight to hell. Still another, back from a weekend in Kansas City, reported that he had met a girl who knew me. "Who was she?" I asked. "She told me not to tell you," he said with a smirk. The reminder of the narrow gap between my feckless undergraduate days and my shaky current status was disconcerting.

The amount and variety of material I had to teach was also daunting. Kitzhaber's fifty-seven page syllabus for the freshman and sophomore courses was very specific about my assignment. I had to give students a review of grammar, or in many cases teach it to them, and like many English majors I hadn't thought about that since high school and had to learn the formal terms before I could teach them. I had to demonstrate to the students how to recognize unity, coherence, and emphasis in the reading assignments and how to achieve it in their own themes. I had to lead discussions of essays on topics thought crucial at that time—nature, men and women, schools, religion, democratic freedom, race (x-ed out in the table of contents of my anthology, which meant either that I wasn't supposed to cover it or that I was), crime, and "The Age of Danger." I was supposed to assign, mark, return, and read corrections of a total of 320 papers, plus quizzes and examinations, for my section of composition.

In grading the papers, I was supposed to be judicious about which errors I chose to mark, give appropriate praise and blame in marginal comments, and end with a summary comment which justified the grade, "telling the student what things he is doing well and what he needs to pay more attention to. Even an F paper will have something about it which is not quite as bad as the rest...." (We called this the "neat margins" clause.)

Kitzhaber's section on theme grading describes the ideal critic of writing, student and otherwise. The letter grade, he says,

> epitomizes in a single symbol innumerable value-judgments. As you read through a paper you pass judgment...on an almost infinite number of things. You decide whether the subject of the paper is properly adapted to the capacity of the student and to the scale of treatment; you try to discern and evaluate the purpose of the paper, and to judge whether the material used by the student is appropriate to the purpose and full enough to accomplish it; you try to discover and evaluate the pattern of organization used; and in addition, you examine closely every word, phrase, clause, sentence, and paragraph, both singly and in their combinations, to decide not only whether they are mechanically correct but also

whether they are rhetorically effective. You look at all marks of punctuation to see whether they meet standards of conventional correctness; and if they do not, whether the meaning or rhetorical effect of the particular passage in which they occur justifies a departure from convention. Every time you pass judgment...you are setting this particular piece of writing alongside your recollection of everything you have previously read, and measuring the theme against your total experience with written English.

It is a wonder not that English teachers try to get out of teaching composition as soon as possible but that anyone is ever willing to teach it.

The syllabus contained my official job description. What I actually did in the classroom is, after more than fifty years, obscure. I can say confidently that what I almost certainly did, more often than not, was fail. That's what I've always done and what most teachers do. A friend who teaches middle school says it's a good day when nobody gets hit or sent to the principal's office. Teaching college is easier, but, especially though not exclusively in required courses, students often lack motivation or basic skills or both. They are faced with new challenges and distractions that seem more pressing than next week's assignments.

Moreover, first-semester freshmen sometimes have an inflated view of their abilities. The worst class I ever taught had three self-proclaimed high school valedictorians on the roster. And all teachers are familiar with the kind of student who shows up for a conference, woefully inadequate paper in hand, tears in the eyes and furrows on the brow, and says, "But I got all A's in high school." A teaching assistant at the University of Oklahoma supposedly replied, "Sally Ann, those people were lying to you."

She had more experience and more nerve than I had in 1955 or for some years. Dealing with students was more difficult than dealing with their papers. Not that I had exalted ideas of my role or romantic ideals about the young minds come to be formed in my classroom. I had been an indifferent student, in several senses of that term, but except in math classes I had always or almost always realized that a mediocre grade was the result of mediocre performance. When I was interested, I could work very hard; when I wasn't interested, I never thought it was the teacher's job to spark my interest.

Or to boost my self-esteem. After I'd been teaching for twenty years, an honors student complained that I didn't make her feel smart. That puzzled me, and still does. My best teachers made me feel inadequate (not stupid—that's the unforgivable sin for a teacher) because I didn't know as much as they did and couldn't think as fast or as subtly. I watched and listened and tried to figure out how they did it. I may not have realized this when I was a student or a beginning teacher, but at some level I thought that it was my job to prepare each class as well as I could. And, of course, survive from one class to the next.

As far as I can remember, I didn't make two mistakes common among beginning teachers: I didn't regard my students as an outlet for my feelings (or, as my mother used to say, take them to raise), and I didn't get drunk on power. The first and most common error can be observed during registration for the second semester: new graduate assistants want to overload their sections with students from the past on the understandable but fallacious view that more students mean more love. The second error brings, or should, the intervention of a supervisor and in many cases abrupt termination.

My first experience in the classroom was occasionally stressful but not terribly demanding. I vaguely remember giving grammar exercises and discussing essays. But the only specific discussion I can remember is a unit on paragraph structure, and that because it made me think about my own writing enough to sit with my little finger frozen over tab key as I thought for the first time about whether I had written a unified enough paragraph to end one and begin another. Probably I tried to enlighten them by teaching them what I had been taught, ignoring whatever their real needs were because that is the way I had been treated. Probably I was somewhat priggishly superior to their views on art, politics, and life, not having encountered Diana Trilling's observation that having liberal opinions doesn't necessarily make one a good person. But the veterans were used to official nonsense, and the rest were eighteen years old and still uncertain of themselves as college students.

In some ways, it was the easiest class I taught until I got my own graduate seminar: as at Rockhurst, the students were all male; they had the same general background; and the ex-petty officer unobtrusively kept things in order. I don't have that grade book; I think he earned an A.

19

If so, he and the Texan were the only sure bets. But no one threw anything, no one complained during or after the end of the semester, and this was long before the days of teacher evaluation. So I felt some sense of accomplishment and a great deal of relief. Grading papers was, I discovered, something like editing newspaper copy, I could think of enough to say every class and could usually answer or deflect questions. Assigning grades, which agonize some beginning teachers, was not a problem to an eldest child and a Virgo. When a young woman aggressively questioned how I could justify judging other people, I answered "Because the state of Kansas hires me to."

The second semester was more difficult. For one thing, as I have discovered over the years, second-semester freshmen are difficult to teach because they have survived a term, because they have some basis of comparison ("Miss Smith didn't do it that way!"), because they have become acquainted with the available fleshpots—because, in short, they have recovered their eighteen-year-old feelings of invulnerability.

Moreover, I was teaching them literature as well as composition: *The Odyssey*, Sophocles' Theban plays, Conrad's *Victory*, Shaw's *Pygmalion* and *Saint Joan*, a poetry anthology. Since I had barely heard of these books and writers and had not heard the supposed response of a veteran teacher, "Read it! I've never even taught it," I dived into secondary sources and tried to become an instant expert. As a result, I overloaded them and myself, and the paper topics I assigned (comparing Shakespeare's *Anthony and Cleopatra* and Dryden's *All for Love*, for example) produced the expected dismal result. And, at the end of the semester, a visit from a student's father, far older and more prosperous looking than I, who suggested that because the topic was so difficult that I should consider raising her grade in the course. I remember how I felt—on the edge of panic—but not what I did. I think I had the presence of mind to point out that the grade on that paper was not inconsistent with her other work.

(That was the last contact I had with a parent for a quarter-century. Then a student spoke so highly of me that his mother called to ask me out. At first I didn't have any better response than I'd had in 1956, though ultimately both sides were better satisfied.)

Moreover, the second-semester class had a mix of men and women, which naturally, and especially for eighteen-year-olds, causes distractions, though not as many as the couple playing footsie in the back of the room in my second year of teaching. Besides, I had two athletes in the class, and they were diverted by other interests and occasionally by minor injuries. Beginning teachers at schools with big-time athletic programs, unsure of how much influence coaches have, are leery of athletes. I was lucky: on the blank for "Attitude in Class" on the progress reports from the athletic department, I wrote "Quiescent" for one and "Lethargic" for the other. The older and more experienced of the two sought me out a day or so later. "Man," he said plaintively, "what did you tell those people? They had us in and sweated us for an hour! You have any beef, you talk to us first, ok?" (At least they were fed; years later I turned in a tennis player for excessive absences. He showed up even more promptly because he was barred from the athletic department dining room until he brought a note from me.) Obviously I had all the leverage I needed. An athletic department might not care if its people graduate—one KU All-American reportedly flunked remedial English five times—but it does try to make sure that they stay eligible.

But most students did not and still don't have much support. A freshman girl I had known as a beauty queen and champion majorette in Great Bend showed up one day in the Fraser Hall office to confer with her instructor. When I spoke to her afterward, she was almost in tears because her teacher had not been able to reassure her. Another girl was more enthusiastic about her conference. The instructor, flanked by two desks, the wall, and the buxom young woman, fidgeted nervously as she edged towards him, pulling down on her sweater and repeating, "Oh, Mr. _____, you make everything so clear!" Those of us still in the office acted as though we were going to leave, enjoying his frantic signals for us to stay.

Sometimes problems were better left alone. A timid blonde girl in one of my classes wrote this sentence: "Women are prone to enjoy certain things." I held the red pencil over the margin. And hesitated. And finally could think of nothing to say. But usually I did think of things to say, though I wasn't and in fact have seldom been sure that my advice was even comprehended, let alone taken, or how effective it was in the long term. Occasionally a former student will mention that he or she was influenced by something I said, but these rewards are rare and belated. A teacher who lives on these alone won't last very long.

Of course, teaching was, as Kitzhaber reminded us, only part of the job. It is hard for students to realize that their teachers have any professional or personal lives outside classroom and office hour. (It took me a long time to do so, partly because I had very little personal life.) This first struck me one night in the library where, surrounded by piles of reference books, I looked up to see one of my students looking at me in surprise. "Gee," she said, "I didn't know you had work to do too!"

That was during in the spring of 1957, my last semester at KU, when I was doing very hard and seemingly pointless work that later turned out to be indirectly useful and when I had begun to look, if not for something else to do as a teacher or researcher, for somewhere else to do it.

III

At some point in the previous term, I had begun to want a different if not a wider setting, and I looked for ways to leave Lawrence and KU, more or less in that order because, while I was not tired of graduate school, I was tired of myself in that setting. Part of the reason was the fact that Jim still seemed to think of Kansas City as his chief base of operations, while I didn't have a base. Or I may have felt the need to strike out for myself. At any rate, I took two contradictory initiatives: applying for an instructor's job at a two-year branch of the University of Tennessee and for assistantships at the University of Washington and the University of Wisconsin. Why I thought of Washington I can't remember. Perhaps Seattle sounded exotic. Perhaps I had seen and been impressed by some work by Robert B. Heilman, the department head. But Wisconsin was an obvious choice: Frank Nelick had done Ph.D. work there. Paden and others had degrees from the Ivies, but those seemed far out of my reach financially and intellectually.

My decision to leave KU was not exactly usual—one friend said that he had to be pushed out—but neither was it original. One of my predecessors at KU was convinced by his fiancée that a Ph.D. from KU was far less marketable than one from Wisconsin because Wisconsin's department had a dozen or so faculty members with international reputations.

Her decision was based on careful analysis. I chose Wisconsin because it offered me three-fourths of an assistantship and a small fellowship; the two-year branch turned me down for the instructorship; Washington put me on the waiting list. Nelick's Wisconsin connection, like Knickerbocker's Kansas connection, may have compensated for my record. However, it had improved: I had more A's in eleven courses at KU than I had in my whole undergraduate career. A different grading scale may explain some of the disparity, but I had also worked a great deal harder than I had as an undergraduate.

Of course, there was still a good deal of work to do: write a thesis and take enough courses to retain my assistantship and my income. I had satisfied the course requirements for the M.A., but I realized that I needed some background in Victorian literature, and since nothing was being offered that semester, I was advised to approach Paden about a directed reading and became an unwitting and fairly useless appendage to his research. Instead of giving me a reading list, he sent me to the special collections room to look at some recently acquired letters from, to, and about Arthur William Edgar O'Shaughnessy, a very minor post-Pre-Raphaelite poet. This taught me that the library held more than books.

O'Shaughnessy lived in the pre-telephone period, when every nuance of social intercourse took place on paper, resulting in letters something like this—I have to make this up because I read them almost sixty years ago—"Monday, February 10. Dear Paddy, Come to tea on Thursday and bring Willie, but on no account mention it to Sam because we have quarreled over Charlie's review of George's book."

Even someone far better versed in Victorian literature and culture than I was at the time would be confused by this sort of thing. I was thoroughly bewildered, and instead of working on my M.A. thesis, I spent hours in the library surrounded by dusty volumes of the *Dictionary of National Biography, Who's Who,* and *Who Was Who,* wishing fervently for a reference book giving the biographies of otherwise unknown men. At the end of the process, lured by Paden's suggestion that I might actually publish something, I wrote a rather breezy account of O'Shaughnessy and his circle that made little use of the letters.

Only then did I discover that Paden wanted something like an annotated edition of the letters as background material for his own research. He was so disappointed that he gave me a grade of Incomplete that I did not discover until I had been at Wisconsin for a semester and consciously taken an Incomplete there too, so that I am one of the few people to have that grade at two different universities, a rare and unenviable distinction.

I felt that Paden had, if not misused or misled me, counseled me poorly. Now I realize that if he had not had some confidence in me, he would never have given me the material to work with or left me to work independently. But the experience should have taught me several lessons, including "find out where you are supposed to be going before you begin." I also felt for the first time the almost indecent thrill of looking at something that almost no one else has seen, even if I had not yet figured out what to do with it. Archival research was not a substitute for sex, but it provided a guilt-free alternative.

I didn't have access to archival materials for my M.A. thesis, but the research and writing was even more absorbing because I had chosen the topic and had to work through for a longer period and more independently than I had ever done.

From the moment I knew that I would have to write a thesis, I decided to work on Aldous Huxley. As an undergraduate, I admired his early novels for their ironic tone, wide erudition, general air of sophistication, and absence from any syllabus at my Catholic college. I had read, and re-read, his books more thoroughly than those of any other serious writer. The summer after my first year at KU, I read most of his nonfiction books and began to keep a list of words I didn't know before I realized that I could either look them up or write the thesis.

Because Frank Nelick taught the course in the modern English novel, where I had read *Point Counter Point* for the first time, I asked him to serve as my director. He agreed, but he didn't give much direction, nor did I ask for it.

By the time my work for Paden came to its mutually unsatisfactory conclusion, my final semester at KU was almost over. In order to complete the research and write the thesis, I had to stay in Lawrence, and I arranged to share a sub-let of the Dennistons' apartment with the Lawrence scholar, which from an intellectual point of view like pairing a Dostoevskian and a Tolstoyite, a Northern Irish Orangeman and a Dublin Sinn Feiner, a cat and a dog. But we seldom clashed because I spent most of my time in the library.

Having absorbed the implied lessons of the bibliography course and the Keats seminar, I felt obliged to read everything by and about Huxley I could find as well as writers like Joris-Karl Huysmans, Anatole France, and Ronald Firbank mentioned as analogues or influences. Fortunately, there was a great deal less written about everything in those days, but Huxley was incredibly prolific, and only a small percentage of his essays and reviews had been collected in volume form. Because I decided to trace the development of Huxley's ideas at least until he left Europe and irony for Los Angeles and mysticism, the uncollected material seemed at least as significant as that between hard covers. So I descended into the lower depths of the library to deal with the dusty files of the *Athenaeum* and other bound periodicals which contained his work and reviews of it.

I learned a number of things. For one thing, that kind of research is very dusty work. For another, paging through the dry leaves of old periodicals dries and cracks the fingertips. And finally, there are few better ways to acquire an appreciation of mutability than to look at week after week of book reviews. Books and writers now forgotten are canonized; books and writers now valued are dismissed or ignored—in both cases, by reviewers one has never heard of. I found at least 142 books and articles about and reviews of Huxley's books. Since I cited only eleven of these in my notes, it is clear that I overdid the secondary research, but at least I had enough sense of self-preservation to let most of it stay on note-cards. A student today would find far more articles and books but would probably, and wisely, ignore the reviews and a good deal of Huxley's uncollected material. And, though I regard this as a sign of seriously weakened scholarly and intellectual standards, even some of his books.

That was one of the most spartan periods of my life. The apartment was not within walking distance of a decent grocery store, so I lived off sardines, crackers, and cottage cheese from the nearby mom and pop store and occasional meals at the Union cafeteria. Socially I was even more isolated. Most of my friends had scattered for the summer, and in any case, I was leaving Kansas for the University of Wisconsin and felt emotionally detached from my surroundings and from the few colleagues who remained. It was also the first summer I had spent away from my home town, but the previous summer I had worked second shift at a liquor store, so that I saw few of my old friends and little of my family, stayed up much of the night, and did not play ball for the first time in ten years. As a result, I already felt so detached from Boonville that I didn't even think in those terms.

There was some social contact with a motley group of summer school waifs: a very bright Colombian graduate student; some black students, the first I had ever tried to have a serious conversation with; and a white undergraduate woman whom I tried to attract with a discussion of the geometry of baseball. That led to a wary and inconclusive relationship. But none of these people were colleagues, and my distance from them showed how insular I had become.

On the whole, I was not unhappy. I had a task which I had chosen, the successful completion of which—unlike teaching—depended solely on my effort and ability. When things were going even moderately well, the ability to make connections, see patterns, put my ideas into words and the words into a larger form made me, if not exactly happy, satisfied in a way I had never experienced. Even now, paging through the thesis for perhaps the third time in five decades, I find a great deal to modify but nothing to be ashamed of.

Midway through the summer my college girlfriend wrote to ask me to drive with her to a wedding in mid-Missouri. Since Lawrence was well out of her way, her excuse was transparent, but, lonely and in all but my work disoriented, I agreed. Face to face, she was more direct. Why did I want another degree? The implication, of course, was why not get on with a life, preferably with her. Although I was still attracted to her and uncertain about my future, at some level I knew that I was making the right decision. And that I could never explain my newly-found passion to her. We parted as inconclusively as ever, and I never saw her again, though years later we reconnected on e-mail.

Back in Lawrence, where I had enjoined my roommate not to leave me alone in the apartment with the woman, I got back to the thesis, finished a draft, and submitted it to Nelick. Even if he had read it with unprecedented speed, I had neither the time nor the emotional energy to revise it before I left. So I went back to Boonville to get ready to leave for the University of Wisconsin, larger, more remote, and far more intimidating than the University of Kansas had ever seemed.

On Wisconsin

I

Generalizing from his experience at Eton, Cyril Connolly maintained that the life at an English public school was so intense that the rest of life was anti-climactic. Since tougher and more experienced friends like Evelyn Waugh and George Orwell jeered at this, I won't make a similar generalization about Ph.D. programs at major universities. But I still have dreams about trying to find my way around the warren-like corridors of Bascom Hall because I have had to return as a temporary instructor and finish writing my dissertation. Secretaries and faculty are brusque. The halls are narrower. Nothing is where it should be, and I can't find my mailbox or my office or my teaching schedule. After I wake, sweating, it takes a few moments for me to realize, "I have a Ph.D."

(Another dream deals with my taking, in a large group, a written test for a second Ph.D. from a Polish university, administered by Professor Shiv Kumar. I realize that the whole thing is a shuck, but before entering the examination room, I check my shirt pocket to see if I have enough cigarettes to get me through the hours ahead. I haven't smoked in almost fifty years, but I did when I took preliminary examinations at Wisconsin, and I can't decide whether the anxiety is about graduate school or nicotine.)

Obviously the Wisconsin Ph.D. program left a lasting impression. But I never dream about KU. That department certainly had standards—one half-admitted reason for my leaving was that German was inescapable—but they were not strictly codified and I was too anxious about being in graduate school at all to test how strictly they were enforced. Some people failed exams; some left the program. But the atmosphere was fairly relaxed.

If I had left KU because I wanted a more challenging atmosphere, I made the right choice. The program at Wisconsin had regulations designed to move people through. Teaching assistantships, the only real form of financial support, were given only to Ph.D. candidates and could be held for not more than five years: typically three for course work, one for a minor, and, very theoretically, one for the dissertation. When—or a very big if—the candidate passed prelims over five periods of English and perhaps American literature, she or he had five additional years to complete the dissertation. Failure to do so meant that the candidate had to re-take prelims. The head secretary of the department, an incredibly powerful being, had reportedly led an unfortunate man in this situation through the teaching assistants' offices to encourage diligence.

Later, when I directed a graduate program where a student had been a teaching assistant for fourteen years and had begun taking dissertation hours before I did, I saw the value of these regulations. But in 1957 they inspired more dread than respect.

The physical transition to Wisconsin had not been difficult. My mother, always glad of a chance to take a trip, had driven with my younger sister and me to Madison, where I would share an apartment with another man from Rockhurst. He had higher housekeeping standards than my previous roommate Jim Scott—high enough that he thought it better, not knowing my mother's relaxed housekeeping standards, that she not see the conditions in which I was going to live.

He was as unlike Jim as possible: dour, reserved, balding, and, though probably not yet thirty, middle-aged in appearance and demeanor. (Jim, now eighty and energetic, is still none of these except balding.) Of course, he may have seemed old because he had taught me modern drama at Rockhurst. During the year we roomed together, he never exactly pulled rank, but he planned so well that it was easier to follow his lead. And he was a much better cook than Jim.

But he wasn't a companion. Nor, because he was married and had a small child, was a man whom I had known at KU. Besides, he had a casual approach to the Ph.D. program that, I realized, was better for me to stay away from.

However, the location of the apartment, over a drug store on a busy commercial street, meant that there was plenty of activity in the neighborhood. (Sometimes too much: one night I was awakened by a loud noise and heard a man shout, "You son of a bitch! I'm bleeding!") And unlike Lawrence, there was someplace soothing to walk to. Two blocks away was the book co-op, with more books for sale than I had ever seen, on topics I had barely heard of, just around the corner from the university library, larger even than KU's, which faced the equally impressive Historical Society building. Even more impressive than the number of books were the comments—not defacement but annotation—that their readers made in the margins and sometimes along the bottom of several consecutive pages to contest or develop an argument. Clearly this was a more contentious and exciting place to be.

The student union was not as cosy as KU's, but the view—of Lake Mendota dotted with the boats, sail or ice, depending on the season—was a lot better. It also had tanks of tropical fish that were more colorful and soothing than the lake. The Union was more famous among under-graduates across the country because it sold beer, but we rarely drank there.

Bascom Hall, home of the English department and a number of others, was larger and more labyrinthine than Fraser Hall at KU, but most of the departmental offices and all of the important ones were on the third floor, a stiff climb after the already stiff climb up Bascom Hill. It was so crowded that not all of the associate professors had private offices, and all of the teaching assistants were assigned two to a desk in the large bullpens. You had to have urgent business or be really important to see the department chair—in my time it rotated from Helen C. White to Ricardo Quintana—and possibly even more important to see the head secretary of the department, who did have her own office. For the first week or so, I didn't encounter her or any of the faculty.

I couldn't see as far from the top of Bascom Hall as I could from the Fraser Hall tower at KU, but what I saw—the capitol building at the other end of State Street to the east, and glimpses of Lake Mendota to the north—was far more inspiring than the Kansas fields which surrounded Mt. Oread, though the jumble of buildings at Wisconsin contrasted unfavorably with those of KU, spaced effectively along the sweeping drive on the hilltop. But unlike Lawrence, Madison was a real city. Most important, Lake Mendota, the north boundary of the campus, was a soothing presence during my years in Madison.

There was more spiritual room as well. Madison had a larger Catholic population than Lawrence. The priests at the Catholic student center were far more interesting than the parish priest in Lawrence and not sentimental at all. If I wanted a change of scene, I could go to the Italian church on what was called Spaghetti Corner and kneel before statues in niches outlined by 15-watt light bulbs.

More secular and even more heartening was the bar just down the street where some of the older English graduate students went after they finished the evening's work, and for a while they provided the only context in which I could laugh and relax.

Next door to our apartment lived an older woman who worked as a medical receptionist and acted as a kind of den mother to the students who lived on the floor. One night she hosted a gathering made up of leftist undergraduates from Milwaukee, a man with a guitar who was the first person from Norman, Oklahoma, I had ever met, and me. He obligingly played accompaniment to protest songs from the Thirties. These didn't seem to be very good songs, and the singers certainly didn't seem to be workers, and I was getting bored and a little annoyed. During a break, I said to the guitarist, "Do you know 'Moving On'?" He grinned and said "Oh, yes!" And off we went, astonishing the natives with material they had never heard before.

But though I was glad to find someone who shared something of my regional culture, I hadn't come to Wisconsin to sing country music. In fact, I wasn't sure why I had come, but it didn't take long to find people who would tell me and show me what I needed to do. I could see not only the example of people just ahead of me but share the intellectual and emotional experience with a clearly-defined cadre who came and, we hoped, would leave at the same time. This was very different from KU not only in rigor but in the way we thought about time. Five years did not seem forever even to a twenty-three-year-old, but it was too long to think of as an interlude. I didn't know what I wanted to do with my professional career, let alone my personal life, but it was clear that most of my seniors and even some of my contemporaries were getting on with both.

The senior graduate students felt obliged to let us know how academic matters stood. On my first day in the large third-floor T.A. office where I shared one of perhaps twenty desks, an older graduate student pointed to a sturdy and alert-looking woman across the room. "That's Joan Webber," he said. "She just got a straight A on her prelims." I must have looked puzzled, for he explained that, as for graduate courses, A and B were the only passing grades for prelims, and pluses and minuses were used to make further distinctions among the candidates. The result, as I realized more clearly as I approached the exams, was to make them not only stressful but competitive. A-minuses were uncommon; straight A's were rare enough—I can think of four during my five years in residence—to inspire awe.

Competition and awe seemed to be the point. Graduate students at Kansas were encouraged to think of jobs. At Wisconsin, we were encouraged to think of careers. To give an example: in each program, I overlapped with people who later became department chairs. The ones from Kansas chaired Saint Louis University and Emporia State. The ones from Wisconsin chaired Rice and the University of Pennsylvania, and another served as Executive Secretary of the Modern Language Association and chair at UCLA.

This attitude sounds, and was, hierarchical and elitist. No one at Wisconsin apologized for terms which weren't then in common use. If they had been used, the professors would probably have said, "Of course. That's the point." The system demanded that we share this attitude. One naturally got A's in course work—those who got too many B's were given reduced teaching loads and therefore reduced income. (Years later, after I became member of a graduate faculty, a serious young man asked me if a student with a B average should feel confident of passing the equivalent of prelims. He was nonplussed by my answer: "A student with a B average shouldn't be in a Ph.D. program.") One was either an M.A. candidate or a Ph.D. candidate, and M.A. candidates were outside the pale. Joyce Carol Oates, preceded by her fame as winner of the writing contest earlier won by Sylvia Plath, was the only M.A. candidate any of my friends had ever heard of, and we were less surprised that Ray Smith married her than that he knew an M.A. candidate at all. And she was denied admission to the Ph.D. program.

Teaching assignments, like everything else, had a clear structure.

Required freshman classes were the lowest. Intermediate composition and introductory creative writing classes were a rung and rung-and-a-half higher. Highest of all was assisting a professor as section leader and grader in one of the large sophomore courses or, at the most rarefied heights, in an upper- division course, though these assignments were usually given to instructors who had received the Ph.D. elsewhere.

It took me a while to learn all this. As at Rockhurst and KU, I was involved at first with my peers. I can remember a far higher proportion of them than of my group at KU, partly because there were more of them, partly because the ones I remember stayed together for five years and went through prelims together, but partly because they were more vivid than most of the people who entered KU with me.

There were at least five women in the group, a high percentage for that time. (Two of them married other graduate students while at Wisconsin; two dropped out, one before and one after taking prelims.) But the Wisconsin English department was, if not a gynarchy, well-staffed with internationally recognized women scholars—Ruth Wallerstein, Helen C. White, Madeline Doran—who could hold their own against men like Merritt Y. Hughes, Ricardo Quintana, and Frederick J. Hoffman, and while the department had a nepotism rule so strong that a graduate student couple could not both have assistantships in the same department, women did not seem to be openly disparaged and were often mentored by the department's senior women. (Though, now that I think of it, no women I knew were picked to assist in the literature courses.)

There was also a relatively high proportion of Roman Catholic graduate students, including, in my later years, some priests. Catholics had been rare enough at KU that, after I knew that I was leaving and that another student was coming from Rockhurst, I half-convinced a stuffy and rigid Protestant that the Jesuits were sending him as my replacement in the vast Roman conspiracy. But at Wisconsin Helen C. White was not only a prominent scholar but a prominent Catholic laywoman, and she had strong connections to Boston College and other Jesuit schools in the east. Moreover, as my graduating class at Rockhurst demonstrated, Catholics were just beginning to enter graduate schools in large numbers.

There was an equally large contingent of Jews, and we joked that if you didn't come from Boston College or Brooklyn College, or a generic equivalent, you just didn't count. But in practice gender and religion had little influence on the relationships we formed. Nor did specialization in a literary period (the only conceivable kind of choice at the time). Region was more important. One group, mostly from the east, had very liberal views on politics and behavior for 1957 and was rumored to practice cohabitation if not free love. Most of the people I associated with were midwesterners, with a few conservative or conventional easterners.

Some of these were women, far more intellectual than those I had been attracted to as an undergraduate and far more attractive than the ones I had met at KU. Or perhaps I was wearier of celibacy or more ready to pair up than I had been two years earlier, so I made clumsy overtures to one or two of them that didn't go very far.

The new graduate students first learned about each other in meetings about teaching freshman English. Compared to the ones Kitzhaber ran, the training was elementary. Like many other schools in those days, Wisconsin turned the freshman program over to people who had to rely for tenure on service rather than scholarship and who would not be missed from the graduate program. They gave little advice and less training about teaching, perhaps on the assumption that if we were bright enough to be there, we were smart enough to keep the freshmen subdued. When I brought up points from Kitzhaber's sessions, I got suspicious looks. The people in charge at Wisconsin lacked Kitzhaber's sense of humor as well as his interest in and knowledge of composition theory, and the courses they supervised were unenterprising at best and stultifying at worst. In the first semester course, one whole class period was devoted to terminal punctuation. I may have taught duller classes, but I hope not.

After the first year, whether it was because I was regarded as a troublemaker or because I had more experience, I was handed over to George Rodman, the coordinator of intermediate composition, under whom I spent four relatively happy years teaching students, some of whom actually cared about the process, to write research papers, and explaining to new assistant professors why their ideas wouldn't work because we had tried them back in ought-fifty-nine. Rodman, easy-going and tolerant, was also in charge of extension—correspondence—courses, and he took me on as vacation fill-in during two pleasant and, by my standards, lucrative summers to grade lessons in a variety of courses that kept fresh much of the information I acquired in studying for prelims.

The people who ran freshman composition did have good beginning-of-the year receptions for faculty and 120 teaching assistants at a private home with a lawn sloping down to one of Madison's lakes. I always felt a little stiff and uncomfortable, but I appreciated the chance to see faculty members in a social context and even have them speak to me. It was a little awkward at the beginning of my third year when one mistook me for Paul Davis—several inches shorter, some pounds lighter, and far blonder than I—and congratulated me on his success in passing prelims a year before I took them.

After we enrolled—the department chair advised all Ph.D. candidates—and went to our first classes, we began to meet other graduate students who were still taking course work. The ones I encountered seemed very different from my elders at KU. For one thing, they were not as old. Some had done peace-time military service, but they were not veterans in the sense I was used to. For another, they didn't try in any obvious way to one-up us or make us feel inferior. (We suspected Alan Grob of one-upping because he would cite, by page, a reference to something in our area until we realized that he had a photographic memory and didn't understand that not everyone else did.) Of course, when they talked about what they were reading and what they thought about it, I did feel inferior, and was, because I lacked the gravity and intellectual maturity as well as the knowledge of the graduate students who would obviously be stars in the profession.

A few people were openly competitive and even nasty, but the program was large enough that they could be avoided. Others seemed distant, like the man whose desk I shared in the T.A. office, until he invited me to a party at his house.

Until then, I had little social life. Fortunately, I became friendly with a woman from my Shakespeare class, and for the rest of the term we went to movies and parties and studied together. That was very useful, for she had an uncanny ability to predict what questions would be on the examination. My roommate was also in the class, but he took a sour view of my social life and of women in general. His misogyny was punished: my friend and I got A's; he got a B because, he said, the teacher was prejudiced against drama majors.

As far as I could tell, the faculty operated at Olympian levels far above petty concerns like this. Most senior members had published widely—though, if the rumor about the dean's pressuring Helen White to produce another book was true, not widely enough—and others used the Modern Language Association's "Work in Progress" listings to maintain the illusion that they were going to publish. Even dead faculty members like William Ellery Leonard, known publicly for his poems and his auto-biographical *The Locomotive God* and privately for his annotation of the copy of Norman Douglas's collection of dirty limericks locked away in the special collections room of the library, lived on in department myth.

Not all of the big names were effective in the classroom, but in my first semester I was lucky to have courses from two of the best teachers I encountered in twenty-two years as a student. Madeline Doran and Frederick J. Hoffman not only taught me more about their subjects than I thought I was capable of learning but also about what kind of scholar and teacher I might become.

Although I now know that Doran was then in her early fifties, I didn't think of her as any particular age. She sometimes dressed oddly— plaid knee socks, tweed skirt, striped flannel shirt—and she seemed to have little reverence for Shakespeare and none at all for scholars. Once, when a graduate student quoted Lily Bess Campbell to support his argu-ment, she put her head on the table and howled with laughter. In class, she seemed merely to page through a play, scene by scene, summarizing and commenting as she went. But somehow she conveyed a thorough sense not only of the plays' backgrounds but of their dynamics. I did a good deal of extra reading and wrote a paper on the sources of Shakespeare's *King John*, and though I didn't plan to specialize in Renaissance drama, I did so without much of strain because I felt that Doran would be a sympathetic audience.

My relations with Fred Hoffman, on the other hand, were always strained and never sympathetic. Where Doran made scholarship look easy, Hoffman made it seem hard, and as hard for him as anyone else. He was supposed to have bought at least one book in every town in which he had spent the night, and graduate students joked that he was on vacation when he was only working ten or twelve hours a day. I had heard that he had been raised as a Catholic, which figured, but I didn't know until I looked it up just now that he was a Virgo. I should have guessed. His attitude towards the job and towards me, I realize now, was a lot like my father's—except that I could count on my father's bailing me out if I got into real trouble.

Hoffman had published what I thought was a staggering number of books and was to publish more—twenty, written or edited, by the time he died in 1967. By 1957, when he was in his late forties, he had published *Freudianism and the Literary Mind* and *The Twenties* and the collaborative *The Little Magazine: A History and a Bibliography* and was publishing in article form material that would be incorporated in *The Mortal No: Death and the Modern Imagination*. He was the first scholar I knew of who built journal articles into books; after I had known him a year or so and got over the most paralyzing awe, I called the process "Hoffmanizing."

His 1957 seminar on modern American criticism was so difficult that I would have considered leaving graduate school if I could have imagined anything else to do. At the first meeting, I could see that I was in trouble. At KU, Bill Paden had taught me to look analytically at scholarly and critical analyses of particular work, but I was not prepared by training or temperament to deal with abstract questions, and Hoffman's brusque and confident outline of the semester's work did nothing to reassure me. But when he asked for a volunteer for the first report—on Irving Babbitt—I raised my hand, thinking that I would be judged less harshly because I would have less time to prepare.

The choice of Babbitt was probably the best I could have made. His reasoning and conclusions, among those of the critics covered in the seminar, was closest to the kind of thing I had learned from the Jesuits, so I could at least understand what he was saying and, in the week or so I had to prepare, summarize it.

Hoffman's method of conducting a seminar would have unsettled a more confident student than I. He would begin with a succinct introduction to the work being covered, which in the best case anticipated most of the points that the report might raise and in the worst completely undermined them, making the student feel superfluous or stupid. After the report, he would summarize and expand on what had been said, making the student feel shallow and short-sighted. (There were worse possibilities.

After one very weak report, he stared into the open space which the seminar tables surrounded, silent for what seemed like ten minutes. The rest of us sat there, not daring to clear a throat, waiting to be hit by the fall-out when he detonated.) Then he would ask for questions from the other members of the seminar. They frequently removed what skin Hoffman had left. It took me almost ten years to recover the nerve to give an oral presentation to an audience of my peers.

But after the sessions, Hoffman would sometimes go for coffee in the Union—the only faculty member in my experience to do so—and would unbend a little. Joe Riddel, later a Stevens scholar and theorist, once asked him how he dealt with foreign graduate students who had a shaky grasp of English. "Have you heard of the Chinese home run?" Hoffman asked. Most of us knew that meant a home run down the very short foul lines in the Polo Grounds, in those days home of the New York Giants. We nodded. "Well," Hoffman said, "we have something called the Chinese B." (In 1957, I should add, racial and ethnic sensitivity was directed exclusively toward Jews and Negroes.) Asked about the book on Faulkner he was writing for the then-new Twayne series, he deprecated it as light-weight and unimportant. I was startled to discover that there were hierarchical distinctions even among books and even more startled to hear him apply them to his own work. He even invited the fiction seminar to his home, where he had the expected number of books and an unexpectedly pleasant wife and daughter.

But that was when he was as off duty as he got, and I still feared that Hoffman thought little of my abilities. Nevertheless, the next semester I enrolled in his seminar in modern American fiction and his course in backgrounds of modern literature. For one thing, I heard rumors that he might leave Wisconsin for another university. Also, I sensed that he was the kind of teacher—more like a drill instructor than a mentor—I needed. Most important, I realized at some level that to be able to become a serious student, perhaps even a scholar, I would have to follow his example. If I could not be brilliant, perhaps I could be diligent.

Not diligent enough to suit him, it turned out. The fiction seminar went better than the one in criticism—I had at least read some novels, though not, as Hoffman pointed out, the right ones. The bibliographical training at KU—Wisconsin required and indeed offered none at the time—enabled me to do a competent survey of criticism of *The Great Gatsby*. But Hoffman was so brilliant at surveying criticism of an author or area that I couldn't possibly live up to his standard. Still, I enjoyed doing something like that kind of work. And his course in the continental roots of modernism was the best organized I have ever experienced.

But I was handicapped not only by my intellectual shortcomings but also by some external factors. At Thanksgiving, I had a hernia operation, and on New Year's Eve my appendix ruptured. I may have been out of the hospital before the semester ended in mid-January, but I was in no shape to teach, and other graduate students took my classes. (One thought I was an exceptionally rigorous grader until he met the class.) And I was obviously in no condition to finish the first-semester paper for Hoffman, so I took an incomplete. During the second semester, I was taking three courses, auditing French for my language requirement and, after the beginning of Daylight Savings Time becoming seriously involved with Barbara, another graduate student of my cadre. These activities didn't leave much time.

Well before the semester ended, I realized that I would not be able to do an adequate job on three papers for Hoffman, and I was afraid to aim any lower. So I went to his office to explain that I could finish either the paper from the fall seminar or the paper for the current one. (I did not emphasize my medical problems, since in earlier conversation, where I had mentioned burning my writing hand just before an examination at KU, he looked at me in Freudian speculation as though he knew what I had meant by that. It would never have occurred to me to mention my personal life.)

After a pause, during which he looked at me appraisingly, he said, "Tell me, Mr. Davis. Does your income depend upon your academic record?" Then he granted me an extension on the Babbitt paper. It took three weeks for my stomach to settle and ten years for me to realize that he was not threatening me. He was merely curious to know if I was a dilettante with independent means or a person with serious aspirations. A few weeks later he praised my paper on Sartre for his backgrounds course by contrasting it with everything else I had ever done for him.

I never had another incomplete, and I never took another course from Hoffman. But he helped me to focus more clearly on where I wanted to go and, by example, gave me a pattern for my scholarly career. Perhaps most important, working for him was like doing a different kind of work for my father: after those experiences, everything else seemed easy.

One more experience with Hoffman provided a climax and a form of resolution for my relationship to and feelings about him. In the spring of 1959, my second year at Wisconsin, I audited his seminar on death and the modern imagination. That was the most exciting group experience in my graduate career, not because Hoffman was in the process of finishing his book on the subject but because he was willing to debate issues arising from it with the most impressive group of students I had been associated with, most of them older graduate students, most of them auditors. Only Joe Riddel and I were modern specialists. David DeLaura, obviously on track to become a distinguished Victorianist, and Arthur Schwartz, subsequently a linguist, sat in because the topic was exciting. We did all of the reading as overload, and one week I read *The Brothers Karamazov* and *Middlemarch* as well as teaching two classes and studying for a History of the Language course. I was quite impressed with myself. Now, perhaps more so.

Once I was brave enough to challenge Hoffman and convincing enough to carry my point. In a discussion of E. M. Forster's *Howards End*, I argued that the hay was a sentimental symbol. Hoffman bristled and demanded to know what I meant. Well, I said, Forster makes the Schlegels superior to the Wilcoxes because they don't have hay fever. Hoffman raised an eyebrow and said, "And?"

And, I said, the only contact the Schlegels have with hay is to carry around wisps of it. Hoffman looked threatening, so I added, "Did you ever buck bales?" "Yes," he said, and though I don't remember that he said I was right, he did not pursue the discussion. And he didn't say, as he did in praising my paper on Sartre, that my comment had "the fuzziness and the willingness to bring everything into a discussion regardless of relevance."

(Years later, teaching *Howards End* in Canada, I found a quotation that would have clinched the argument. Margaret Schlegel walks round the fields of Howards End and comes across a little piece of ground which she thinks of as "a sort of cows' powder closet." Frigging Forster indeed, as the character says in *Educating Rita*.)

I should have learned from this exchange that my semi-rural, middle-class, mid-western background could be an asset as well as an obvious handicap in dealing with the world I was trying to enter. But the condescension I encountered or merely suspected made it difficult for me to reveal much about where I came from. I was trying to escape my background, though not my family, but sometimes, as in the songfest with the Milwaukeans and the discussion about Forster, I would be irritated enough to use my experience as a weapon and actually get away with it. And at least once, when I mentioned having done manual labor to a very elegant Anglican, so high that he celebrated feasts of the Virgin Mary at the aesthetically deplorable Roman Church in the Italian community, he clearly regarded me as exotic for actually having sweated. But more often I hid behind what a woman friend called my "very proper butler" pose because Hoffman and others had showed me, painfully, that I sometimes had trouble sticking to the point or even seeing what it was as I tried to fit myself into the ongoing academic discourse.

(Years later, a young woman speaking at a conference said that she had the recurring fear, "What if they find out I'm just a woman?" In the discussion period, I asked why she thought fear peculiar to her or her gender. But I was pleased to discover that I wasn't the only one afraid that I might be found out.)

Things got a little easier after my engagement to Barbara and, after a summer's separation (she in England, I serving as recreation director of Boonville, Missouri, and revising my M.A. thesis), our marriage in December of our second year made it easier for me to act as though I knew what I was doing. She was a comforting if not always soothing presence: she came from my home state and from roughly the same kind of social and educational background, and she had a deep interest in the kind of theology I knew best. She had been a far more serious student than I as an undergraduate and a far more efficient graduate student in her M.A. program. I benefitted from the qualities which made this possible. And she provided social and emotional stability as well as intellectual stimulation. We went to church where, as a convert, she was more curious and more critical than I. We made friends with other couples and entertained modestly. Even at the beginning, however, I now suspect that I was happier in the marriage than she was—most men are—but we had the important bond of our graduate program. Twenty or even ten years later, we might have moved in together for physical comfort and emotional support and gone separate ways when we finished the degree, but that was unimaginable at the time, at any rate for people like us.

Like most newlyweds, we had plans—children, the kind of house we'd buy or build—but we didn't think or perhaps allow ourselves to think about the obstacles facing a two-Ph.D. family. We did realize that one of us (and we both took it for granted it would be she) would have to find support elsewhere because of the department's nepotism rule. Fortunately, she found Helen White as patron, and that solved the immediate financial problem.

The real goal of the first nineteen months of our marriage was getting ready to pass prelims. At that time, candidates had to take five examinations from the following fields: Medieval, Renaissance Drama (required of all candidates, even those in American Literature), Renaissance Non-Dramatic, Restoration and Eighteenth Century, Nineteenth Century English, and either Twentieth Century English or Twentieth Century English and American. American Literature candidates had, I think, two fields, but those areas were under the jurisdiction of Harry Hayden Clark, and those of us in English literature or in Hoffman's orbit regarded them as boring and even suspect. We didn't shun American lit. students—I even played poker with some of them—but we didn't think them really serious.

And God knows the people I associated with were serious. The party at KU in which my friend capered to The *Rite of Spring* was unthinkable in Madison as the conversation about ideal love would have been. Of course, by that time many of the graduate students I knew were married, sometimes to each other, mostly in a stable and responsible 1950s way. What parties we had were dress rehearsals for the academic gatherings most of us would attend for the rest of our lives, though relative poverty kept us soberer than many of us would subsequently be. When we went to movies, we tended to see them in terms of our work, as when Barbara and I earnestly, if excitedly, decided that *The Apartment* fit exactly the Renaissance definition of tragicomedy. One of my friends became a little too serious for his wife. Weary of the graduate school grind—she had, I think, gone to Rollins College in Florida—she bought a glossy women's magazine and settled down to enjoy it. Her husband, a nascent

Wordsworthian, looked at the cover and prowled nervously around their apartment, trying to think of an appropriate comment. Finally he burst out with, "We've got some Dickens you haven't read yet!"

This was excessive but not untypical. We tended to choose courses to enroll in, and audit, which would prepare us for examinations in the fields we had chosen, with areas of specialization a secondary consideration. For example, I planned to write a dissertation in Twentieth Century English literature, but I actually took only one course and one directed reading in that field during my entire graduate career, and none at all in the second half of my Ph.D. course work. Of course, Hoffman's backgrounds course and another in comparative literature were certainly relevant, and I audited the surveys in that field taught by John Enck and Paul Wiley and, like most auditors at Wisconsin, attended all of the classes and did all of the primary and a good deal of the secondary reading expected of all graduate students.

Except for the American lit. people, who reportedly came out of Harry Clark's and Henry Pochmann's seminars with half of their dissertations drafted, we avoided seminars because they didn't give us information we could use on the general examinations. Advisors pushed seminars, sometimes unadvisedly. Wisconsin's hierarchical system extended to the faculty, and few associate professors and no assistant professors were assigned seminars or even lecture courses that included graduate students. Few seminars were scheduled—the reality of enrollment patterns rather than department requirements was recognized—and in a particularly lean semester, Ricardo Quintana wound up with thirty in his Eighteenth Century Literature and Scholarly Problems. He kept repeating, at first seductively and then plaintively, "Wouldn't you rather take the linguistics seminar?" We sat stolidly, avoiding his eyes.

But no one could possibly take or even audit enough courses to prepare for prelims. Of my thirteen courses at Wisconsin, six would not be directly relevant to the periods I had elected: English literature from 1500 to the most recent work my examiners had read, including major secondary works. I had taken Doran's Shakespeare class and audited selected portions of Mark Eccles' drama including Shakespeare course, so I had major gaps in that field. In Renaissance Non-Dramatic, I had taken Helen White's early seventeenth century survey and Jim Wortham's class at KU. In the Eighteenth Century, I had three courses at KU and Quintana's seminar. In the Nineteenth, Romantics and the novel from Carl Woodring and courses in Victorian prose and poetry from Robert Doremus (unfairly called "Dormemus" by some Jesuit products who'd had Latin). In Twentieth, where I opted to exclude American literature, fearing Hoffman (unnecessarily—he left for the University of California-Riverside the summer before I took prelims), wider coverage, and the absence of support from fellow students, I had one KU course, some audits, and a fair amount of independent reading. Allowing for differences in emphasis and background on the M.A. level, my situation was much like that of the twenty-six others facing the examination with me.

By this time, I had become a much better student—more diligent, more attentive, and more willing to explore background material without being prompted—than I had ever been before. But I was still a student, and then and since I have seen many students who for various reasons could not face or did not have the flexibility and stamina to deal successfully with the final written examinations for the Ph.D. For me and my contemporaries, they were the test that separated mere readers from scholars. Years later, many of my colleagues seemed not to agree, but I still think so. In 1960, I was not at all sure that I would be successful, but, typical of my generation, I doubted myself rather than the system.

Farther Along

"Farther along, we'll know all about it.
Farther along, we'll understand why."
W. B. Stevens and J. R. Baxter, Jr.

In the 1950s and through much of the 1980s in Ph.D. programs at most big state universities, the process of getting ready for prelims was both competitive and, as in any contest, necessarily collective because we faced the same questions on examinations in standard fields. At Wisconsin we were less like combatants than like candidates for knighthood or holy orders or other forms of initiation into a select group. No one had to lose. On the other hand, no one might win. All faced the same ordeal in which some would probably fail and others would pass. In the prelims, it would be with varying degrees of success. But it would be bad form among those who did pass to begrudge someone else's A- to their B+.

This spirit of camaraderie did not preclude various mind games. For example, two close friends were studying the material in tandem; one would read ahead and send his wife to ask the other a question about something on the next day's list. A ploy like this was regarded as legitimate and funny. Not kosher was the tactic, reportedly used by a few graduate students, of using a secondary work in the library and then mis-shelving it so other graduate students could not find it. Of course, if some students could not find their way around the Wisconsin library, which was in the process of moving from the arcane and idiosyncratic system named after Cutter, its inventor, to the Library of Congress system or did not know that multiple copies of important secondary works—i.e., those written by Hoffman, White, Quintana, Wiley, and other star Wisconsin professors—

were kept in a special section on one of the lower decks, then that was a defect in their education. Telling them was an act of kindness, not obligation.

But we were not usually like the characters in the joke, "How many pre-med students does it take to change a light bulb?" The answer is two: one to turn the bulb and the other to pull the ladder from under him. (How many graduate students? One, but it takes him seven years.)

Instead, some of us formed study groups and, with the best intentions, drove one another crazy. My wife and I joined with the woman who had studied with me in Doran's Shakespeare class and another Midwesterner. During the summer of 1960 we studied, individually and collectively, English literature from 1500 through and a little beyond the modernists in chronological order, two weeks to an exam period. We re-read class notes and exchanged them. For example, I had summarized the material assigned in the anthology of Victorian prose, made a digest of that material, and then a digest of the digest that was so thorough that the rest of our group, who had not taken the course, and later a man at another university passed the test largely on its strength. We also read and took notes on secondary sources and studied previous examination questions to try to spot tendencies. Each time the examination was given, we knew, one professor wrote the questions and another graded them, and a Merritt Hughes exam in Seventeenth century or a Carl Woodring exam in Nineteenth Century would be very different from and probably a lot harder than ones written by Helen White and Bob Doremus or Alvin Whitley. But though we could guess who had written what past exam, we could not be sure who would write ours. The one constant was Eighteenth Century: Ricardo Quintana always wrote that, and though the arrangement might vary, the questions had a reassuringly consistent pattern.

Every two weeks we would meet for an evening to ask one another questions. Some were factual, as in "Name five malcontent figures in Renaissance drama and distinguish among them." I remember this field the best because we would reward ourselves for diligence by allowing ourselves to read another play by Shakespeare. Other questions, somewhat to incredibly general, are harder to remember. The purpose of these meetings was to broaden our knowledge and force us to make connections. The usual effect was to make us even more depressed and anxious than we had been.

Mid-way through the summer, I dreamed that I was taking a seminar from a shadowy professor in the room that Hoffman had used. Assigned the topic of Conrad's poetry, I fast-forwarded through the process of compiling a bibliography, reading criticism, making notes, and drafting a paper. As I walked into the seminar room to deliver my report, I thought, "But Conrad didn't write any poetry" and woke up sweating. At that point, I began to drink more heavily.

As prelims approached, the panic level increased. We knew well a man who had, on the eve of his first exam, packed his belongings and, on his way out of town, stopped at the English department to notify the secretary that he wasn't ready. In contrast, another man had, or said he had, walked in with the attitude that if he passed three—the minimum number—he could always retake the other two. (The first man returned a year later, and both men passed all five examinations on the first try.) While secretly we would have settled for passing three, we could not share his insouciance, and the longer we studied the less sure we were either that this was possible or that we could go through the ordeal again.

So we devoted the time remaining to review our notes on each period, make summaries of summaries until we didn't quite get the whole nineteenth century on one 4x6 card, and try without success to take deep breaths and relax.

Fall exams were scheduled before the beginning of classes (spring exams during the vacation period), three hours each day, with an extra hour permitted which almost everyone built into their strategies. My group's exams were scheduled five days in a row, better, we agreed, than having to wait a day or, worse, a weekend between stages of the ordeal. People who had those schedules argued that they would get some rest and have time to review. We knew better.

I had heard people say that the reality was much less worse than the anticipation, the race easier than the training. That is true of some athletic events, but it was not true of prelims.

The week did not begin well for me. People writing answers in long-hand were distributed among several of the large T.A. offices. The rest of my group was using this method, so I decided to try it. And locked up. Fortunately, I had brought my portable typewriter, so the head secretary, who became more important and more helpful the farther along one got, put me in Henry Pochmann's office because he taught American literature and his books would be of no use to me. I rolled a sheet of paper into the platen and, my brain and fingers perhaps remembering the pressures of a journalistic deadline, began to type.

After years of moving the exam file from job to job, I finally got rid of all but the Twentieth Century British exam. I don't remember the Renaissance Drama exam, so it must have gone fairly smoothly. But we were loaded for that, partly because it is easier to prepare for an examination on plays than on poetry or even on discursive prose. Helen White had apparently written the Renaissance non-dramatic exam, thank God, because there was only one question on Milton, on light and dark imagery in *Paradise Lost*. I hadn't studied Milton since Rockhurst, where we had used Merritt Hughes' edition, and then had written a review of Evelyn Waugh's *The Loved One* instead of a term paper. But I remembered the KU bull-session in which we had created the all-purpose set of transitions for a graduate paper for a man writing a paper on Milton's imagery. I came out of the exam not exactly confident but not totally depressed about my performance.

We had looked forward to the Eighteenth Century exam as a mid-week breather. We walked in to our exam rooms to discover that the Greeks were right about hubris. Quintana had written a whole new examination. I couldn't see anyone else's reaction, but I do know that when we got home, Barbara threw up what little she had managed to eat the past three days. Fortunately for me, Q. had included a major question about irony in Swift's "A Modest Proposal." Aside from the fact that I liked irony, I had not only read and taught the essay a number of times but, because it was not included in many of the anthologies we used, I had typed the whole thing onto stencils. If Xerox had been available, I might still be trying to pass prelims, because it was the only question I was confident of answering.

The other questions, none of which we had anticipated, ranged from difficult to impossible. Near the end of the examination, confronted with a choice of short answers to identification questions, the best alternative I could find was Christopher Smart. I knew only that he had written "A Hymn to David" and had prayed in the street. That is hard to stretch into five minutes. It may have been that night, though probably it was earlier in the week, that I began to wash down a non-prescription sleeping pill with a quart of beer in order to get four hours' sleep. Barbara and the others were getting less.

The next day was almost as bad. Carl Woodring had obviously written the Nineteenth Century exam. He was, to understate considerably, less predictable than Bob Doremus. It was said that he had already written about every book published in the century and had started on the illustrations. In lectures, he would dart from one subject to another by associations known only to him. In taking notes for his Victorian novel course, I had skipped a line every time he changed subjects, and a page of my notebook looked like sheet music.

His questions were not unfair. They were even interesting, as in "Compare the use of irony in Byron and Thackeray." Yesterday, irony had been my friend. Today it had turned on me. To a graduate student used to periodizing everything, questions like this, crossing from Romantics to Victorians, seemed impossible to answer. I rolled a sheet of paper into my typewriter and stared at it. I might still be staring at it if I had not seen another graduate student, whose announced period of specialty was the nineteenth century, rushing down the hall tearing at her hair and moaning, "Aaah! Aaah!" Montaigne said that in the misfortune even of our best friends there is something that does not entirely displease us. And this person had always seemed overly competitive with and dismissive of others. So I smiled to myself, took a deep breath, and began to type.

On the final day, covering the twentieth century, I was more thoroughly prepared than I had been all week, but since it was my period, I was under pressure to show the examiners, one of whom would undoubtedly direct my dissertation, that I was worth their attention.

By contemporary standards, the questions were amazingly comprehensive. In the first question, we were asked to choose four or five of sixteen titles and discuss, in fifty minutes, their "distinguishing characteristics of form or structure." Some of the works—by George Barker, Christopher Fry, Louis MacNiece—reflected Paul Wiley's obsession with the 1930s, and no examiner would now expect a Ph.D. candidate to know or care about Shaw's *Back to Methuselah*.

The second question was more standard. It required us to spend another fifty minutes on five or six of eighteen topics—such as Joyce and the Daedalus myth, pursuit in Graham Greene, polarity in D. H. Lawrence —identify and define the issues, mention an example or two of other works or relevant evidence. These were compressed essays, followed by forty minutes on one or two discussions of seven topics like "principles, value and significance of the literary theory of any one: Ford Madox Ford, Virginia Woolf, Wyndham Lewis, Herbert Read, C. S. Lewis."

Then an hour discussing "themes or issues that have emerged in contemporary writing and on any other features of style or content, in relation to author or literary developments," in three or four of six quotations from Eliot, Joyce, Yeats, Auden, Woolf, and Edith Sitwell.

In the home stretch we had first to discuss a scholarly or critical book on an individual writer and another on a broader topic and then to write a sentence or two describing the type or nature of seven of sixteen works. This must be one of the last preliminary examinations to ask for knowledge of a Galsworthy play or a Robert Bridges poem, and only now, with the help of Google, can I identify *The Card* as a novel by Arnold Bennett, an author most of my juniors probably never heard of.

We were enjoined to "Allow sufficient range...so as to show your acquaintance with different genres, especially as regards poetry and prose fiction." Although I was loaded with information on Yeats, I kept putting off using him for better opportunities and don't recall writing about him at all. The low point came when, writing about Huxley's *Brave New World*, a novel I had read at least a half-dozen times and discussed in my thesis, I could not remember the name of the principal female character, Lenina Crowne. But I circumlocuted my way around that gap, and finally the ordeal was over.

The other woman from our group and I went to a beach on Lake Mendota—Barbara had gone to find a present for my twenty-sixth birthday —and I immersed myself up to my nose and hung there, too weary to move. When Barbara and I got back to our apartment, we looked at the piles of books covering the floor and the dust and other clutter that had accumulated over the past three months, laughed a little ruefully, and collapsed.

Between the end of the exams and the announcement of the results—not more than two weeks, I think—those who had taken the exam avoided one another and the professors and other graduate students. If one failed all, or any, of the preliminary examinations, one would have to go through the whole process all over again. And, I began to realize, there was the distinct possibility that even if both of us passed, it was possible that Barbara might get a grade higher than mine. It was even likely: she had a far better undergraduate record, she had a smoother and more successful career at Wisconsin; and she had clearer and more ready answers to every kind of question than I did. I could live with that result, but I hoped I wouldn't have to. Given the choice between a spouse who shared the experience and one who stood on the sidelines, however supportive, I was pleased with the one I had made. I kept my anxieties to myself. We did agree that, like the other twenty-five people who took the exams, we would be glad to settle for B-minuses.

Results were announced by mail, but the head secretary called each candidate before the letters went out, and most people came in to pick up the envelopes. One candidate had thanked the secretary but said that he was busy and would wait for the mail. That was generally felt to demonstrate an excess of confidence or stoicism. Most of us were properly anxious. Bascom Hill had never been as steep as it seemed that day. Barbara and I got the envelopes and realized that we couldn't, as a couple, use the traditional place—a booth in a rest room, both secluded and convenient—to open them. Rather than separate, we went down to the corridor outside the Spanish Department on the second floor, where no one knew us, breathed deeply, and opened our letters. Both of us had received the grade of A-minus. All these years later, I let out almost as long a breath after I typed the last sentence as I did when I read the results. And, in revising the chapter, I realize that the experience represented the highest and in some ways the last moment of intensity in our marriage.

Everybody we knew had passed, a half-dozen with A-minuses and one, later a novelist, with a straight A. We were a little shy around people who had lower passing grades, except for the man who, with his wife, had gotten B pluses and was sure that his wife got a lower grade because the examiners had wanted to keep couples on a par. The implication was that Barbara had pulled me up and he had pulled his wife down. We thought it more gallant of him to believe it than professional to say so, but after a while our friendship resumed.

Success after a shared ordeal is a great bond, and in the round of parties that followed, we became temporary friends with people we'd hardly spoken to before. We agreed that we would never have as much knowledge of a broad range of English literature or be able to communicate with each other about it as we did now, and we justified prelims on the grounds that anyone who passed them could teach a survey of English literature without having to look at a secondary source. In a fit of partial modesty, we concluded that prelims were a test of character rather than intelligence. I sent a card to Fr. McCallin, the teacher, mentor, and confessor at Rockhurst who had addressed me as "young Davis," to tell him that young Davis had passed prelims and now felt considerably aged. He didn't respond. In the general atmosphere of relief, I thought about writing a Western novel based on a Jacobean revenge play, but got no farther than a page or so.

I had the same kind of trouble gearing up for the rest of my Ph.D. program: taking a minor and writing a dissertation. I had originally planned to minor in comparative literature and had even taken one course. But near the beginning of studying for prelims, I realized that comp lit required a preliminary exam of its minors, and even at that stage I realized that I could not endure another of those, however lightly my contemporaries regarded it. So I switched to drama. The one course I'd had at Rockhurst turned out to be more rigorous than the UW drama department's two survey courses in English drama, 1660 to modern. By the standards of the English Department, the teacher was competent but undemanding, the competition weak. Working with trained actors in the course in dramatic interpretation, I fared less well, having delivered nothing to an audience since my role as a leprous thirteenth century church architect in my freshman year at Rockhurst. But I enjoyed the performance and got some badly needed practice in reading aloud. In contrast, the seminar in dramatic theory was a breeze because I had far more experience that the drama majors in the library and was used, as I ungenerously put it, to reading without moving my lips. Most of my contemporaries had similar attitudes, complaining, for example, that philosophy didn't even have an annual bibliography of secondary sources, for God's sake!

So I did well enough in the minor, but the prelims had left me with a feeling of lassitude, similar to my experience of being newly sober twenty years later, and I felt that I was not being very productive. But I decided to indulge myself and try to get back in some kind of shape, and I played city league basketball during my last two years in Madison. That was the first real exercise I had gotten—except for a few softball games the summer before my marriage, when I was athletic director in Boonville, Missouri—since I had graduated from college. As an athlete, I had been dogged rather than talented, and I realized how much I had missed the physical competition as well as the exercise. Barbara came to some of the games. She had never seen this side of me, and she worried when I was the last out of the locker room—I couldn't stop sweating—and was shocked when, in front of her seat, I threw a hip into an opponent who, unknown to her, had just shoved me from behind under the basket. There was a lot we didn't know about each other.

After I finished the required twelve-hour minor, I had to start work on the dissertation. I had found a topic, or at least the corner of one, purely by accident. When Paul Wiley's Conrad seminar was canceled in the fall of 1958, each student was asked to pick an author and wait for assignment to a suitable professor who would give us a directed reading. For want of an alternative, I chose Evelyn Waugh, then still alive and producing work. He was not unknown—Wiley assigned *A Handful of Dust* in, I think, the New Directions edition—but he was not highly regarded. I was sent to talk to Ricardo Quintana, who taught a course in modern satire as well as the eighteenth century. His initial response to me was repeated every time I went to see him.

"Mr. Quintana?"

"Yes, yes, yes! Come in, come in, come in!"

"My name is Davis."

"I know, I know, I know! M.A. candidate or Ph.D. candidate?"

In that first meeting, he said, "I don't know much about Waugh this semester," a remark I found astonishing until I had been teaching a variety of courses for a number of years. He gave me minimal directions which amounted to "go out and read some Waugh and come back and then write something about it."

I did; he read it and wrote "Altogether first-rate, or so it strikes me

(I've made it clear that E. W. is not one of my specialties.)" That was his only comment, and I didn't expect him to remember it once it left his hands. But early in the next semester Alvin Whitley, younger than Q. but a tenured professor, invited me to lunch at the University Club because Q. had mentioned my paper to him. This was the first positive notice I had received at Wisconsin, and I was as startled as I was pleased. And Paul Wiley read the paper and praised it. Unfortunately, Frederick J. Stopp's book on Waugh appeared shortly thereafter, and I couldn't imagine adding anything to his lucid and, for a first book, thorough account of Waugh's career.

But part-way through the summer of preparing for prelims, probably while I was reading the section on genre in Northrop Frye's *Anatomy of Criticism*, it occurred to me that I could examine Waugh and some other writers and develop an extended descriptive definition of the fictional sub-genre he helped to establish.

Despite the fact that Paul Wiley had a reputation of stretching out the writing of a dissertation, both in time and in physical bulk, he was the obvious person to direct the dissertation because he was the only professor at Wisconsin who had published a book on modern English fiction. I approached him—at the time I was teaching five discussion sections of his sophomore course in modern English and American literature—and at first he agreed. Then, one day as I was leaving his office, after discussing the possibility of using Waugh and Nathanael West, who had begun their careers as cartoonists, he said, "Wouldn't you rather write about irony in Conrad?" It sounded a lot like the speech Anse Bundren makes to his young son Vardaman in Faulkner's *As I Lay Dying,* "Wouldn't you rather have a banana [than the model train he'd seen in a window]?" Vardaman and I had the same undelivered response. I said, "Let me think about that," and went down three flights of stairs, out the door of Bascom Hall, and over to the Liberal Arts building to see Whitley, who directed dissertations on English literature from the mid-eighteenth century to the modern period. He agreed.

(When the next school year began, I discovered that I had not been re-assigned, as was the normal practice, to assist in Wiley's course. I went to ask the man in charge of teaching assistants what had happened. I'd have to talk to Wiley, he said. So, very nervously, I did. "Oh," he said, "I thought you were leaving to take a job." Paul Davis again. But I suspected that he was upset at my defection, though my only recourse was hurt feelings. As I said from the vantage of a tenured professorship to a graduate student who asked if he was being paranoid, "Of course you're being paranoid. You're a graduate student.")

Whitley was not the most distinguished scholar in the department, but he was by far the most polished lecturer. A Wordsworthian whose dissertation Whitley directed complained that Whitley refused to read any more of his dissertation and made him stop writing and that, had he been allowed to think through the issues more fully, he would have had a better book. This seemed a strange view to take, even after I had long since finished my own dissertation. I was grateful for the tact and efficiency with which Whitley handled it.

Whitley had a Ph.D. from Harvard and an enviably and, to me, irreproducibly crisp accent that was not quite British. I was told, though I never saw evidence, that he came from San Antonio, where his father was a barber. The point, aside from pure snobbery, seemed to be that he had created a facade. Since I was trying in a less ambitious way to create one for myself, I admired his artfulness.

First, he said, I had to write a proposal. Not to worry, he and others told me: one could propose a dissertation on Lawrence and turn in one on Joyce. The point was to have the proposal approved because thereafter the department was obliged to furnish a new director should something happen to the original signatory. By that time I had discovered links among the novels of Ronald Firbank, Carl Van Vechten, and Evelyn Waugh. Whitley made it clear that I would know more about the topic than he did and that his job was to insure that the final product was coherent and readable enough to send to the dissertation committee. And, considering what he had to work with, he did, as expeditiously as possible. In the later stages, I would send him a draft from Chicago on Monday and get it back, with careful comments, on Friday. As a director, I was more brusque and more critical than he—the Hoffman influence?—but I have tried to match his efficiency.

Whitley's style was as crisp as his speech and clothing. On a 45-page graduate student paper—not mine—he had written, "A. Sensitive, intelligent, and, God knows, thorough." When I asked him if I should begin the dissertation with a survey of scholarship, he said, "Put all the guff in the footnotes. You'll have to put it there anyway when you turn it into a book." When the process was over, he advised me to write a book on Waugh rather than on Ronald Firbank, whom I preferred less because he was interesting—he was—than because almost nothing had been written about him. I didn't take his advice and still have the unpublished manuscript in my files. He may have thought my Waugh material far better; he almost certainly knew what I didn't find out until later: my friend and Wisconsin contemporary Jim Merritt had a contract for the Twayne English Authors Series book on Firbank. Whitley was the ideal advisor for me at that time. If Fred Hoffman had frightened me into working hard, Alvin Whitley helped teach me how to avoid showing the strain.

Because I was dealing with three figures, I had or thought I had to do three times as much research as I would have had to do for a single-figure dissertation. After I finished writing about one novelist, I would have to go back to taking notes and outlining. As a result, it took three years to finish a workable draft of the dissertation, the last two while teaching three sections of composition and one of literature every semester. I wrote the last sentence on a rainy night in Chicago. "Beat the Devil," which I had never seen, was playing at an art house near Lincoln Park. With a full-time teaching job of her own, Barbara had papers to grade and couldn't take time to celebrate with me, so I went by myself, somewhere between satisfaction and melancholy, watching the lights gleam off the wet pavements as I waited for a series of buses and feeling that scholarship was a very lonely enterprise.

I felt the same way when, a few months later, I returned to Madison to defend the dissertation. When I ran into a bureaucratic glitch, the head secretary made a phone call, barked some orders, and sent me to the proper office with instructions to tell them she had sent me. But even the people who remembered me after two years' absence had their own concerns, though they were cordial enough.

The defense was, as predicted, an anti-climax. Three of the five committee members had never seen me or I them. Students were finishing dissertations at assembly-line speed, and committees had to be formed without regard to faculty members' interest or even competence. Only Whitley and John Enck had any knowledge of the authors I was treating, and the most memorable comment from the notably capricious Enck, on a dissertation about formal qualities, was "You don't seem to like these characters very much." I was injudicious enough to say something about realistic dialogue, and the committee demanded to know what I meant. Well, I said, I can give a good counter-example, and I remembered, from *The West Indian*, a play I had read for my minor, the worst seduction speech in the history of drama: "Oh give me love—free, disencumbered, anti-matrimonial love!" That deflected them.

The committee didn't cause much trouble, and if they had been inclined to do so, Whitley would have pulled them back into line. A friend told me that, at his defense, he, Whitley, and Murray Fowler the linguist were the first to arrive. Fowler, anxious to get on with it, said, "Tell me, which of the three following sentences is a metaphor, and why or why not?" The candidate sat, appalled, until Whitley stood up and said, "Murray, if you're going to start that kind of crap, I'm leaving!"

After what seemed hours, Whitley led me to the door so that the committee could reach a decision. "Don't go far," he said quietly. When I was called back for congratulations, I expelled all of my held breath. "Surely it wasn't that bad," someone said. "No," I replied, "that was for the whole process."

Looking back, I am reminded of a conversation I had with a colleague in a locker room. He was complaining about how expensive his divorce had been. "Was it worth it?" I asked.

He looked puzzled and said, "What?" "Well," I said, "usually when you spend a lot of money on something, sooner or later you try to figure out if you got your money's worth." He thought a moment and said, "I guess I did."

Money wasn't the main issue for Ph.D. candidates in English at the University of Wisconsin, for teaching assistants were paid enough to live at a poverty level, even in modest comfort. But we expended a fair amount of time and even more effort. The question is, was it worth it?

Probably, in most cases; definitely, in mine. Over the years, the value of a Ph.D. from the University of Wisconsin (I refuse to add the hyphenated "Madison" to the title) has remained high among all universities and at or near the top among state universities. The degree made me more marketable in the days when it was a seller's market.

After a while, of course, a professional academic has to stand on his or her accomplishments rather than where the degree came from, a lesson that some people from the Ivies find it hard or impossible to learn. The Wisconsin program was valuable because department chairs could be fairly sure that its graduates would be engaged in the critical and scholarly dialogue of the profession and that there was a good chance that they would be productive scholars. What employers could not predict was what kind of work they would do—unlike graduates from the University of Chicago, for example, where dissertations that turned into books bore the unmistakable stamp of Aristotle's *Poetics*. Wisconsin Ph.D.s were expected to have a more or less common body of knowledge in order to pass prelims, but they were given little direction about what topics or approaches to use on their dissertations. For example, William Spanos, who did a dissertation on religious verse drama in England in the 1930s, later founded *Boundary 2*, a militantly anti-humanist, ultra-post-modernist journal. Harold Fromm, from the same era, has mounted an effective counterattack against many of the positions that Spanos represents. Although I had no training in bibliography at Wisconsin and no training anywhere in textual study, the program taught me that I could teach myself what I wanted and needed to know and, by forcing me to read more, and more coherently, than I had done before, took me another step in the process of transforming myself from an addict, drifting among enthusiasms, to a scholar and critic. And, though some academics wonder about the personal cost, into a functioning if by no means confident adult.

Was it too hard? Years later, I saw this slogan on a t-shirt at a swimming meet: When the going gets tough, the sprinters get out. The Ph.D., especially the written examinations and the dissertation, is a kind of training—not for a semester or a year or even the probationary period that leads to tenure, but for a whole professional life. It embodies a social and intellectual and in a broad sense moral commitment. That commitment doesn't always last, but that doesn't mean that the process is flawed. In other words, it wasn't too hard for me.

Was it worth it? I think I got good value. Of course, I still had to learn how to use what I had acquired.

To Market

When I began graduate work at the University of Kansas, I had been acculturated by an undergraduate liberal arts major not to ask what I would do with a Master's in English. It didn't take long to learn from the older graduate students that you tried to find a teaching job, and to do that, on anything like a secure basis at any rate, you had to have a Ph.D. And the better the school from which you got it and the better connected your dissertation director, the more likely you were to get a good job—defined then at a starting salary between $3000 and $3600, at best under eight hundred dollars a year more than I had been making as a beginning newspaper reporter. But the other graduate students were somewhat vague about how one looked for a job and what constituted a good one.

At Wisconsin, the process and goal were made quite clear to us by the students ahead of us, partly because the five-year limit on assistant-ships established one's position in the pipe-line, partly because the graduate students had definite if not always precise views about what it took to succeed in the profession. New students learned from overheard conversations among their seniors about which new Ph.D. was going where, for how much, on the strength of whose recommendations and what credentials. As a result, we didn't need the formal workshops on the job market that became popular, and largely futile, when the fat days ended.

But even the most professionalized graduate students at Wisconsin were not fully aware that the market was changing by the time we were completing our degrees. We should have been alerted that something was up when Quintana brought to his seminar a questionnaire about willingness to take jobs in Southern universities. This will startle a generation grateful for jobs anywhere, but this was only six years after the Brown v. Board of Education decision, state officials and less public forces were opposing de-segregation orders and civil rights marches, and the whole region was generally regarded as an intellectual backwater. Most of us, perhaps all, said that we would not even consider working under those conditions. One student took the opportunity to raise questions about a recent exposé of working conditions for untenured people. "Those people are nothing but whiners," Q. huffed.

In fact, conditions were getting better because even schools in more enlightened areas were having trouble recruiting enough teachers. This was partly a demographic problem: the first baby boomers were due to arrive on campuses in 1963, and the new crop of Ph.D.s had been born at a time when the birth-rate was at its lowest in the country's history. Moreover, the economy created rising expectations among people who would never before have thought of sending their children to college, so a larger percentage of the larger pool would have to be taught. One effect was that even large schools could no longer hire new Ph.D.s at the rank of instructor for limited terms. When the market collapsed and I proposed reinstituting the practice, a colleague who had been a member of Students for a Democratic Society argued that the very rank of instructor was immoral. It had disappeared, I pointed out, for reasons that were historic and economic. Surely a Marxist should understand that.

I didn't understand historical and economic conditions, but I was ready to go on the market—the term Wisconsin people used—at the 1961 Modern Language Association meeting, then and now the hiring hall for the profession. So I joined the association. Membership gave me a subscription to PMLA, the association's learned journal (which published, and still does, four issues a year of scholarly articles; one listing members, departments and names of chairs, and names of publishers and foundations, all with addresses and phone numbers; the annual bibliography; and the convention program) and the right, for an additional fee, to register at the convention, always, in my time, beginning on December 27.

During the fall, I scattered blind letters of application—the Association didn't begin publishing a job list until 1966—to as many chairs as possible, including, out of nostalgia and the feeling that I could survive better there than in a secular context, most of the Jesuit colleges and universities, waited for responses, compared notes with other job-seekers, wondered how to get to Cincinnati, that year's site, taught my classes, and tried, with what attention I had left, to work on my dissertation. As a result, when the MLA announced that the convention would be held in Chicago because Cincinnati did not have enough hotel space, my only reaction was relief because it was a cheap and easy trip from Madison. I did not have enough experience to understand that this was a watershed for the profession—only New York and Chicago were big enough to hold us.

Not that it made much difference to me, for I spent much of my time standing wide-eyed in the Palmer House lobby, impressed just to be there, fighting to get on an elevator or trying to read the badges of people who might be famous or looking among the jostling hordes for a familiar face (and found Jim Scott, also on the market, and the man with whom I had shared the desk in the Wisconsin bullpen). The rest of the time I was being interviewed by at least fourteen different departments. Today, only a potential super-star would have come even close to having that many interviews. Then, I was a fair-to-middling student with recommendations from solid but not prominent people who clearly was not going to complete his dissertation by the beginning of the following academic year. Several of these interviews were solicited by chairs of small departments who had seen my dossier on file at the location provided by the association and had put my name on one of the chalk boards in the large interview hall used by people whose hotel rooms were too remote to be convenient for or too shabby to impress the candidates.

After more than five decades, those interviews have blended with the dozens I later participated in, but the process is the same. Nervous candidates line up at house phones trying to locate their interviewers and set times. Then they line up at elevators trying to get to the right floor. Then they pass other nervous candidates in the hall until they find the right door, whereupon they wait for the previous anxious candidate to come out. After the interview—getting out is more awkward than getting in—they pass another anxious candidate waiting to enter. Inside the room, the interviews cover the same ground: topic of your dissertation and when it will be finished; what the candidate is prepared to teach and what else he or she might able to teach with a little preparation; what the department, school, and area are like; when one might expect to teach upper division courses; salary range (around $6,000 for people with degree in hand that year—Helen White, people said in the halls, had broken the market; and any other incentives that might induce the candidate to consider the position. Meanwhile, the candidate is trying to remember the names of the interviewers, store away details in order to distinguish between this job and all the others, and not say anything outstandingly stupid.

I remember only a few details about that year's interviews. The woman chair of a Protestant denominational college—she'd called me, clearly ignorant of what my Rockhurst degree implied—said doubtfully, on learning my religious affiliation, "Well, we never have hired a Catholic," with just enough tinge of doubt to indicate that she might be desperate enough to consider it. Saint Louis University was willing to interview me for a position in Victorian literature, with a little modern on the side, because I had taken four courses at Wisconsin and possibly because I had a Jesuit background. But I knew that Jim had also applied, and I told them that, if it came down to the two of us, they should hire him because he was a real Victorianist. Back at St. Louis, the chair was asked if he'd hired that hotshot from Wisconsin. (Either my references were better than I imagined or the intervening years have inflated them.) He looked a little puzzled and said, "No, I hired his roommate." The chairman at Wayne State, at the end of a long day, was frank: he'd give me a three year instructorship if I wanted it, but I wouldn't want it. The interview team from Loyola University of Chicago saw me over the remains of what looked like a lavish lunch on room service carts.

I returned to report, wide-eyed, to my dissertation director about my interviews and about the famous names I had seen. Whitley was known for having belonged to the MLA for years but never having gone. He listened patiently to my excited revelations and said, "Ah, yes. I suppose it's all right if you like finding out who has gone mad in Pennsylvania." I hadn't thought of that motive, but it seemed quite reasonable to me, and did for years.

Years later, I have come closer to his view. If one isn't looking to find or fill a job or giving a paper (and, some of us said, the real reason to be on the program is that your friends will know where to find you), the chief point in going is to see one's friends, talk to journal and book editors about work in progress or prospect, and find out who had done what, moved where, or gotten divorced, gone bananas, or, increasingly, fallen ill or died. Of course, initially it was exciting to listen to papers delivered by academic stars or to sessions on exciting new topics or to people one wants to meet. But since most professors rapidly settle into one of two modes, talking or waiting, and shifting fashions in criticism sooner or later render the topics unintelligible or offensive to all but the most trend-conscious among the ageing generations, these do not for most people remain sufficient motives for going to the MLA.

But in 1961 I had all of these motives, especially wanting a job. So I came back full of awe at the size and energy of the meeting. And then waited. Today the wait would probably have been a lot longer, what with an oversupply of qualified candidates who have already finished the dissertation, many of whom might have published several articles and even a book or two. But before the end of January, I had been offered five positions and had to make a decision. Since I was married to a woman with a Ph.D. in English long before the concept of spousal hires was conceived, I had been careful to apply only to schools in metropolitan areas with other colleges nearby so that Barbara could find a teaching job. It wasn't fair to put my career first, but in 1961 we agreed that this seemed the only reasonable thing to do.

The only on-campus visit was to a small Catholic college in a very small town that was anxious to hire both of us and even lend us money with which to buy a house. We visited the school, and though I was flattered at the attention, I was a little uneasy about their hesitation when I mentioned teaching James Joyce, and it was easy for Barbara to convince me that the job would be a dead end.

The other jobs were in major metropolitan areas. One chair told me I could teach graduate courses right away, even before I finished my dissertation. I had a little more confidence than at the beginning of my program at Wisconsin, but I knew that this was ridiculous. The only state university to make an offer was a long way from Wisconsin, and not only didn't I feel ready for the east, I wanted to be close enough to get advice on the dissertation. The University of Detroit was not as far, and it was a Jesuit school. I didn't have a good feeling about Detroit, but I might have accepted (if I had, Joyce Carol Oates wouldn't have gotten the job). Then Loyola University of Chicago made an offer which seemed to fit all the specifications. It was also a Jesuit school like Rockhurst, but it had a Ph.D. program like KU and Wisconsin; it was close to Madison; and two other men from the Wisconsin graduate program, one of whom I knew fairly well, were already teaching there. Most important, one of the faculty members was married to a woman on the faculty of the Catholic women's college next door which offered Barbara a job for as much money as the man in our study group who went to Yale.

So now I was a full-time college teacher. But while I would be paid a good deal more than I had been as a graduate assistant, I would have to teach four courses instead of two, find my way around a new department and a much larger city than I had ever dealt with, and finish my dissertation. Two years had already passed since I had taken generals, so that I had only three more until I had to finish or be paraded before a new generation of graduate students as an object lesson.

Wisconsin graduate students believed that everyone hated the first job—note the underlying assumption—because it wasn't at Wisconsin and therefore probably not as good, because everything was unfamiliar, and because one discovered that having a Ph.D. did not automatically make all problems disappear. I didn't have time to hate Loyola. I enjoyed being in Chicago, except that I was too preoccupied to take full advantage of clubs where Lenny Bruce kept getting busted and now-legendary blues men played. But I could enjoy just walking along the street among a fascinating if bewildering variety of people, buildings, and vistas.

Loyola was less inspiring. Although it was a university and won the NCAA basketball championship while I was there, its physical plant at the Lake Shore campus was not much more impressive than Rockhurst's. It adjoined Lake Michigan, but whoever had laid out the buildings ignored that feature. Although the student union was larger than the Rockhurst cafeteria where I had eaten (and which had been replaced by a handsome modern building shortly after I left), it was recognizably the same kind of architecture—World War II surplus—and the food was about as bad. The English Department was housed in a war-surplus temporary building that reminded me of the barracks I had lived in at Rockhurst, and most of my classes were in another temporary building except for one or two in the field house, next to the tracks of the El. But I could go and look at the lake when I was weary or stressed.

And there was some stress. I still had several chapters of my dissertation to finish. I was teaching twice as many classes with almost twice as many papers to grade, and I was far more worried about making a good impression on my chair and colleagues than I had been under the easy-going and supportive George Rodman. Barbara and I quickly learned to find our way around Chicago, but socially we had a good deal to learn about a lot of things.

One was the Catholic Church. It was more difficult than I had imagined to come back to a Jesuit school. Like Rockhurst, Loyola had a show Jesuit—the one the media thought of when they needed a quotation or a quick and easy ethical opinion. I had been able to ignore Rockhurst's, except when I had him in class, because I saw newspapers rarely and television never. Loyola's was a recurrent embarrassment to the more liberal-minded faculty, priests and laymen alike. And the local parish church, huge, gray, and neo-Gothic, was so large that it didn't feel like a community to a newcomer. But like many Catholics before the Second Vatican Council, we privately dismissed or ignored pronouncements, even orders, that we disagreed with.

Socially, we spent more time with a few of Barbara's colleagues than with mine, who were older, staider, and more conservative. One of her male colleagues introduced me to some of his very Irish friends from undergraduate school, and for one or two summers I tried to continue my modest athletic career by playing softball—the peculiar Chicago variety, with a sixteen-inch ball and no gloves—on the team sponsored by a local bar.

Loyola didn't have as many students or as distinguished a faculty as the University of Wisconsin, but it spread out much farther, for, widely separated from the Lake Shore campus, it had a medical school, a dental school, a Rome branch, and a downtown campus. (A columnist in the student newspaper asked how the Jesuits could claim to educate the whole man when they couldn't even keep their campuses together.) The English faculty was split only between the Lake Shore and the downtown campus on the near North Side, between the historic Water Tower on Michigan Avenue and the night clubs of Rush Street. Senior faculty stayed at one location; juniors like me often commuted downtown to teach our only literature classes at night or on Saturday morning.

My downtown students were almost uniformly older, more pre-occupied, and generally tireder than their more traditional counterparts to the north, and I don't think I ever saw one of them outside of class, even in my brief office hours in the basement of Loyola's building. I felt a little closer to the Lake Shore students because, except for ethnic and gender differences—Rockhurst had no women and its student body was heavily Irish, while at Loyola Italians outnumbered Celts and Germans—they reminded me of my classmates at Rockhurst. Many of them were the first in their families to go to college; they worked hard; and, just out of Catholic high schools, most of them were tractable. Occasionally one would surprise and delight me, like the young man who looked ruefully at the misspellings circled on his paper and said, "Spelling has always been my bête noire." I was more comfortable with him than with the very pleasant but dim student with the same name and from the same suburb as a high-ranking Mafioso. On the other hand, I had my greatest success with a young man who sat in the front row and was always first to raise his hand to call attention to himself and would offer oral prolegomena to his wordy and pretentious papers. One day I snapped and said, "Just give me the paper without the commercial." He stepped back, shocked. Next class he moved to the back row, glared at me, and on his next paper tried to destroy me with his language. He became a much better writer.

Except for him and some nuns who plagiarized their papers (the whole order did, a colleague told me), the Loyola students were the easiest group to teach I have encountered, for if there was a lot they didn't know, they all knew the same things, so that I could count on a common frame of reference. And they seemed to think me a raging sophisticate because I had gone to a Big Ten university and even read things like *New Republic,* took them to hear Dick Gregory talk about civil rights, and used James Baldwin's essays in class. (One student looked at Baldwin's phrase about the third sex and remarked that it worried him because Baldwin seemed to know something he didn't.) For the first time, I felt somewhat like a role model. But like Rockhurst, Loyola was a street car college: most students commuted, so that by five o'clock, the campus was deserted. As a result, I didn't get to know them as well as I'd have liked. And stuck in freshman composition as I was, I wasn't likely to see them in another class.

The faculty also dispersed at the end of the day, except for the Jesuits, and there weren't many of those in the English department. Most of the laymen had commuted either to Northwestern or the University of Chicago for the Ph.D., and they seemed to identify themselves more with their native city than with the profession at large. They tended either to be single and live with a single aged parent or to be married to women named Mary something: Ann, Sue, and so on. I can think of four men who attended professional meetings and published regularly, though a few others either had edited textbooks or were to do so in the boom years just ahead.

My colleagues were good for my shaky confidence. Almost immediately I saw that they were of a different order, professionally speaking, not only from the professors at Wisconsin but many of the graduate students. They seemed content to transmit received information rather than to break new ground, and some of them were not very critical of the information they had gathered. The chairman implied something like this when, after visiting one of my freshman classes, he took me to lunch. Over martinis and cigarettes, his in an elegant holder, he said that, while my comments were probably over the heads of the students, I seemed to be very intelligent. I thanked him and said, "I hope so. After all, I'm a college teacher." He didn't quite sigh or grimace, but he did say, "You'd be surprised."

One episode convinced me that some of my colleagues lacked, if not intelligence, the critical acuity I had been led to value. In one of the department meetings devoted to discussing a particular work—much better than most department meetings—we were asked to read and prepare to discuss an excerpt from Thomas Merton's *The Seven Storey Mountain* in the anthology used for freshman English. I read it as I would any essay, to see what students could learn from it about writing. The more I read, the more I was annoyed by Merton's taste for redundancy and anti-climax. When I pointed this out, a layman who taught the advanced and graduate courses in my field said indignantly, "What do you have against the man Merton?" "I don't have anything against the man," I said. "Just the writer." Years later I was pleased to discover that Evelyn Waugh, who had cut Merton's book by about a third, agreed with me about

Merton's prose, but I didn't need the confirmation and it wouldn't have made my colleagues any more comfortable with the unaccustomed sharpness of the argument. I was uncomfortable because the dialogue in my graduate programs, in and out of class, and for that matter my training at Rockhurst had taught me that the intellectual life was conducted in that way, even when, as was usually the case, I was overwhelmed by it.

My colleagues were good people and no doubt effective teachers, and some were obviously very bright, but I began to realize that I didn't want to be anything like them. For the first time since I began college, I had no one to regard as a model, and at twenty-eight, I was still unformed enough to need one. One night, after a general faculty meeting in which I beat even the Jesuits to the open bar (a sure sign, which I ignored, about an incipient drinking problem), I proclaimed that I wanted to measure up to Jewish intellectuals. Since that was a few years after Norman Mailer set about trying to be a "White Negro," trying to be a Catholic Jew wasn't totally ridiculous, even if I was one jump behind. (Twenty-five years later I was pleased when a friend remarked that I was the blackest white person she'd ever known.) What did I mean by that? I'm not sure I knew, but it had something to do with an approach that was objective, thorough, and probably superior expressed in a witty, direct prose style that was as clean and sharp as a well-tempered blade. I wanted to be an intellectual and a man of the world.

In other words, someone I wasn't. And definitely not someone like two of my colleagues, one decent but dim, the other dim but dumb and given to making inappropriate remarks. Fortunately, two other colleagues showed me that I didn't have to live in that way or even in this world. One was really a couple, David and Jeffrey Spencer. He had a Ph.D. from the University of California-Berkeley and had come to Loyola from Oregon State, where he had Bernard Malamud as a colleague, and she taught at the women's college with Barbara. In departmental gatherings, they looked happily out of place. She was rangy and tweedy enough to fit into a Katherine Hepburn movie; he was dapper in an eighteenth century way and looked as though he might be carrying the sword cane to which he aspired. They had three bright, handsome children and a spacious apartment near their work. Barbara and I wanted their life and did get an apartment like theirs.

Dave was not the leading scholar of the department, but he was active, and he had some name recognition because he had edited some textbooks, the best known on drama. Possibly in order to have someone to talk to, he helped recruit his collaborator Stan Clayes, who was lean, fit, divorced, and not even Catholic. I didn't exactly want to be like them, but they did represent other approaches to the profession.

A year or so after I came, I encountered still another in a new office-mate, Tony LaBranche. Tony had a Ph.D. from Yale, where he was legendary for the oral exam in which he replied to W. K. Wimsatt's "Tell me, Mr. LaBranche, would you like to compare Dr. Samuel Johnson and Charles Baudelaire?" with "No I wouldn't. That's too hard." Cleanth Brooks had agreed, and the rest of the committee had turned on Wimsatt to explain a connection that only he and God understood.

Tony was and I hope still is a diminutive man with bad hair—in the Sixties sense—before most black people had bad hair. He was one of the most consistently alert people I had, or have, met, with a kind of enthusiastic skepticism I found very appealing. He questioned me about my methods and motives and frequently mocked the answers. At a time when I was taking myself very solemnly, he was very good for me. His wife Carol had gone to a Catholic grade school, for which her Jewish mother sewed the finest altar cloths in the circle. Later he took to driving sports cars in amateur races and publishing articles on philosophy. When I checked years later, he was still at Loyola, so outrageously unsuited to its personnel and ethos that he was in danger of becoming an institution.

I could have stayed at Loyola—the chairman told Dave he was delighted with my work but doubted they could keep me—but I was ready to move on. For one thing, I finished my dissertation on the rainy night I mentioned earlier, feeling empty, alone, and somehow complete, though I had no real idea about how to write a book or even an article, let alone to embark on a career of research like those of my best teachers at Wisconsin. However, released from the pressure of the deadline, I had a burst of energy and wrote my first real scholarly article on a Katherine Mansfield story that had puzzled my class and began to mine the dissertation for material to turn into articles.

I also began to search *Forthcoming Books* to find titles related to my work that I could request for review from tolerant editors like the one at

Books Abroad (which, as *World Literature Today*, still responds to my queries). To complete these reviews of no more than three hundred words I had to learn to write not like a diffuse, diffident, or querulous graduate student but directly, in an authoritative tone, like a scholar. The tight rules of the form resembled those of the headlines I had written as a journalist: both make the writer conscious of the smallest elements of language.

I also had to learn where my efforts could be published. Since I had read hundreds of scholarly and critical articles over the past eight years and referred to them by the initials used in the MLA Bibliography (JEGP, PLL, TSLL, PQ, and so on), it may seem that I had not been paying much attention, but I was reading more to see what these exalted beings said than how they said it. Now I began to look at the rows of new journal issues for the possibility that they might accept something I had already done or might do in order to appeal to their special emphasis.

This was a good time for a beginning scholar, especially in twentieth century literature, because in the mid-1950s a number of new journals were being founded: *Modern Fiction Studies* and *Twentieth Century Literature* in 1955, *Critique: Studies in Modern Fiction* in 1956, *Modern Drama* in 1958, *Texas Studies in Literature and Language* and *Extrapolation* (dealing with science fiction) in 1959, *Studies in Short Fiction* and *South Dakota Review* in 1963, *Papers on Language and Literature* in 1965, *Western American Literature* in 1966, *Journal of Popular Culture* and *Southern Humanities Review* in 1967, *Genre* in 1968, *Journal of Modern Literature* in 1970. Subsequently I published in most of them. Far from having backlogs of articles, these editors were actually soliciting them, and they did not always apply exacting standards. One editor warned me off his next issue because he was gritting his teeth and publishing material he had accepted in the early days. For a while, so many of my pieces appeared in these new journals that Tony LaBranche, who maintained an amused detachment at my efforts, asked when I was going to publish in one that somebody had actually heard of. Though I never published in the most formidable-sounding of all, *Journal of English and Germanic Philology* (1897), I was pleased to send him a copy of an article that appeared in *Philological Quarterly* (1922).

But it was difficult, given the Loyola teaching load of four courses a semester, much of it composition, to make the kind of progress I wanted.

Other universities, I heard, had lighter loads, and I decided to try to find a job at one of them. And perhaps more challenging colleagues. I missed the critical and competitive attitude I had known at Wisconsin and was occasionally reminded of during visits from friends like the one who, relaxing in our apartment the morning after a strenuous MLA meeting, sipped his Bloody Mary and said, "Just think. At this very moment, X [a contemporary at UW] is vomiting in the back of a bus on the way to Des Moines, Iowa, which proves there's a God."

Besides my personal tastes and ambitions, there was another reason to be dissatisfied with Catholic higher education. Barbara seemed to enjoy teaching at Mundelein, the women's college that was a block closer to our apartment than my office was. She had been to a women's college, and she was an excellent role model for her students and a far better scholar than most of her colleagues. Perhaps she was too good. She was asked to write a critique of and propose revision for the curriculum at her college, and she did so in her efficient and uncompromising fashion. Shortly thereafter, she was informed that her services were longer needed.

I didn't understand for years that she had been fired summarily, perhaps because I didn't probe behind the formula in which she had been terminated and certainly because I began immediately to think of what the loss of a second income would mean to us and what she might do instead. This was more ignorant than insensitive, but it may have accounted for her inability to join my celebration on finishing the dissertation. At the time, I thought that it was a good thing I had, because supporting us was now up to me.

Barbara could undoubtedly have moved to another college in the area, but we had begun the process of adopting our first child, I was finishing my dissertation, and we were facing up to cares of adult life we had been able to ignore. She was disillusioned with teaching, and neither of us was sure that we wanted to raise children in a third-floor walk-up, however spacious. Our daughter arrived in June and happily distracted us from other concerns.

As a result of these changes, I decided, just after my thirtieth birthday in the fall of 1964, to go, with Barbara's consent, on my second jobhunt. This time I pared down the list to universities that might offer what I wanted—no Catholic schools were on it, and a place where she might teach was not a consideration—and flew, for the first time in a jet, for my first visit to New York.

Because I already had a job and because I had fewer interviews, I had more time to talk to old acquaintances and make new ones, attend some sessions, at most of which I did not find the level of discourse as intimidating as before, and catch up on who had gone mad in Pennsylvania. Even more enlightening was a conversation I heard late one night in the hotel bar between the chairs of the two most prestigious departments on the west coast, men whose critical work I had read and respected. Sure that they were discoursing about the cutting edge of criticism, I listened to the one say, in slurred tones, "The trouble with you, Mark, you old sumbitch, is you're hiring all the best people."

"Nah, that's noh true. Lemme look at your list." He ran a finger down the piece of paper. "Yeah, I'm going to hire him and him. You can have him. You don't want him."

Beside that memory my interviews have paled. I remember only two. The one with two representatives of the University of Southern California, both of whose names I had encountered in journals, was hectic. They took turns answering a series of phone calls and talking to me. When asked when I expected to finish my dissertation, I said casually, "Oh, I finished that last year." The man on the phone heard this and, said, over his shoulder, "Hire him!" The interview with the University of California-Santa Barbara didn't produce any good lines, but Philip Damon, the chairman, was intelligent, charming, and persuasive.

Back in Chicago, I played with my daughter, who had been puzzled by my unaccountable and unprecedented absence, and waited for the results. USC made an offer in mid-January, but I was not sure that I wanted to bring up children in Los Angeles. So even though UCSB was less well known, I called Damon to ask if Santa Barbara had made a decision, a legitimate practice in any kind of marketplace, even academic. He said that he would have to check with some colleagues, but within the hour he called to offer me a job and somewhat more money and far better surroundings than USC. I accepted immediately. I never saw or spoke to him again, for as I was moving to Santa Barbara, he was moving to Berkeley to join the classics department.

As soon as I got the written offer, I told my chairman. He mentioned a possible counter-offer and a somewhat nebulous plan to reduce the teaching load, but he could not promise me upper division and graduate courses in my field. Finally he offered suitable regrets and congratulations and accepted my resignation.

Damon and I were not the only ones on the move. Two of my colleagues, energized I think by my attempt to better myself, also went on the job market. The Chicago native got a considerably higher salary at a new state-supported college on the northwest side; my Wisconsin contemporary found a job at a liberal arts college in Indiana, where he later became chairman and had—I was going to say taught—Dan Quayle in a freshman English class. A year or so after we left, Loyola went to a three-course teaching load.

California Dreaming

"You haven't got a chance, kid....They hate Jews."

"But I'm not Jewish...."

"It will make no difference," Yossarian promised, and Yossarian was right. "They're after everybody."

Catch-22

In the summer of 1965 I finished teaching summer school at Loyola, helped Barbara pack, and saw her and the children—we adopted a second daughter only weeks before the move—off to stay with her parents while I dealt with the movers, closed the apartment, and for the first time experienced the thrill that comes when the only key left in the case starts the car. I had a sense that I was going to an entirely new life in an entirely new world, unconscious for a while of the irony that, because my father had made a deal with his Boonville colleague Joe Jeff Davis, my new car had the words "Davis / Boonville" affixed to the trunk lid.

Route 66, or what had not been subsumed into the Interstate system, was more or less familiar until I reached Albuquerque, home of my aunt and her many descendants. After that, the territory was unknown and, since the Watts riots had broken out while I was en route, probably hostile. As far as I knew, the only way to Santa Barbara was through Los Angeles, and I had no desire to drive through the middle of a riot. However, in Seligman, Arizona, a friendly gas station owner traced on my map the route he called the Palmdale cutoff which took me across more desert to the first citrus groves I had ever seen, incredibly green after two days in arid land and finally, from the top of a hill, to my first sight and smell of the Pacific. Then, and again when, early one morning in Santa

Barbara when I saw my first pelican diving into the harbor, my sense that I had discovered a brave new world seemed to be confirmed.

But as I drove around Santa Barbara proper and up and down U.S. 101 and Hollister Avenue looking for a place to live and then getting oriented to the social as well as the geographical layout of a new town, I realized that it was even stranger than it was brave. If I had a problem in Chicago, whether with the government or with Sears, I might have to make a few phone calls, but if I said the magic words "Let me talk to your supervisor" often enough, I could get to someone who could take care of it. In California, though the people were far more relaxed, nobody seemed to be in charge. And after living in a city so racially and ethnically mixed that I could spin the FM dial and not be able to count on getting even the same language twice in a row, Santa Barbara seemed so up-tight that I could laugh with the disc jockey on the only AM station that didn't play terminally white bubble-gum rock ("XERB, Mighty ten-ninety over Los Angeles; rhythm and blues and racing news") at the idea of someone phoning in a request for a soul tune from there. I was less amused at a conversation among a group of teenagers about going down to Los Angeles to get in on the white-is-right side of the Watts riots, making history as the first American civil disturbance to be televised. More humorous, though with disturbing overtones, was the play of some neighborhood boys ducking behind trees and walls and making shooting noises at each other. An older girl came out of the house and asked if they were playing cops and robbers. "No," one said, "cops and niggers." "That's Negroes," she said, and left them to their game.

But Santa Barbarans were less racist than clueless. Hispanics made good house servants. Asians were industrious and docile. Blacks were, as the story indicates, on television. Santa Barbara was cut off by mountain range from reception of all but the single local TV station and, as far as long-term residents were concerned, all of the problems of Los Angeles to the southeast. Periodically a letter to the newspaper would concede that while Santa Barbara might have haze now and then, it definitely did not and could never have smog. And the realtor who showed me rental housing said that of course Santa Barbara had no slums. I had driven around by myself enough to see that while there were no projects or tenements, some of the housing was pretty shoddy, however vivid the flowers on the surrounding vegetation, but for a change I didn't argue the point.

Years later, I was back in southern California, east rather than north of Los Angeles, and one evening I drove out into the foothills with some colleagues who were seeing the area for the first time. One looked at the flowers and the evening light that seems to outline the hills with purple neon tubing and said, "It doesn't look real." "Oh," I replied, "it's real all right. It's just not serious." But that was a better counter than it was analysis. Finally, after years of teaching Thomas Pynchon's *The Crying of Lot 49*, a fantastic and convoluted novel published while I was living in California, I realized that it was not so much an example of black humor but, as far as setting, character, and ethos are concerned, an historical novel.

But at the time I was more concerned with the exciting possibilities of my professional future than with analyzing my surroundings. The lean Texan from Pampa who drove the Mayflower van reinforced my illusion by remarking, as we paused from unloading, that he hoped to move me back East when I got an even better job. When I said something modest, he added that they sure wouldn't move me all the way out here if they didn't think highly of me. Neither of us knew that a dozen other assistant professors of English were on their way to Santa Barbara or that roughly the same number were leaving it. Or that hundreds of other men and women with recent doctorates were criss-crossing America to teach the hordes of Baby Boomers cramming their way into all of the old and an increasing number of new or upgraded institutions of higher learning.

The University of California-Santa Barbara was one of the upgrades. Until 1944, it was known as Santa Barbara State College. At one point it was located physically on one of the hills midway between Los Padres National Forest and the Santa Barbara Channel three thousand feet below and structurally between the University system at the top of the California hierarchy and the State colleges—now called universities—below which the junior colleges rested at academic sea level. Then it was promoted to university status and moved to what had been a training base for Marine fighter pilots on a bluff which descended into the Pacific.

The campus looked like the set of a 1930s Hollywood musical, with lush vegetation I had never seen before clustered around the homogeneous if not distinguished buildings and almost hiding the survivors from the military past and dotted across broad lawns traversed by students who sometimes seemed exclusively blonde and tanned and who came to class with feet covered only by the tar that had sweated up through the sand on the beach a few hundred yards away. (In fact, since the students had to be from the top 12 ½ percent of their high school class, they were very good, and two of the five brightest I've encountered in forty years of teaching were in my classes that first year. I also got to teach real literature—and in the daytime). The Union, though not as large as Wisconsin's, had an even better view of bluffs arcing out into the ocean.

The faculty had a good deal in common with the buildings. Some, who had been there since the days when it had been a state college, were functional but not designed for current needs. They had been hired primarily as teachers, and they were overmatched and overshadowed by the few men with nationally recognizable names who had been hired after World War II and by most of the younger men, many of them disciples of Yvor Winters at Stanford, who had recently been tenured or were clearly about to be. One woman had been my contemporary at Wisconsin, another instance of the incestuous nature of the academic world. But the most memorable was Scott Momaday, who had recently published an edition of the poems of Frederick Goddard Tuckerman, exalted by Winters and unknown to everyone but his disciples. Scott's Indian ancestry was a matter of interest, even of curiosity, but it did not seem especially important.

None of my group was that exotic, though one was a woman, which was at least unusual; one claimed to be part Cherokee and was married to the daughter of an oil company executive; one was Jewish; and one was a Scotsman. We had solid, commonplace first names: two Roberts, Jane, Donald, John, James, Frank, Arthur, Dennis, Gerald, Bruce, and, a little unusual, Joel. One parted his name in the middle, a good move considering the precedent of a past chair, W. Hugh Kenner, and a subsequent one, H. Porter Abbott. One was from a blue-collar family in Michigan; one was probably upper-middle-class, from St. Louis; I was mid-mid, from Missouri; one was an Oklahoman; one was from Texas and was thought by the rest to talk even funnier than I did after a few drinks. Most of the others were born into professional families, and many of those came from somewhere in the East. Two were probably related to me, if we had bothered to look far enough back, through the Cary connection. Of those whose birth dates I can find, one man was born in 1932, one in 1940, others between 1933 and 1938. Judging from appearances, the rest probably fell within that span. All but three of us were married, four of us to women who had or were working on doctorates, one of whom now has the most prestigious scholarly appointment of the whole group. (None of these academic marriages survived the seventies; one other barely made it into the decade. I don't know about the others, but if only four of nine ended in divorce, we didn't hurt the national average.)

Our doctorates came mostly from predictable sources: three from the Ivy League; three from the Big Ten; two from the Pacific Coast Conference; one from a place I never knew or have forgotten. The others had degrees from smaller, if solid, programs: University of Connecticut, Washington University in St. Louis, and Claremont Graduate School. With the spread of our major fields, we could have started a solid upper-division and graduate program: two in medieval literature, three in Renaissance, shading back to earlier drama; three in Eighteenth Century; one in Nineteenth Century; three in modern, nicely divided among poetry, fiction, and creative writing, English and American. Most of us were very ambitious.

Though we didn't think of the years at Santa Barbara in this way, and I didn't until now, they were like a post-doctoral fellowship in the sciences, designed to introduce new Ph.D.s to systems and methods different from the ones they were trained in and to acculturate them to professional life. There was one difference: we learned not from the senior professors in the department but from each other. On campus, we talked about what we were writing, to which journals we might send the results, where to find useful material for new work, what we had seen that the others might be able to use—in short, how to manage our careers. In a way, it was like being back at Wisconsin, except that we had the confidence of those who had gotten through prelims and dissertation, we had a better idea of where our professional lives were going, and we had more disposable income. As a doctoral candidate, I had felt that my colleagues set a standard I could not attain. At Loyola, I had felt that the standard was set too low. But at Santa Barbara, it felt just right: enough to push me to work harder and better but not impossible to equal.

It may seem surprising that our ambition did not make us competitive, though we were often exacting and sometimes mischievous. Some of us exchanged drafts of work in progress, getting peer review in the literal and best sense. A friend said of a piece I had written, "It was very interesting on page 16 and from page 32 on." I said of his, "Did you use an outline?" "No." "Well, you should." Cut and structured, respectively, both pieces were later published. Some people had thinner skins, like the Renaissance specialist who handed me the draft of an article on Shakespeare. I scanned the first page and noted that the argument didn't seem to be going anywhere. "Well," I said, "I think you need to...." and almost got paper cuts on eight fingers when he snatched it back. (He subsequently re-tooled in linguistics, perhaps because he thought that it was a less crowded and exacting field. He seemed to have an eye for the main chance that made even some of our group a little nervous. One of my friends predicted that he would be a dean some day, and he did become an associate dean before taking up with lawyers.)

Besides critiquing each other's work, we kept tabs on submissions, sympathized at rejections, and rejoiced at acceptances. One of my most ambitious and subsequently most successful peers and I played games with each other. We were both terminal mail junkies, but my office was closer to the departmental boxes. If I saw a tell-tale envelope in his slot, I would dial his number and, without saying hello or identifying myself, say in hollow tones, "There's a large brown envelope in your mail box." Soon I would hear the sound of his characteristic footsteps coming down the hall, pass my office, return, and stop at my door. "You son of a bitch," he would say, and depart. Once my phone rang and I heard the fatal words. I went to the box, opened the envelope, and returned to pick up the phone. "An editor wants me to evaluate a manuscript for him," I said, holding the receiver at an angle to protect my hearing from the expected response, "You son of a bitch!" But he was resilient, energetic, and talented, and soon he was working on a parody of "Briggflatts," the poem by Basil Bunting, the most prominent of several Englishmen-in-Residence that the department seemed to be able to hire at will because of the unfilled positions, referred to as FTE (Full Time Equivalent) lines, that it and every other department in the university system had squirreled away.

Some of us enjoyed other forms of competition. Every noon, this friend and I would lunch at the union and then go to the pool tables for games that, like the ping-pong in *Catch-22*, became so interesting that they were ridiculous. He once confided that his ambition was to get tenure, move to a house in the hills rising above Santa Barbara, quit the Modern Language Association, cash in some stocks, and buy a pool table. He did quit the MLA, but he moved on to another ocean, and I don't think he got the pool table.

He and I and several others who felt the need for more physical forms of competition played faculty intramural basketball and volleyball and, with some of our older colleagues, entered a team in the city softball league during its season and played pickup games at the university at other times. After all of these, jock camaraderie required a few beers after the contest.

Not everyone shared the illusion of the ageing jocks, but everyone could and most did go to the numerous parties we gave among ourselves and attended at the home of the very hospitable chair, Bill Frost. There was a great deal of drinking but, at that point, not many signs of drunkenness—though the child of a nursing mother showed hangover symptoms on at least one occasion. Some UCSB undergraduates waged something like a holy war over the respective virtues of marijuana and LSD, at least until several acid-heads reportedly burned out their corneas by staring oh-wow at the sun, but none of the faculty seemed to be using controlled substances (we still did not think of alcohol as a drug) or even tobacco. And since I had quit smoking the day after the Surgeon General's report early in 1964, I would have noticed that. Nor, as far as I could tell, which at that stage was not very well, was anyone engaging in extramarital sex. Dr. Samuel Johnson is supposed to have said that a man is seldom so innocently employed as when he is making money. We were more interested in professional advancement, but the line seemed to fit us.

Mostly we worked. Santa Barbara had a fairly good library considering its short history, and a daily shuttle would bring books from UCLA or take faculty members there to browse the stacks. Support for travel to professional meetings and for research was plentiful. My trips to New York City and to the Humanities Research Center in Austin to look at Ronald Firbank's unpublished notebooks helped me to learn something about archival research and to give me other kinds of experience that would not lengthen my vita but would enrich my life.

At the time, I just did what everyone else seemed to be doing. But I had an additional incentive. Barbara had given up her career to raise children—we adopted our son in California in a process much more relaxed than the ones in Chicago—and I had the burden not merely of supporting the family but of representing it in the academic world. She complained only once, when, to save money, I failed to renew the Modern Language Association membership for both of us, which meant that she didn't appear in the annual membership list. That was symbolic to her in ways I should have understood.

She was left with the children, toddlers at best, and the society of the other wives, at least one of whom envied her education and assurance. She couldn't even drive, having given it up after her first look at Chicago traffic. There were few other outlets. The Catholic Church was in those days under the control of the very conservative Cardinal McIntyre. The local parish was notable chiefly for its large crying room where parents could take unruly infants, and for its pastor, who got laryngitis every time a topic came up which might attract McIntyre's attention. The only other schools in the area where, theoretically, she might ultimately teach were a conservative religious institution and a junior college, neither of which she would have considered. For one quarter in our second year she taught a section of freshman English, and even that wasn't using her training and talents.

But at the time, I accepted the situation as normal, helped (more than most men but never enough) with the children and enjoyed it, and worked as much as I could. If all this seems too good to be true, it was. At some level, we knew that the department wasn't going to tenure two eighteenth century people or two modern poetry specialists out of the same year, and we had heard the names of people who had come and gone before us. Besides, I had seen instructors and assistant professors come and go at the University of Wisconsin, including one who was not even considered for tenure because, the senior professors were supposed to have said, his book already in press would not get good reviews. Others had moved to other jobs without leaving rumors among the graduate students.

And Loyola had lulled me. It was possible that the nerdiest of my colleagues would not get tenure, but in looking around, I found it difficult to believe that the department had ever got rid of anyone before. At Santa Barbara, I could see that my friends were exceptionally able and intelligent and thought that it would be a waste of time and talent to let any of us go. What I hadn't counted on was the university's desire to boot-strap itself to a level parallel with Berkeley and Los Angeles. There was plenty of money and plenty of unfilled positions, and it must have seemed to the senior members of the department that they could keep looking until they found just the right person for every available slot. I also hadn't realized that the department had an unofficial policy of filling tenure lines with people brought in from outside—at least two at the beginning of our second year and, I later realized, a number of others in the recent past.

This was happening all over the country. Wealthier or more upward striving departments—especially new ones like the University of California branches at San Diego and Irvine and the State University of New York at Buffalo—could try to achieve instant prominence by raiding their slower neighbors. To put it another way, though the money involved is very different, they didn't have time for the farm system (tenure-track assistant professors) to produce; they went to the free agent market. In the process, which boomed in the mid-1960s, a lot of money changed hands and a lot of full professors changed places.

So those of us at Santa Barbara were not just competing with other assistant professors but with people who had a running start. But when we did consider the possibility that we might move on, through choice or necessity, the job market was so good that, as a classicist said, the money piling up in the retirement fund almost cried out to be used to pay a moving company. But some of us thought that we had found a home.

Cannier than I, my most worldly colleague wanted to call our softball team the Flobots, short for "floating bottom," the term for expendable lower ranks who came and went at the bidding of tenured faculty at the largest and most prestigious universities. And privately, like the audience of a Hollywood platoon movie, we may have speculated about who might get it first—the Southerner with the funny accent and the big ears? The wise-cracking kid from Brooklyn? The slim aesthete who seemed too frail for battle conditions? But as in combat, the situation was tolerable only if we believed that if something bad were to happen at all, it would happen to someone else. And perhaps it wouldn't.

The boom atmosphere in American higher education, especially intense in California, conspired with our own hopes and illusions to make us feel that there was room for everyone. The UCSB chancellor, Vernon I. Cheadle, consistently forecast almost unlimited growth in the best of all possible state university systems. Not only would there be more and more students but enrollment would be capped at UCLA and Berkeley so that the student body at the other branches, UCSB more than others, would rise until our campus was the equal in size, with quality not far behind, of the two flagship schools. The corollary, not always subtly implied, was that departments would have to double in size and there would be enough tenure to go around. In context—which included pundits at all levels and in all fields, including the Association of Departments of English—and allowing for administrator's windage, he did not seem off the mark.

This optimism was further inflated by what seemed like weekly visits from publishers' representatives asking about possible textbook ideas— nothing vulgar like a freshman English textbook, of course—and producing contracts for the barest outlines. Several of my near-contemporaries at Wisconsin edited anthologies, one of poetry, one of what would now be called urban studies, one of essays on existentialism. The Loyola graduate student who had been a colleague of Barbara's produced one, perhaps two, and left the academy to become an editor. I was given a contract to produce a collection of essays on theory of the novel in the innocent days before Francophilia spread like a virus through the American academy. And I had published several articles, had been commissioned to write another, and was doing research that would lead to still more and, I hoped, to a book. So a fairly rosy view of my tenure prospects, if things kept going this way for another four years, was not unwarranted.

Some people decided during their first year that whether or not the department might think them desirable, they wanted no part of it. The two single people departed for newly-founded branch universities located in cities where they had done doctoral work. One of the nicest and most sensible of the married men in the next year's cadre had been informed by the chairman's wife that he was living in a part of town inappropriate for a university professor. That soured him, and he took a job in Canada before the Viet Nam war heated up and the Canadians grew weary of

Americans moving across the border and taking the best jobs.

But the rest of us, and certainly I, thought that if we worked hard and successfully we would be safe. That revealed our ignorance of the official system and even more of the department's private and unwritten rules of evaluation. We didn't understand the first because our position was equivocal. We taught some large sections of freshman literature courses, but the real scut work went to the graduate students, relatively few by Big Ten standards, and to Associates, at that time mostly people with M.A. degrees, who mostly taught non-credit courses in a sophisticated version of remedial composition (called Subject A) on renewable one-year contracts. The assistant professors didn't teach graduate or even the core upper division undergraduate courses, but we assumed that those naturally went to the senior staff. I was content because I found it far more reasonable to stand in line behind Hugh Kenner than behind his virtually unpublished and not otherwise professionally active counterpart at Loyola. After all, we were asked to serve on M.A. oral examinations, and we were given copies of the proposed revision of the graduate program.

Coming from a dozen different graduate programs, each of us naturally thought that the program should be more like the one he had successfully completed. Our most competitive member called a meeting at a favorite bar in order to prepare our responses to the draft over a few beers and a few games of pool afterwards. Only one man refused the invitation outright, and we didn't think highly of his future in the profession. He turned out to be politically more astute than the rest of us, for he was the only one of my cadre to be tenured in the department at UCSB.

The trouble with some of us, as the department's leading scholar was reported to have said, was that we were too visible and too audible. The former chair put it another way: if you don't publish, the dean gets you; if you do publish, we do.

My competitive friend and I had published most, so we were the first to get the chop. The news created panic or depression, depending on the temperament of the recipient. If it could happen to them.... We weren't fired, exactly; we were merely told that we had not been recommended for merit increases at a department meeting held early in November of our second year. This apparently didn't mean that we would have to leave at once. Probably we could have finished out our probationary period,

85

another four years, but neither of us was inclined to slink down the corridor walls shaking bells and crying "Unclean, unclean."

The chair—the third and least distinguished since I was hired—made clear to me, at any rate, that I had no future in the department. The reasons: I was older than some of my cadre with less time to develop, and I was publishing on minor literary figures. Later I heard that I had been approved for a merit increase until an associate professor asked that my case be reconsidered. He had been tenured on the strength—everything being relative—of a slender monograph, issued by an Yvor-Winters friendly chapbook publisher, consisting of his few articles on the same topic. When I heard of it, I innocently asked when he might expect reviews, and he may have thought I was trying to get at him. He was wrong about that but not about the fact that, from his point of view, I was insufficiently deferential to his rank. Or he may have been acting, some of my colleagues thought, as the agent of a senior professor.

Probably this had nothing to do with my being...discouraged from staying...and I shouldn't have taken it personally. But even if I'd realized the economic and other factors that led to rapid turnover, I would still have felt like Yossarian in *Catch-22* who, asks why he refuses to fly, says it's because people are trying to kill him. Why does he think so? Because every time he flies people shoot at him. They're not shooting at him, the reply comes; they're shooting at everybody. "What difference does that make?" he asks, with what still seems impeccable logic.

Whether they were shooting at me or whether I had run into some flak, it was clear that I needed to find a more sympathetic department. There was not much time to apply for jobs, but the first MLA job list had appeared, and, in far more panic than the first two jobs, I sent out applications and got two interviews at MLA. Fortunately, I had managed to secure a place on the program for the first time, and UCSB paid my way. The session, to discuss the feasibility of compiling a book-length list of critical terms for fiction, was pleasant, though the project went no further. The sympathy and indignation of people I had known at Wisconsin, Loyola, and Santa Barbara were both welcome and painful. Given the chance, I would have crept back repentantly to Loyola, but there was no opening for me.

The interview team from the University of Oklahoma did not seem as high-powered as the one from UCSB two years earlier, but its members seemed a great deal more pleasant and far more impressed with my dossier, and in my emotional state that seemed far more important. I was invited for an on-campus interview which went so well that I came away remembering the names not just of the inevitable Wisconsin Ph.D.s but of everyone in the department, the first and only time I have possessed that skill. When the chair called to offer me the job a week later, I accepted. With more time, I could probably have gotten a job at a more prestigious university, but I wanted to be settled; Oklahoma, closer to my home in the Midwest—my mother's death the previous summer helped to make that look more desirable than before—seemed a potential refuge; and from the Oklahoma department's reaction to my research, published and in progress, tenure seemed virtually certain.

Back in Santa Barbara, I struggled through a bout of Asian flu with my family and most of my colleagues, spent the research money I had been awarded, and endured the condolences of my friends. My competitive colleague had found a job in a much better department; another had secured a fellowship that was his ticket out. I remarked to my second and most sociable chair that the department was like the old Kansas City Athletics, who supposedly had great depth at every position: one team going, one team playing, and one team coming. Too much so, he agreed only a little regretfully. When I told the current chair the salary OU had offered—higher than UCSB was paying—he asked me to put that in my letter of resignation so that he could use it to get more money from the dean for his new squad of assistant professors. Sensitivity was not his greatest virtue; I had already decided, and told my friends, that he was like the manager of the Central Station in Conrad's *Heart of Darkness* who "inspired neither love nor fear, nor even respect....He had no genius for organizing, for initiative, or for order even....He had no learning, and no intelligence. His position had come to him—why? Perhaps because he was never ill...."

One of my friends said, to try to mitigate our distress, that all of us would get tenure somewhere, someday. Two I cannot trace; the rest of us did, at schools at least as good as UCSB, though some hung on there for as much as another seven years, and have had active and productive careers. One man won the first MLA prize given for the outstanding scholarly book of the year; another, after years of being a scholar and biographer, wrote a memoir so good that I am not even envious. Collectively we have written and edited several dozen books and published articles into three figures. So I guess we weren't permanently damaged.

Even had we known the future in the spring of 1967, we would not have been much consoled. I at least felt like Dante Gabriel Rossetti when Holman Hunt's departure signaled the end of the Pre-Raphaelite Brotherhood: "So now the whole Round Table is dissolved." If none of us was Arthur or Lancelot, we felt that there were plenty of Mordreds to go round.

A few years later, one of us arranged a cash bar meeting of former Santa Barbara assistant professors of English at a MLA meeting in San Francisco. My competitive friend was still too bitter to attend, but enough people did to make the gathering bigger than most publishers' free cocktail parties. People hired after our group had not been as lucky on the job market as we had been.

By the early 1970s, hard times had fallen on UCSB and the whole University of California system. Ronald Reagan, elected governor in 1966, fired its chancellor. Stunned faculty liberals mounted a protest which, because they had never anticipated anything like it and had therefore not bothered to form an organization or even to support the American Association of University Professors, was feeble and belated. Reagan's attack on the university was popular with a large segment of the voters, and the number grew when the Free Speech movement at Berkeley turned into the anti-war riots of the late 1960s that led to the burning of the Bank of America building in Isla Vista, the student community adjoining the UCSB campus. Proposition 13 passed, cutting property taxes and putting further strains on the state budget. For a while, the University system coasted along on the surplus FTE positions it had piled up, but by the mid-1970s, about the time I was promoted to professor, I looked at a UCSB catalogue and saw that the English department had achieved the final solution to the assistant professor problem.

In 1967, of course, I didn't know any of this. We sold the house on which we had closed the day the chair informed me of the department's decision; Barbara and the (now three) children flew to stay with her parents; and I dealt with the movers and handed over all the keys. The last night I slept at a friend's house and left before anyone else was awake.

XERB wasn't on at that hour, so I listened to KRLA playing the Mamas and the Papas' hit "California Dreaming. When XERB began its broadcast day, I switched to it and listened until, as I entered the low mountain range west of Palmdale, the signal faded.

"Find the Excellence"

—Bumper sticker for OU fund-raising campaign

The move to Oklahoma didn't at first go as smoothly as the move to California two years earlier. When I stopped for gas on the south side of Route 66 in Seligman, Arizona, a gas station owner just as friendly as the one on the north side who had steered me around the Watts riots two years earlier told me that I had a bad alternator and he just happened to have one to replace it. It was Saturday afternoon, I was in a hurry, and I wasn't aware that I had a choice. I watched the needle on the charge dial swing back and forth until I got to Tucumcari, New Mexico, where an even nicer gas station owner said that the real problem was my battery. The rest of the way to Oklahoma, the needle behaved itself.

I had been through if not exactly to Oklahoma several times and had less unfavorable impressions of it than most Americans. It certainly looks arid when approached from the east, but everything is always compared to what, and I was making my second approach from the west, and in contrast to most of the land from the coastal range through the Texas Panhandle, it looks positively lush. My grandfather had spoken scornfully of the natives—"Sooner? Sooner steal than work!"—but he had a delightful tendency to exaggerate. When I was shutting down utilities in Santa Barbara, I gave my forwarding address for the final bill. Everyone I talked to said, "Norman! My parents/uncle/sister came from/still lives in Tulsa/Checota/Ardmore." They seemed pleased that I was moving to the land of their ancestors.

I even knew a little about Norman besides what I'd seen on my interview visit. Four years earlier, driving from Chicago to visit Barbara's parents in Texas, we had spent the night in Norman and gone to Mass on

Easter Sunday. Having left winter in Chicago and driven into late spring, we were struck not only by the contrast between the tanned and healthy-looking natives and the pasty winter complexions we were accustomed to but also by the simplicity of the church building, which looked more like a Congregational church than like the large and ornate structures in the Chicago diocese. On our way out of town, we had driven by the north edge of the university and seen mostly grass and the upper tiers of the football stadium.

I'd lived near the University of Missouri and been a fan of the University of Kansas long before I went there. I did not have good associations with the OU football team, which casually rolled over the other teams in the Big Eight season after season. But now, in the post-Wilkinson, pre-Switzer years, the team was, from an academic's point of view, encouragingly if uncharacteristically mediocre. Besides, there had been considerable fan-fare, even in *Time* magazine, about the search for a dynamic new president to replace the venerable George Lynn Cross, longest-sitting president in the school's history, who would raise OU from the comfortable swamp of regional respectability into the fertile fields of national prominence. They found J. Herbert Holloman, former Under-secretary of Commerce in the current Democratic administration and before that an executive in a major corporation.

And the English department had found two other assistant professors and me in the biggest hiring year since the post World War II boom. A few years earlier, an unidentified but nationally known scholar was supposed to have said, at an unspecified event at an undisclosed location, that the department was the most underrated in the country. True or not, the department had recently lost three prominent members to raids by wealthier and more ambitious departments.

When I arrived in Norman in June, 1967, to wait for the movers and my family, to phone in the grades from my courses at Santa Barbara, and to prepare to teach three summer school courses, I should have realized how badly the department needed bodies, but I was too harried to look at structural matters.

I had wanted to be taken seriously as a scholar and to be able to teach advanced courses, but it was surprising and a little disconcerting to realize, during the on-campus interview, that I was regarded—to use a term then popular among younger scholars on the make—as a fast gun. (Today my five years of full-time teaching, five articles, and a textbook contract would possibly, though not certainly, get me to the preferred pool of job candidates.) I was assigned to teach a literature survey course, a senior-graduate level course in the modern English novel, and a seminar. I was not sure that I wanted to be taken all that seriously.

When I had the leisure to look at who was doing what and why, I could see that the department not only didn't have a floating bottom, it barely had a bottom at all. It was top-heavy (with more tenured than untenured people) and, from my perspective, showing signs of age. The people who had moved on had not been replaced, but my two new colleagues and I filled the lines vacated by retirements. Several women who had been hired during the male teacher shortage of the Second World War were about to retire. When I interviewed, the department had only three (male) assistant professors with doctorates, two (female) with M.A. degrees, and a permanent instructor who wasn't quite tenured because, married to another member of the department, she was ineligible by reason of the university's nepotism rule. The other woman was an associate professor who had received the doctorate from OU. Since none of the four taught graduate or even, except for Methods of Teaching English, advanced undergraduate courses, they were not regarded as real faculty members.

There were other survivals from an earlier age: in the campus telephone book, married faculty members had an asterisk before their names, presumably to indicate the necessity for "Mr. and Mrs." on social invitations, and the organization for faculty wives was called University Dames. At least I think so; I'm not going to stir up trouble by asking any-one. The first faculty wife to speak to Barbara invited her to a sorority fashion show. So when, a few years later, the department interviewed its first woman candidate since Germany invaded Poland, I adapted the line from a song and apologized for the department's awkwardness because we'd never done this with "a real live girl." She and I were friends for a quarter century, so for once I judged my audience correctly. The fact that the most senior professor, until the day he retired, addressed her only as "Miss," despite her doctorate, may have made my attitude look good in contrast.

The department was more liberal in its attitude towards blacks, for though it had none on the faculty (and the first black man allowed or brave enough to buy a house in Norman joined the faculty when I did), several black students had successfully completed the doctoral program well before most other departments began to recruit them. And there was if anything the reverse of anti-Semitism: four of the five chairs I served under were Jewish. The most senior professor, a staunch Presbyterian, had reservations about Roman Catholics. But he put a high value on connections with Cornell, where he had studied with Lane Cooper, and on publishing scholars. The most productive of his immediate juniors, another Cornell man, and I were both Catholics. That brought his value systems into conflict, but he managed it quite gracefully.

Even after the department hired a woman, it remained a men's club. During a discussion of what specialties we most needed to fill, a colleague said impatiently, "What's the problem? We just find the best man and hire him." Another, arguing for the virtues of direct English instead of scholarly jargon, said, "Take Davis. He writes stuff a wife can understand." And for years, candidates were asked if they played golf, and search committees were clearly biased towards scholar-athletes, though the hyphenated terms could be reversed and the first subordinated if the candidate looked physically active. The English department might not publish more than the History department, but we could over-run them on the softball field. Of the three men hired in 1967, for example, one had played baseball for Yale, one still played rugby on the national level, and I had plenty of hitting practice at Santa Barbara.

The assistant professors in place were less physically competitive than the newcomers, and they took a more leisurely attitude towards publication than I was used to. For that matter, so did the senior faculty. Only three had published scholarly books (two of them had also published textbooks), though another did so on the verge of retirement, and another had collaborated on a freshman reader. Most of them had never had a tenure-track appointment anywhere but Oklahoma, and their view of academe seemed to me quite limited.

All of the faculty had doctorates from solid programs—in their days as graduate students, there were at most three tiers, as opposed to the current multiplicity—and they gave good training to their own graduate students. In fact, the advisees of a man in modern literature who published very little had been hired at places like Wisconsin and Washington and some who had gone to lesser schools were publishing scholarly books. When I began to read graduate exams, I could see that students of a Victorianist who published only a little more than his colleague were getting very good training.

Clearly tenure cases did not depend heavily on publication, though not often as lightly as the successful candidate who presented a single book review as evidence of scholarship. Most candidates had stronger cases, but though some cases led to hand-wringing and division of opinion and required last-minute reprieves in the form of book contracts, the department rarely voted to deny tenure, and one of those decisions was rightly overturned at a higher level. As a result, at the end of the twentieth century the department had fewer assistant professors than it did in 1967.

My experience at Wisconsin and Santa Barbara had taught me to think in terms of the profession at large, and I had brought enough momentum with me so that the relaxed atmosphere of the OU department did not cause me to nod off. As I explained to former colleagues prepared to sympathize with my exile to this backwater and to students at Oklahoma who wondered what I had done to get sent here, there were many kinds of climate, psychological as well as physical. No one threatened me; when I expressed concern about gaps in the library's holdings, I was put in charge of book orders; and period lines and seminar assignments were reshuffled to accommodate my talents and preferences.

I was still close enough to the rigors of the Wisconsin program to be a little shocked at the attitude towards the performance, or non-performance, of graduate students. When I asked why we didn't require students to take the Graduate Record Examination, the response sounded a lot like, "We'd rather not know." And when I sat in on some really appalling oral examinations, at one of which the candidate could barely remember his own name, it was disturbing to hear my older colleagues vote to pass candidates with the excuse that someone would hire them. Or to hear a dissertation director say defensively about a marginally literate final draft, "You should have seen it before I fixed it." I was sure that I would never be reduced to saying anything like that. (I was wrong.) But I protested only mildly, and my colleagues seemed able to tolerate my youthful enthusiasm.

The town seemed equally ready to accept me and my family. Barbara and I chose to attend the local parish church rather than the Catholic student center because it had better programs for the children and because it offered a more stable community. One of my Catholic colleagues scoffed that the parish was full of mechanics. Carpenters, too, I pointed out.

This was in the days just after the Second Vatican Council, and there was so much enthusiasm and good will that I was named to the liturgy committee, though the very liberal director of Christian education was stunned when I offered to lead a rosary and nonplussed when, asked what to sing at the folk Mass our new bishop was to attend, I suggested, "I've never been to Heaven, but I've been to Oklahoma." Barbara began teaching Sunday school and for a while was content to do that until new appointments at the parish brought a post-post-Conciliar backlash and the children refused to attend the rigid catechism classes under the direction of an old-fashioned nun.

We didn't interact much with my colleagues, partly because few of them were our age or seemed otherwise compatible, especially after the camaraderie of Santa Barbara. But mostly it was Barbara's decision. She said, quite rightly, that most of my colleagues were sexists. And this was before the chair of the department called me into his office and asked why I had let my wife apply for a job even though the nepotism rule had been abolished. "Let her?" I said. "Have you met her?" This annoyed both of us, especially Barbara, who was growing increasingly discontented with the university's and Catholic church's attitude towards women and with her inability to use her talents. But at the moment she was involved with the children, and as they became increasingly involved in school and other activities, both of us could support and enjoy them.

For the most part, however, I was still working hard at teaching and scholarship, so hard that my most senior colleague told me, gently, that he and others were worried that I was injuring my health. I laughed, thanked him, and couldn't wait to tell my father, who at one time despaired of my accomplishing anything.

Anyway, going to work was a real pleasure. These were exciting if not always comfortable times for the whole university. The new president had little academic background but had brought many new ideas—and vice presidents and other functionaries—from Washington in order to create a local, academic version of the Great Society. He organized meetings with small groups of faculty to lobby for support of his ideas, some impractical, some grandiose, some dependent upon ignoring or transforming human nature. Perhaps responding to the early stages of the student protests at Berkeley, he was especially interested in student opinion.

Faculty were supposed to talk with and, even better, listen to students. I was prepared, by temperament as well as experience, to believe their injunction not to trust anyone over thirty, even though I was past that limit, but I thought that they had stopped short of the necessary skepticism about the rest of the population. For example, I overheard one young idealist say—this was about the time that anti-war protests had begun to have an impact on Oklahoma—that he'd be willing to give up his U.S. citizenship if he could get a good job with the U.N., an interesting variation on Jack Kennedy's injunction to ask not what your country could do for you or for that matter the theme of *The Man Without a Country*. Some were less self-deceived than he and less pompous than the outdoor orator who proclaimed his generation the best educated and the most enlightened in history, and I talked to some of them, though I didn't understand that I was supposed to agree with them. After one nice young man proposed a scheme that, as far as I could see, had no reference to human frailty or to verification and asked what I thought about it, I replied, "I think it's a crock." Later, a young woman asked, as confronta-tionally as a prosecuting attorney, what I thought the most important job I had as a teacher. I knew that I was supposed to talk about encouraging courageous and independent thought or something equally windy and idealistic, but I thought that I'd stick with basics. "Fill fifty minutes," I said, and, aghast at what she thought cynicism, she was about to relay this to the president until a friend dissuaded her. A few years later, someone told me that she had done some teaching and had revised her opinion of me.

I had a more immediate effect on a young man high in student government. He and a number of others in one of my courses had a habit of strolling in late, often accompanied by wet dogs. One day I locked the door at the scheduled time and began my lecture. About ten minutes later, the door rattled. The student seated nearest it looked, said, "It's locked," and reached for the knob. "I know it's locked," I said. "I locked it. Leave it alone." At the end of the hour I opened the door, almost causing severe damage to the leader's groin area. He sounded aggrieved. "Why did you lock the door?" "Because," I said, "I am tired of this shit." After he enrolled in another of my classes, he told me that this had been a pivotal experience in his political education. After he graduated from law school at Texas, I spoke to him, over the phone, after I had to go through two secretaries at a corporate law firm in Dallas. (When I told the story to a black colleague in another department, he practically jumped in glee, recalling a meeting in which he had counseled moderation and the student leader had said, in astonishment and indignation, "Why...why...you're nothing but a house nigger!") Now he's one of the few former students I have contact with.

Once I was cast in the role of house nigger myself. When student activists protested the acceptance of ROTC courses for graduation credit, a committee was appointed to study the issue. I don't think it had a student representative, rare in those days of student demands for a place in the power structure. (When they got a chance to participate, they tended to be first puzzled and then angry. All right, you could see them thinking, where is the exciting, hidden exercise of power really going on?) But it did have me as the token young or anyway untenured person. The committee came up with a compromise that satisfied neither the radicals nor their opponents: no more credit for things like drill; continued credit for military history and other courses that had a clear or at least potential academic slant. That was the closest I got to the protest movement. I did decide, when the senior ROTC officer (famous primarily for not shooting back when Israeli planes mistakenly strafed his ship during the Six-Day war) tried to crush my hand while shaking it, that it was time for me to get back in shape. So I played basketball at noon until a knee gave out and then took to swimming, first for exercise and then for competition, as a way of keeping my weight and my increasing frustration level down. That was the most positive result of any committee I have served on.

When we presented our report, the president of the university didn't object to the committee's findings, perhaps because he was more interested in vision than in details and in students than in faculty. Having been around politicians, he had apparently decided to concentrate on the largest and most easily swayed part of his constituency. He did not seem to realize that students did not put him in power. Or that it takes the cooperation of the permanent staff, in this case faculty, to make things run well enough to keep him there, an oversight that raises some questions about how well he functioned as a bureaucrat.

It was not entirely fair of me to say that he operated on the carrot and stick approach: the students got the carrot and the faculty got the shaft. For a while, there were bread and circuses all round, or, in the case of the English department, booze and visiting writers. Within two years we played host, for several days each, to writers like Robert Penn Warren, Gary Snyder, Brother Antoninus, John Barth, John Hawkes, Joseph Heller, and Anthony Burgess.

This was a pleasant time to be a member of the department, the university, and the profession. But for a variety of reasons, it was brief. Locally, the president's position grew increasingly shaky, only partly because of his shortcomings. He had avoided violence during the anti-war protests, but some Oklahomans, including some politicians, seemed disappointed that the scenes at Kent State and Jackson State had not been repeated. One colleague, as close to being liberal Eastern establishment as the department could boast, returned from the barber shop in shock. The other customers, talking about campus unrest, had said, "Them goddam hippies try to burn down our ROTC building, we'll shoot the sons-a-bitches." He had not known there were such people. I replied that this was a defect in his education, the kind fatal to the students at Kent State. "I grew up with that kind of people," I said. "I'm related to that kind of people. Sometimes I am that kind of people."

Of course, I could see that the president had acted responsibly during the crisis, and he was an intelligent man. His problem was that he didn't seem to think that anyone else was intelligent, including the Board of Regents and the faculty, and support from both groups was eroding. Finally the regents made their displeasure known. This was in the summer, and student organizations were dormant. The president called the only summer meeting of the general faculty anyone could remember. The hall was packed. He came out, said, like a standup comedian, that he was certainly glad to be here, and waited for a laugh. The audience was completely silent. The next day he resigned.

But that was his problem. I was coming up for tenure with an impregnable case; I had agreed to help compile information for a new edition of *American Literary Manuscripts* in exchange for the commission to catalogue the Evelyn Waugh collection at the University of Texas, a rich source of material for further research; I had been asked to serve as external examiner for a dissertation on Waugh at the University of Toronto; and the University of Missouri English department, twenty miles from my home town, had invited me to interview for a job there.

So I prepared to go to my fifth Modern Language Association meeting with the most confidence I had felt, and for the MLA's first trip to Denver. Originally the convention had been scheduled for Chicago, but many of the Association's members were angered by the behavior of Mayor Richard Daley and his police force during the riots at the 1968 Democratic convention. Enough of them, including members of the newly emerged Radical Caucus, came to the general meeting where they passed the resolution which denied Chicago the income from 10,000 visitors.

I don't know why Denver was selected. It was certainly less convenient than Chicago for most of the Association's members, especially the east coast radicals. Certainly the meeting had the lowest attendance in recent years. I heard a rumor that, realizing this after the fact, the leaders of the Radical Caucus asked that the Executive Council move the meeting back to Chicago and were turned down.

Denver had enough hotel rooms to house those attending the conference, but they were scattered over the downtown area. And no hotel or hall was large enough to house both the meetings and the book exhibit. As a result, it was the healthiest conference I remember because members had to walk from their hotels past the Hari Krishnas whirling on the sidewalks to meetings and from meetings to the exhibit and back again in crisp, cold mountain air. But the meeting took a toll. One of the most confirmed MLA-goers I have known said, wearily, "It's another day longer and I'm another day older." But he was happier than the publishers' representatives, stuck in the convention center where they had little traffic and thus little opportunity to push their wares. Lonely and desperate, they were open to all kinds of suggestion, and I came away from the meeting with two book contracts.

I also had a double pleasure in seeing friends from Santa Barbara days: first, because I liked them and enjoyed their company; second, because it was clear that my situation, emotionally and financially, was better than that of the ones who were trying to hang on. And it was pleasant to go to the Missouri cocktail party to be courted rather than court. When the wife of an assistant professor said, rather snippily, "I hear you're looking for a job," I replied, "No, one is looking for me."

Very few people were in that position. The Radical Caucus had been institutionalized in a number of large sessions and small workshops and, in campaigning for equal opportunity for women and homosexuals (not yet "gay"), made their presence felt in the general meeting. But the real action was in impromptu meetings, which evolved into the Job Seekers Caucus, of people who had come expecting interviews and found few or none.

While I saw notices of meetings and heard rumblings, I did not realize how bad things had become until a young man with a badge which gave his affiliation as Kent State saw my Oklahoma badge and asked if my chairman had come to the meeting.

"There was no reason for him to," I said. "We aren't hiring this year."

"Not hiring? I got an encouraging letter from him."

"Well," I said, "I don't know everything that goes on, but I try to keep up. What did it say?"

His brow furrowed as he began to recite a message that went something like this: "Thank you for your interest in the University of Oklahoma. We have not determined our needs for next year, but we will keep your letter on file. If we decide to look for someone in your area of specialization, we will get in touch with you."

I muttered something noncommittal and, I hope, soothing, but I had been on the job market enough to realize that if he regarded that as an encouraging letter, the profession was in a lot worse trouble than I or anyone had anticipated.

It took a while to understand the causes of a disaster as profound as, if more limited in scope than, the stock market crash forty years earlier. As usual, catastrophe had taken a long time to develop, human effort played only a part, and that effort was misdirected. In 1965, the Modern Language Association had asked chairs of major graduate departments—all men—to consider ways to alleviate the colleges' and universities' "hunger for Ph.D.'s" that began in 1958 and increased throughout the period of the study. Under the leadership of Don Cameron Allen of Johns Hopkins

University, the group identified two major problems. First, the Ph.D. process took too long. It should be streamlined by cutting course, language, and examination requirements, by encouraging more limited dissertation topics, and by abandoning the notion that the degree had anything to do with producing men (and, one infers, women) of culture. Second, one-fifth of the more than 100 graduate English departments produced two-thirds of the Ph.D.s. On the model of industry, the solution was to get more production out of the other four-fifths and to encourage, responsibly of course, the creation of additional doctoral programs.

Many of the recommendations were adopted, with disastrous effects. But it is easier to forgive Allen for mistakes founded on the assumption that the future is going to be exactly like the past than for his tone, which is occasionally sexist, as when, in a rare glance at gender issues, he maintains that the nine of a hundred Ph.D.s who do not enter teaching "probably end up grading their husband's themes" (17); sometimes cynical, as when he dismisses figures about the falling birth rate, evidence that very soon there would be far fewer students for those new Ph.D.s to teach, as "probably not worrisome unless the national income falls more rapidly than the desire to breed" (81).

The report, *The Ph.D. in English and American Literature*, was issued in 1968, but some leading departments had already streamlined their programs. Rumor at the 1969 convention held that Indiana University had helped to break the market by turning out sixty new Ph.D.s, thirty under the old program, thirty under the new. This may have been truer of the profession at large than of a particular department, but it was certainly true that the number had been swelled by those like the unhappy young man from Kent State and many more from schools like it.

The profession at large was slow to see what had happened and what would happen to many of the students in the assembly line or being recruited to doctoral programs. One friend from Wisconsin agreed with my analysis but maintained that "the top four or five people in the profession each year won't have any trouble getting jobs." This was too Olympian for me. Later I tried, with a little success, to persuade my colleagues to reduce the number of people in the doctoral program and to replace them with instructors hired from the ranks of the unemployed.

But at the 1969 MLA convention my attitude towards the jobless was rather detached. I was employed, and I might be offered an even better job. So a few weeks later I flew into the small airport near Columbia, Missouri, with a sense of anticipation, but also of apprehension because I was not at all sure it would be a good idea to move that close to my father and the people I had grown up with. The department seemed cordial, with a number of people about my age and level of professional development, and one of my friends from Santa Barbara was about to join them. But the temperature never got above zero, I would have had a hard time selling my children on the move to a town where they could not get "Sesame Street" on television, and the office and support facilities did not seem as good as Oklahoma's.

By the time I got to the group interviews—English department and administrators—I knew that only an exceedingly attractive offer would induce me to call Mayflower again. In any case, I had decided that it made life simpler, even if I got the job, to let them know what I was really like, a strategy which may explain why I spent the rest of my career at Oklahoma. The departmental interview went well enough, since I had learned that if you keep talking, they can't ask you another question. But when I outlined my plans for future research, a young man who was probably afraid that I was going to take his tenure slot asked truculently, how I could be so sure of myself. "If you don't know what you can do by the time you're thirty-five," I said, "then you're probably never going to know." We were both right: I completed all but one of the projects I had mentioned, but I also did a number of things that I couldn't have imagined then. Still, that was the wrong thing to say in the wrong tone if I had really wanted the job.

The interview with the administrators was more enjoyable because by then I didn't care. When they tried to tell me something about the region, I told them I had grown up in Boonville. Oh, they said, one of our highest-paid mathematicians is from Boonville. "I used to deliver his mother's newspaper," I said, "and I wouldn't want to do anything to hurt the average." When they asked if I had questions about the university, I wondered about the admissions standards. A little man who looked like a caricature of an assistant dean, a dried-up, rule-bound gofer, said, "I'm sure they're higher than Oklahoma's!" This was the rudest thing I've heard in forty years of interviewing. The rest of the group was silent, either stunned or interested in what I was going to say. Which was, "I wouldn't be too sure of that. You not only let my brother in, you gave him a degree."

Then the grownups took over.

During the very pleasant department reception at the house of the chairman, the cold weather knocked out Columbia's telephone system, the modern poetry specialist mentioned that he had received an offer from Michigan State, and the chairman found out how much I was being paid at Oklahoma. The last two revelations made him realize that he could fill a more important gap more cheaply with someone else, and he hired a man I had known at Wisconsin.

Although nothing came of the visit, I enjoyed the trip, most of the people were stimulating to talk to, and being the center of attention was pleasant. Most important, looking at other people's conditions made me appreciate my own.

I returned from Missouri to sign contracts to edit a collection of modern short novels, which was in my area, and a collection of essays on John Steinbeck, which was not; and to prepare to dig into the Waugh materials in Austin, Texas, from which, professionally, I would not emerge for nearly ten years. And to learn that I had been granted tenure, which meant that, short of a felony conviction or other evidence of moral turpitude or insanity or total disability, I was guaranteed a job as an English teacher at the University of Oklahoma for as long as I wanted to hold it. My seniors were forced to retire at seventy; I and my contemporaries and juniors can never, under federal law, be forced to do so.

Now, of course, I had to learn how to function without anxiety, now that I had full membership in the guild.

Job

"...peaks are always found, or assumed, in the academic career."
Caplow and McGee, *The Academic Marketplace*

The *Bildungsroman* is a highly dramatic, even melodramatic, form because it starts from the position that the central character is engaged in a unique and heroic struggle to assert his or her unique talents and identity and to find a way to carve a place in the world. Moreover, it has a natural progression in the movement from one stage of consciousness to another, marked in Western culture by the educational system and other social structures—family, religion, country—which provide the hero with arenas and antagonists. Typically this kind of novel ends on a high point when the hero recognizes and embraces the true vocation. Showing the person actually following the vocation seems unnecessary because the book itself serves as evidence of success.

Would-be protagonists of this story envision adult life as uneventful and stultifying because it seems to lack the obvious crises that face the apprentice and point him or her towards the next. In the academic world, these are represented by the heart-wrenching series of examinations and the tenure decision. After those ordeals, the tenured professor appears to tread the tranquil circle of the academic year, chewing the cud of old yellow lecture notes delivered in a drone that echoes down the years to retirement.

Like all stereotypes, this is both unfair to individuals and based on superficial observation of a class. A friend who free-lances in Hollywood said, a little enviously, that I always knew what I was going to be doing and when I'd be doing it. That's true: I had my teaching assignments, mostly courses I have taught before, eight months in advance. He was kind enough not to ask how I stand the routine, year after year.

There are different ways of introducing variety into the academic life. Some tenured professors find it in real estate or Amway sales, some, more respectably, in using their expertise as consultants. Some disappear into the hobbies or sports or good civic and charitable works that most academics, indeed most people, consider part of their lives. But when someone is being, in the phrase of my most upright Wisconsin contemporary, "a good academic," his or her activities fall into the categories on which professors are evaluated: teaching, research, and service.

Except in small religious colleges, where the situation is unchanged, service was once more broadly defined and more highly rewarded than it is now. Then people could plausibly list on annual reports things like serving on church, charitable, or civic boards. A former chair of my department was district governor of the Lions Club which condemned *The Grapes of Wrath*. In the more distant past, a distinguished member of another department ranked high in the Ku Klux Klan. These activities theoretically brought academics into the ordinary life of the community. They may still do so, though almost certainly less than in the past, but they are now widely regarded as separate from academic behavior, something one does after hours. Only the most naive or desperate would think of listing them as professional accomplishments.

Today service is defined as activity which supports the academy, whether the college or the university or the profession at large: membership on departmental and university committees, official position in regional or national organizations. Most people regard this kind of civic duty with varying degrees of enthusiasm and cynicism; they do it because, although service ranks lowest in the reward system for tenured faculty and hardly counts at all for tenure, the decisions will otherwise be made by people who do not necessarily consult the best interests of the faculty or, from the faculty's point of view, the institution. That is, by former academics who find the process so interesting or potentially rewarding that they go into administration.

Administrators are not, or not inevitably, bad or stupid people. But they have other agendas and very short tenures. For example, in my first twenty-nine years OU, compared to its 106 year history, I served under more than half of the university's presidents (not counting numerous interim and acting types), seven—eight if one counts a man who resigned and was then reappointed. Also at least five provosts and five deans of my college, Arts and Sciences. One provost and one dean had been members of the OU faculty before assuming their administrative positions. (This changed not only at OU but throughout the higher education system in Oklahoma because boards of regents began to appoint politicians like former governor and senator David Boren who came with a ready-made power base.)

OU is not a special case. Despite the provenance of higher administrators, all large American universities are now governed by a managerial class which has little contact with the faculty and with their original fields of expertise. They come from elsewhere; they don't know anything about local operations. Search committees can't agree about what a university is supposed to do or be, and they are pretty sure that their colleagues don't know. So they look for people who will tell them—or at least sound convincing.

To stay convincing, professional administrators have to be like sharks: keep moving or die. (I'm talking about survival mechanisms, not morals.) Their resumés are constantly circulating, and a lot of what they do in any given job seems to outsiders calculated to pad those resumés. Sometimes a long-term administrator announces that he looks forward to returning to his first loves, teaching and research. No one who has stayed in the classroom believes this for a minute.

Universities adopted the corporate model because everyone had lost faith in the old model, which was never easy to describe. In the most cynical description of the new model, students are raw material; faculty are line workers; administrators are suits.

Some years ago, OU faculty members evaluated administrators on what was supposed to be a regular basis. At some point, consciously or not, the administration stopped sending out the forms. When the practice was reinstituted, there was a rapid turnover of deans and chairs.

Most academic managers are energetic. They produce paper. They especially like grand strategies, visions, plans for whole decades—in the late sixties, a "Plan for the Seventies"; in the late eighties, a "Strategy for

Excellence." These documents take a long time to draft, re-draft, and publish. Even if they are workable, they have probably become obsolete or irrelevant before they reach final form.

But these plans do have a purpose, aside from the laudable one of forcing people to think about what they are doing: they give the upwardly mobile administrator something to show to search committees. Even if the plans produce no results, the administrators who sponsored them have probably moved to better jobs, where they have to devise other plans which will get them still better jobs. But though all academics would welcome better jobs at higher pay and many go looking for them, few of them go so far as to become administrators. Not out of nobility or dedication to teaching and research, but because by training and inclination they are interested in the other two areas, teaching and research.

These two areas are not always incompatible, but there is always the potential conflict. In 1955, Albert Kitzhaber warned new teaching assistants at KU not to spend so much time on teaching that they neglected their own degree programs. Then we wondered when we would get to a point where we didn't feel split between teaching and research. The answer, unless one gives up research altogether, is never. David Lodge dramatizes the conflict fictionally in *Changing Places* by opposing a dim English don, concerned for his students and dead-ended in his scholarly work, to an American careerist totally devoted to advancing his scholarly career through publishing incessantly and attending international conferences. Less dramatic is the testimony of Wayne C. Booth of the University of Chicago, a very good academic indeed, in *The Vocation of a Teacher: Rhetorical Occasions, 1967-1988*. Booth's demonstrable intelligence and energy should make most professors feel lazy and incompetent, but even he suffers from the recurrent guilt that comes from trying to balance preparation for classes, counseling students, and doing original work.

Readers may think it odd that, having spent over forty years in the classroom, long enough at OU to have taught the children of former students, I have said little about teaching. There are a number of reasons for my uncharacteristic reticence. Anyone who has taught will recognize them. First, I came away from all but a very few courses with a sense that, because I didn't know enough or plan well enough or motivate them strongly enough, I failed to teach every student as much as she or he was capable of learning. If I did have successes, I rarely saw them. Occasionally a student will thank me—in some cases, for having convinced him or her to find a more appropriate line of work. Second, students are, as Christ said of the poor, always with us. And except for graduate students, they appear and disappear so quickly that it is difficult to know what has happened to them, even if, as with the best or most highly motivated or most individual, one has a continuing interest in them. (I do know that a student to whom I gave a C in a graduate course changed departments and became a college president. I suppose that can be counted as a success story.)

Second, teaching does not provide good dramatic material. It does produce anecdotes, like the one in which an escaped chimpanzee appeared at my classroom door as I was trying to teach Henry James's story "The Beast in the Jungle." But while these can be amusing, they don't reveal much about the nature of the profession. Reading and marking student work is an important part of an English teacher's job, and some students have been grateful for my thoroughness in commenting on their writing. But it isn't very dramatic except when I cursed and shook my fist, as I was doing when a graduate student writing a dissertation with me passed my office. It took him weeks to get over the fear that his work would get the same reception. But I was never able to equal Alvin Whitley's epigrammatic comments; mine tended toward the practical, even banal. And God knows repetitious.

Some teachers spend a great deal of time advising students about life and career decisions. Perhaps because I don't think of myself as a priest or that kind of doctor, students tended to ask me practical questions: how to deal with the college advisors (tell them I said to do so and so; they'd rather do it than talk to me), what to do about inconvenient requirements (knowing rules and loopholes can be useful), which regulations are inflexible, which not. On larger questions, I often felt as though I were impersonating a grown-up. Once a student with a low C average sat in my office debating whether to go into pre-law or pre-med, oblivious to hints that he would need far stronger credentials for either than he had thus far accumulated. Finally I said, sounding like the most banal advisors I could remember, "Well, I suppose that's a matter of the priorities you set for yourself." He looked at me as if I were a holy man on a mountain top and said, in an awed tone, "Wow!" I thought, "Can I be getting away with this shit?" Obviously I was, which was even more discouraging.

But many students are more alert, realistic, self-aware, and amusing to talk to than this young man, and most classes are stimulating, at least to the instructor. Still, there is the distinction we formulated in graduate school between the teacher who teaches the students and the one who teaches the material. Most university professors probably fall into the second group because, rather than merely conveying received information, however eloquently, they are trained to question, to revise, and ultimately to make additions to the existing body of knowledge and to submit it to the evaluation of their peers.

This process helps to explain the difference between an academic and an educated person who knows how to write, in many cases more eloquently and almost always more clearly than someone with a Ph.D. A younger colleague said that another colleague, who had written a nationally-recognized book, had the equivalent of a Ph.D. "There is," I said pompously, "no equivalent of a Ph.D." By that I meant that only in a serious graduate program is one subjected to constant examination by peers as well as professors and required to possess a broad, seemingly irrelevant, knowledge of background as well as the work or idea in the foreground. Besides, I had been in this colleague's company as we talked about a writer on whom she was working and on whom I had done considerable research. I saw her taking notes and joked that I expected to be acknowledged in a footnote. I was not shocked to see that I wasn't.

People coming out of Ph.D. programs tend to have little training in teaching methods in anything but freshman composition, but the process in which they learn the subject matter is parallel to the sequence in which their teaching careers develop. Once past teaching composition, most of my generation began by teaching survey or introductory genre courses. With a little seniority, we moved to courses in our special periods, and finally to seminars that in many cases drew upon material from our dissertations.

To build a career as a scholar, one has to move in the opposite direction. The first and sometimes the only publications probably come out of the dissertation. Then, if there is a then, the scholar begins to work more broadly in the general field of specialization or, increasingly, in theoretical issues connected to the original research.

When I was in graduate school, conventional wisdom dictated that it was prudent to write a dissertation on a single major author because it showed the candidate's willingness to demonstrate that he or she could not only confront a significant body of work but also challenge the work of previous scholars. Second, hiring committees were more likely to recognize the name of Joseph Conrad than of Evelyn Waugh. From this perspective, Paul Wiley was right to ask if I wouldn't rather work on Conrad. (One reason given for my dismissal from Santa Barbara was that I worked on minor figures, though the experience of others indicates that Conrad would not have saved me. In any case, I would still have been too visible and too audible.) Many of my contemporaries at Wisconsin and elsewhere took this route: Jackson Bryer on F. Scott Fitzgerald, Alan Grob on Wordsworth, James Cowan on D. H. Lawrence.

Another tenet of graduate school wisdom held that it was far more efficient to work on one author than on a broader topic. The example of John Vickery's multi-volume dissertation on Sir James Frazier's *The Golden Bough* and modern literature was notorious among graduate students at Wisconsin.

I rejected both theories not because I was brave or perverse but because I couldn't imagine being able to find enough new to say about a single figure. Instead, I attempted to define a fictional sub-genre, using the work of Ronald Firbank and Carl Van Vechten, one a fairly obscure cult figure, the other just obscure, and Evelyn Waugh, regarded at that time as an amusing but probably ephemeral writer. Moreover, I was handicapped by the training at KU to believe that I had to read everything they wrote, everything written about them, and what there was on the theory of the novel as a genre. The wonder is not that it took me three years to finish the dissertation but that I finished it at all.

But I did get a good deal more practice in bibliographical searching; I learned something about literary history from its sources rather than depending on syntheses made by others, and I was forced to make connections and distinctions. But when I finished the dissertation, I thought, rightly, that it was not coherent or searching enough to submit to a university press as a book.

But I knew that to meet the expectations to which I had been acculturated at Wisconsin, I would have to learn, more or less on my own, to what I needed in order to become a publishing scholar. I had nothing as coherent as a research program. It would be nice to say that I found the idea too confining, but the truth is that I poked around trying different subjects and approaches. The first real writing I ever did, beginning at fifteen, was for a weekly newspaper in my home town. Naturally, it was clumsy and pretentious, but the editor, an old-fashioned newspaperman and aspiring novelist, would take my copy, make a few strokes of the pencil which cleared out all kinds of debris and clarified the thought. When I became editor of my college newspaper and then a teaching assistant at the University of Kansas, I tried to use my pencil to help writers discover what they really wanted to say. At worst this may have kept me from the kind of error-hunting prevalent in the mid-1950s; at best, it helped me to learn that a word or a sentence does not stand alone but is part of a whole structure. Although I did not realize it then, the lessons from journalism approached, from the other end of the text, the kind of analysis that had impressed me in Cleanth Brooks and Robert Penn Warren's *Understanding Poetry*. However, I did abandon the notion that every word set on paper was inviolable, that meaning has to be discovered not only by the reader but by the writer.

Of course, even if I had known how to locate the kind of material Gordan had used, I could not conceive that anyone would let me use it. But I got a review copy of Miriam Benkovitz's bibliography of Ronald Firbank and saw that she not only listed locations of manuscript materials but noted variant editions of some of his novels. These I could buy from used book dealers or find at Northwestern and the University of Chicago, and I spent hours doing sight comparisons and transcribing variants in different colored pencils onto 4x6 notecards. In the process, I discovered in the process that I could read two different versions at the same time—not as accurately as a collating machine or a yet-uninvented computer program, but, since I never expected to be able to edit a variorum edition (wrong again), with an acceptable degree of accuracy. I made no immediate use of this material, but by the time I moved to California I had begun to see connections among bibliographical research, textual study, and literary criticism.

By that time I was teaching literature courses and sometimes, when there was any criticism of a work, I realized not only that the critics were wrong or short-sighted but that I had a more satisfactory interpretation. Or, in teaching recent or neglected books, the first interpretation. So my teaching and research invigorated each other, although I have sometimes suspected that the articles that have grown out of my teaching may have dazzled more than enlightened the students for whose benefit I did the research and formulated a new interpretation.

By the end of my career, talking to a colleague who, though he was a very popular teacher, retired as an associate professor because he hadn't published enough, I commented that he had written in order to teach, while I had taught in order to write. There is room for both kinds at a university, and in retirement each of us got to do what he does best: my colleague took another job at a small college in another state, and I get to write and travel.

Career

At lunch with my estranged wife in the relatively amicable period when I had adjusted to living on my own and she and I had not openly contemplated divorce, she asked, "How do you do it?"

"How do I do what?"

"Become an authority on something." Four years earlier, she had resumed her academic career, in a different field, after a dozen years.

"Well," I said, pleased that she thought I might know something about something, "I did one thing and then another and another until one day a few people who wanted to know about Evelyn Waugh think of me." (Not exclusively and sometimes, to my ill-concealed chagrin, in England not always first.)

But you have to start somewhere, and there and several stages along the way I can't even say I was particularly lucky, for Branch Rickey said that luck is the residue of design, and for a long time I wasn't experienced to design much of anything. Put not too simply, I began to read Waugh because he wasn't John Milton. Robert J. O'Sullivan, S.J., not only taught a Milton course at Rockhurst College, but in order to encourage students to enter literary contests, he allowed them to substitute a contest entry for a term paper in his course.

One contest, for reviews of books by Catholic authors, was run by the Catholic Community Library, then housed in an impressive stone converted residence in what was then mid-town Kansas City, Missouri. In 1954, I somehow acquired, more by luck than design, a copy of *The Loved One*, and wrote a review instead of a Milton term paper. The manuscript of my review and for that matter the Catholic Community Library have long disappeared, and the only thing I remember is my delight in Waugh's misdirection in the opening pages where he uses language usually applied to pukka sahibs to a pair of English writers in Los Angeles. Bob Knickerbocker, another English professor, later said, "When I knew what you'd chosen, I knew you'd win." He knew me better than I thought.

I don't know what would have happened if my first encounter had been with *Brideshead Revisited.* Probably the Oxford scenes would have been too rich for a young man living in Spartan conditions and eating even more Spartan food, the Catholicism too overt for someone raised with lots of sexual guilt and weekly confessions, and the style too William Bootish and feather-footed for someone planning to be a newspaperman rather than a journalist.

Luckily, I encountered *The Loved One* at the right place and time, and I won the contest. My ego thus boosted, I found a copy of *Vile Bodies* at a drugstore down the street and thought it thin and tedious. (Years later, I was gratified to discover that Waugh felt the same way.) So, my ear for style not fully developed, I put Waugh aside for Aldous Huxley, seduced by his vocabulary and obvious intellectual pretensions, and wrote my M.A. thesis about him at the University of Kansas.

Mostly for that reason, I decided to specialize in modern British literature at Wisconsin, and I signed up for Paul Wiley's Conrad seminar in the fall of 1958. As usual, I volunteered to give the first report, on *Almayer's Folly.* I can remember nothing about my paper or for that matter the novel, but in the course of hasty research, reading from the indexes of scholarly books, I ran across John D. Gordan's *Joseph Conrad: The Making of a Novelist.* in Chapter IV, "The Growth of the Text," he had combined scholarship and close textual analysis in ways I had never seen. However, I realized, dimly, that Gordan was doing some of the things I had been learning for almost a decade.

As I said earlier, I had first been subjected to editorial revisions of my work and then, as editor and composition teacher, responsible for suggesting them to other writers of varying competence. However, since I did not regard myself or my students as real writers who not only got into print but whose works could possibly become the object of serious study and analysis, I did not make the connection between this kind of analysis and the close textual reading of New Critics like Cleanth Brooks, which I regarded as a much more elevated kind of enterprise. Not until I ran across a book, now unfortunately lost over the years and various moves, in which a poet reproduced successive versions of a poem and analyzed the changes, did I have a glimmer that the two processes might be closely related and that close examination of a text might involve finding out what that text was and how a writer came to discover meaning.

Gordan revealed something about this process of discovery. Transcriptions of text and corrections looked like comments on a freshman paper, but Gordan's analysis went far beyond anything I had seen. Of changes in the abandoned draft of the opening sentences of the eleventh chapter of *Almayer's Folly*, he wrote that

> Conrad continually added to the picture, by turning a non-visual phrase like *small puff* into *light cloud* and by qualifying *eyes* as *wide open eyes*. The cancellation of *cold moonlight* destroyed the too obvious contrast with *warm glow*. The style was tightened when the unnecessary *left by* was condensed into *bygone* and the *great flood* of moonlight into *pouring*.

And Gordan was looking not just at words but drawing inferences from physical evidence: "The nervousness of Conrad's corrections is worth noticing: after beginning the second sentence he suddenly cut the first sentence in half and gave it a new ending" (121).

There were dozens of other examples. Gordan cited some variants without comment, but for many of them he showed why the revisions produced greater economy or variety or sharpness of detail. And while I did not then know what to do with the assertions that the various stages of composition revealed "the gradual evolution of Conrad's plots" (125), I could see that this kind of information could be used to account for a work's final form.

Of course, I didn't know how to find variant states of a work, and at the time there was no one at Wisconsin to teach me. Besides, I suspected that even if I did know where to find manuscripts and typescripts and proofs, the owners were very unlikely to give me access to them.

It took me some years to realize that, even if this was true about manuscripts (and it turned out to be less true than I thought), there were other resources. I should have realized this when Waugh brought out his revised edition of *Brideshead Revisited* in 1960 and, in relative post-prelims leisure, Barbara and I collated it with the earlier (and textually corrupt) Penguin edition, made a list of variants, and speculated on Waugh's reasons for having made changes and, more often, deletions. I hadn't quite forgotten Gordan's example, but it wasn't until eight years and three jobs later that I did any more textual work on that novel.

But I was learning about sources and kinds of textual variants, and although the book about Firbank got parted out into several articles that got me from the compiler of the secondary bibliography the accolade of "one of the few great Firbank scholars," much of my labor never bore fruit. Nevertheless, the skills, or more accurately the habit of mind, led to work on writers as various as Donald Barthelme, Iris Murdoch, Cyril Connolly, and others in order to satisfy my curiosity about what they were up to and why. In the process, working from the ground up, from data to principle, I was forced to think about the best, or at least better, ways to organize an enumerative bibliography. That as distinct from a highly technical and detailed descriptive bibliography and as even more distinct from what a colleague called "a real bibliographer," that is, someone who knows how to make paper. In the words of Clint Eastwood, "A man's got to know his limitations."

Still, to do even the simplest kind of bibliographical work, one has to have certain tools, and even a job badly or incompletely done can lead others to try to improve on it. Furthermore, even in the age of electronic data, a bibliographer has to get out of the office and at least go to a library, local or otherwise. My friend and collaborator Donat Gallagher has been all over Europe, including the Vatican, in search of material by and about Evelyn Waugh, although I'm not sure where he found the physical copy of an interview with Waugh in the *Uganda Times*, and his archival research has corrected misconceptions about Waugh's marital and martial difficulties which lazier or biased biographers continue to ignore. I've covered less ground than Don has, at least in search of Waugh material, but I have met interesting people and examined fascinating documents on the way to preparing an edition of *Brideshead Revisited*, something that, more than fifty years ago, I never thought possible.

But in 1964, I didn't know that. After mining the dissertation for two articles, I couldn't think of anything else to say about him. Then, on

Easter Sunday, 1966, Waugh died, and I regarded this as the closing of a chapter rather than an occasion for mourning. But Nicholas Joost, founding editor of *Papers on Language and Literature*, a conservative Catholic, and a Waugh enthusiast, wanted to mark the occasion in his journal and was impressed enough by the work I had done to ask me to write at length about the nature and significance of Waugh's career. Forced to take a different perspective, I re-read the books, fiction and non-fiction, and, in a title that paid homage to Ricardo Quintana's book on Swift, attempted to characterize Waugh's mind and art in a long and somewhat rambling review essay. Joost, the finest editor I have ever worked with, discerned a structure in it and printed the revised version.

Before that appeared, Joost asked me to evaluate an article on the background of Waugh's *Vile Bodies* by Charles E. Linck, Jr., whose name I vaguely remembered from KU and who had published a bibliography of Waugh's early work that supplemented Paul A. Doyle's pioneering work of the mid-1950s. As this article stood, Joost admitted, it was not satisfactory, but he was fascinated by the material and wondered if I could suggest ways to make it publishable. Not, I replied, without extensive rewriting, and I was willing to do that only for credit as co-author. He checked; Linck was delighted; the article was revised and subsequently published. I turned back to concentrated work on the Firbank book and to less coherent work on Waugh.

Then I moved to Oklahoma, trying to salvage something from the Firbank project, and thinking of what to do next. Then came another accident. At the South Central Modern Language Association meeting in Houston, I was prowling the book publishers' exhibits and at the University of Texas Press booth encountered a senior colleague in the company of a large, self-assured man he introduced as Warren Roberts, director of the Humanities Research Center at the University of Texas-Austin. I had already worked with Firbank materials there; I had just looked at several catalogues of other collections that the press had published; and I knew that the Center had bought a mass of material from the Waugh estate. Two years earlier, while I was still at UCSB, Bill Frost had returned from England with the news it included not only manuscripts but Waugh's library, with annotations. "We can always erase them," Marvin Mudrick said. But Texas, offering cash and a way around paying auction fees, had secured it.

Roberts was in charge of revising *American Literary Manuscripts*, a location list for the whole country, and my colleague had just declined to conduct a survey of manuscripts in Oklahoma. "Would you like to do the survey for Oklahoma?" Roberts asked. "Why not?" I said. "Would you like me to catalogue the Waugh collection?" "Why not?"

One reason why not was logistics. Although I didn't know what was in the collection, I knew that there was a lot and that cataloguing it would require concentrated blocks of time. Austin is almost 400 miles from Norman. But I could use breaks in the teaching schedule and, as it turned out, a series of small grants from OU and a foundation. Another reason why not was that I knew almost nothing about cataloguing. I had used the Firbank materials, but someone had already sorted them out and made a list of them. But I could do what I had done for my whole scholarly career: look at what others had done, try to figure out how they had done it, and follow the example as well as I could. (My awe was considerably reduced when one of the other cataloguers confessed that, in measuring the size of manuscript material, he had failed to notice that the centimeter markings on his ruler began a fraction inside its end, so that he had to go back and re-measure every document.)

Back at OU, a colleague wondered how I could have so much faith in scholarship that I would undertake the task. I wondered, privately, what he thought scholarship involved. (Later he gave up tenure to sell real estate, which in a way answered my question.) I should have used Louis Armstrong's answer to the question, "What is jazz?": "If you gotta ask, you're never gonna know." Instead, I tried to explain that I was being given a five-year lead—this was well before the authorized biography or editions of Waugh's diaries or letters were published—to examine unique materials that could lead to publications far more significant than the catalogue. But anyone who has enjoyed rummaging through an attic will understand my real motives: anticipation of what I might find, curiosity about someone I knew from a very limited perspective, hope to discover the unexpected.

There was and is an enormous amount and variety of stuff: Waugh's first surviving work, a drawing on the back of a form giving instructions for getting a tax refund, ironic in view of his later problems with Inland Revenue; the carnation worn on the day of his marriage, later annulled, to

Evelyn Gardner; all of his surviving diaries and some letters; marginal annotations in books, including advice for embalmers from which he drew details in *The Loved One*; manuscripts of most of his novels and some of his non-fiction books.

Dealing with this material took a great deal of time and enormous concentration. The HRC had not moved to its new, monolithic quarters, and the operation was run in so casual and leisurely a fashion that the reading room closed for lunch. But the staff was cordial, even the formidable Mary M. Hirth. Perhaps I had established the proper tone with her on my earlier trip to examine Firbank's notebooks. Before bringing them to me, she remarked that someone else had looked at them and that I might not find them very useful. "They're useful," I said, "if you know what you're doing."

In looking at the Waugh material, I was gratified and a little surprised to find evidence that I had known what I was doing in earlier speculations: about Waugh's inability to identify with other people and his tendency to classify, analyze, separate, and judge; about the nonsensical reading in the serial version of one of his novels that must have depended on a misreading of his increasingly execrable handwriting. I was fascinated and sometimes touched to see Waugh's habit of ruthless analysis applied to himself. And I was frustrated not only at having to flatten Waugh's barbed and lucid phrases but also at the impossibility of putting something more succinctly than the most precise and economical writer of my century.

I almost disgraced myself when I first read a postcard Waugh had sent to his brother Alec which said something like, "Did H. G. Wells fuck Mrs. Jacobs? I need to know." When I couldn't stop laughing, I had to leave the reading room, splash my face with cold water, and walk around to compose myself. I returned, looked at the card, broke up again, and had to leave. Then I read Alec's note that he had replied that, so far as he knew, Wells had not succeeded in accomplishing his desires. And fell apart again. After I thought I had settled down, I faced the task of summarizing the contents.

When I thought I had finished the job, a staff member told me that the HRC had acquired the files of A. D. Peters, the literary agent who began representing Waugh in 1928—eighteen boxes covering the years

1928-1963, the 1,256 items by Waugh a mere fraction of the whole. This extended my task as well as my knowledge considerably. Aesthetically, I came to regard it as an extraordinarily loose and baggy epistolary/documentary novel, with a central character exhibited in various moods and modes of action. The supporting characters in this episodic tale often have names which Waugh or even Dickens would have hesitated to employ. In a featured role is Augustus Detlof Peters himself, often Sancho to Waugh's Quixote, sometimes Perry Mason to Waugh as hapless client. He tried to mediate and sometimes intervene between Waugh and those who supplicated or demanded his services. He exclaimed in pain and horror at Waugh's desire to buy a painting in which a husband disguised as a priest hears his wife's confession. He bought Waugh's cigars and wine and helped to consume both. He gave advice on the infrequent occasions when it was asked and loaned money on the many more occasions when that was requested. There are minor characters with luminous names. The solicitor Wilfred Ariel Evill established the Waugh Trust, which Waugh established as a tax dodge and used to amass most of the collection which found its way to Texas. Percy A. Popkin tried to handle Waugh's increasingly complicated taxes. S. Benjamin Fisz hoped to film *Scoop*. Peregrine Worsthorne negotiated with Waugh for a series of articles on India until both got too drunk to remember what they had decided. Zane Gertzman wanted to make *The Loved One* as a musical comedy. Not amusingly named but Dickensianly long-suffering was Alex. Mclachlan, Waugh's much put-upon typist, who sometimes wrote plaintively to Peters about his difficulties with Waugh's handwriting.

I was delighted to see this material, but I was beginning to wonder if the HRC would ever stop buying more. One day a reading room assistant came to my table to tell me that he had found an even larger set of boxes full of Waugh material. I wasn't supposed to go into the stacks, but I was so obviously unsettled that he led me back to see what he had found. It was, I thanked God, the files for Alec Waugh.

What I had seen was enough to use for the next two decades of my career. The personal resources were at least as more important, for the HRC widened my circle of friends among the staff and the other students of Waugh attracted by the collection. At one point, there were scholars from France, England, and Australia in the reading room, and all became friends and long-term correspondents.

I also met a Parisian writing a dissertation on Waugh and offered to send her copies of my work, a courtesy repaid many-fold when I was extended two separate invitations to speak at her university. Later she befriended my son during his semester abroad. He wondered how I came to know her. Because, I explained, I happen to be one of the leading Waugh experts in the world. While this was immodest, it was a way of getting one up on my children, who for years thought that Evelyn Waugh was an adult version of an imaginary friend—which, now that I think of it, was a shrewd analysis. I could write about him if not talk to him when everything else seemed to be going wrong.

Of course, I had to—or could—share him with other people, but there has been remarkably little jealousy among us. Waugh was more famous for his wit than for his sympathy, but his work attracts a number of people generous enough to tolerate his vagaries, and for that matter mine. For example, my Australian friend Donat Gallagher and I worked on the HRC material at the same time, but by then I was using the manuscripts to study the way in which Waugh composed his novels and he was working on the intellectual background of the non-fiction. Others, from Poland to Waugh's country house, Combe Florey, where his son Auberon lived, to California, I know only through correspondence, but they have been as generous and supportive as people I have known directly and for much longer periods.

My work at the HRC also had concrete benefits for my professional career. Not long after I began cataloguing the collection, Stephen Goode of Whitston Publishing Company, who published a number of bibliographies, wrote to ask if I had enough material to expand the Firbank checklist into a book. I didn't, I told him, but I could certainly produce enough for the first book-length bibliography of Waugh.

In fact, I couldn't, but by this time I knew the people who could. Charles Linck had put me in touch with Paul A. Doyle, the first bibliographer of Waugh and founder of *Evelyn Waugh Newsletter* after the death of Waugh, who had been notoriously scornful of academics, especially Americans. Paul subsequently complained that I cost him a subscriber every time I reviewed a book for him, but over the years he provided crucial information and loaned me rare books while supporting the

Newsletter out of his own pocket. He and Linck, along with Heinz Kosok, the German scholar who contributed a running list of work about Waugh to the *Newsletter,* were the most obvious and richest sources of material, and with their help I produced the *Checklist* of works by and about Waugh.

As bibliographies go, the *Checklist* was fairly easy to produce. But the expanded *Bibliography of Evelyn Waugh,* which appeared fourteen years later, was subject not only to the vicissitudes of normal life but was complicated by the wild expansion of scholarly publication between the late 1960s and the early 1980s. We have learned to expect and to work around things like mail strikes in Canada; the theft of a briefcase full of original material; the internationalization of scholarship which leads to collaboration with people scattered from the Bay of Fundy to the Great Barrier Reef; a change in management at the publisher; the chief editor's trips to Europe; and the various distractions of the academic life. The index had to be completely re-done because three hundred new items turned up after it had supposedly been completed.

The resulting book was more than twice as long as the *Checklist*, not merely because of the fifteen additional years of secondary material but because Gallagher had discovered 240 new items by Waugh and the Canadian scholar Margaret Morriss had found over 1,000 additional items about Waugh published within the span covered by the *Checklist.*

Of course, a bibliography is obsolete even before it goes to the publisher. In the first six years, 1984 through 1989, after our terminal date for listing material, I found forty pages worth of additional material for a projected supplement. This does not include a two-inch thick stack of note cards, an item per card, to check further before entering. Copies of and references to material from 1990 to the present have gone into a growing series of folders or of files downloaded from MLA and other cd bibliographies which should be, and have not been, sorted and presented in the proper format. I transferred some the information to computer disk, but in the process I realized that I would rather build barbed wire fence barehanded than prepare another edition. So, with the help of a Waugh enthusiast in California, I uploaded the material onto the Internet, where younger scholars can use it as they will.

Long before this, I realized that the HRC material could be exploited for a book on Waugh's habits of composition. However, I kept being interrupted, or interrupting myself when a work or topic in my courses in modern English and American fiction caused an itch that needed scratching or I had the opportunity, following Fred Hoffman's example, to review a cluster of books on a single author or topic.

Finally I pushed through the end of the book on Waugh towards which I had been aiming for nearly two decades, the fourth I had mined from the veins of the HRC. But when I emerged blinking into daylight, I discovered that the novel theory I had read in the 1960s had been rendered obsolete by something called "post-structuralism." "Post?" I thought. I hadn't even heard of structuralism. I had missed a whole movement, and I would never catch up.

But I had a more immediate concern: finding someone willing to read my manuscript. Later a reviewer commented that I worked on Waugh when there wasn't any money in it, apparently on the mistaken assumption that such work is now profitable. But at the end of the 1970s, there was no money and not much interest. Still, after some disappointing near-misses, I managed to place the book that I regarded as the peak and, I sometimes feared, the end of my career, prepared to study Waugh no more, went through a divorce, and tried to think about what I was going to do with the rest of my life.

It turns out that Waugh was as difficult to get rid of as Tar Baby. Catholic University of America Press asked if I could produce a book for a series they were publishing, and with some scissors and paste Hoffmanized previously published material and a push to write new, much of the work done while I was teaching and being a tourist at Dalhousie University in Canada, I produced *Evelyn Waugh and the Forms of His Time* and even managed to salvage bits on Van Vechten from my dissertation. Not long after, Twayne wrote to ask if I'd write a monograph on *Brideshead Revisited*, and after spending a month in a mountain cabin in New Mexico, I emerged to clean up the manuscript and myself.

Penguin asked me to edit and annotate *A Handful of Dust*, so that I could draw upon textual study I had done more or less incidentally over the years. The novel that Sam Marx and I planned to write about Waugh in Hollywood was stalled by Sam's death and postponed by my work on his papers. But I went ahead with a fictional version that publishers and agents found enjoyable but thought no one else would, so it circulated in the capitalist version of *samizdat*. So I retrofitted the story into factual narrative for *Mischief in the Sun*.

Walter Sullivan was wrong: there wasn't any money in any of these books, and very little fame. For example, Valentine Cunningham, who teaches at Oxford, complained that there was no annotated edition of *A Handful of Dust* even though Blackwell's has some copies of my edition at its Oxford store.

More recently, Carlos Villar Flor, a member of a younger generation, invited me to Spain to give lectures that I then had to write. Since the turn of the millennium, I've dribbled out notes and some queries for the resuscitated *Evelyn Waugh Newsletter*.

More than fifty years after I first read Waugh and more than forty after I first published on him, it's fair to ask what I have learned from all this something I asked myself for the first time while writing this. I can think of several things:

1. I learned from careful reading and rereading of Waugh's published writing and especially from working with his manuscripts something about style and rhythm that has affected my writing more by immersion than by imitation. One correspondent thought I was an Englishman; another, judging from my telephone voice and from my writing, that I was short and fat.

2. I learned something, from Waugh as well as from mentors equally unconscious of their effect, of the joys as well as the pains of being deeply engaged with one's work, of never taking one's own words as inviolable—this is from the third draft of a very casual talk—and of the pride in doing work carefully and promptly, though not always as carefully and promptly as I should have.

3. I learned that if I worked hard enough and, more important, long enough, that I would get to go places that I had barely imagined even as a graduate student, and that I could meet a wide variety of stimulating and agreeable people, some of whom don't on the surface seem to have much in common with a provincial monoglot and some of whom very generously seem to take me much more seriously than I take myself.

4. I learned never to say never. Although I don't plan to do any more

extended work on Waugh, except to edit *Brideshead Revisited,* I hope to continue trying to avoid glaring at the computer screen through thicker and thicker glasses while not getting drool on the keyboard. And I do have some more essays on 1930s British writers tucked in my files.

5. To adapt to the scholarly life Alfred Doolittle's remark on undeserving poverty—pace Walter Sullivan again—it's the only life that has any spice to it, like. I wish my successors the same joy that I have had. And if they find joy in revising and extending the bibliography, they are welcome to continue work I have happily abandoned.

6. It is never, at least in my experience, a mistake to share your findings with other scholars. True, some have been reluctant to cite published work on which they have drawn. But I have found that help given pays manifold returns.

7. I hope that I can say, as Waugh did to Julian Jebb, that I have done my best or at least that I have not failed to repay all of those, so many, who have helped, encouraged, and criticized me over more than fifty years and have become a kind of extended family who get a different kind of jokes from my biological family.

8. Finally, or perhaps not, the work of many people has enabled me to meet and learn from a new generation of scholars. I think I can say with my contemporaries and elders that they will know more than we ancients. Perhaps it is not too egotistical, though it may be vain, to hope that we are at least a little of that which they know.

Tools of the Trade

"A good Ph.D. ought to be able and willing to write a doctor's dissertation every year during the rest of his life—a somewhat horrible thought."

Hardin Craig, *Literary Study and the Scholarly Profession* (1944)

Apparently many people who get doctorates in English fail to realize that the skills, however modest, that enabled them to write a dissertation can be used in other areas besides preparing for courses and especially for seminars. When I finished my dissertation, I planned to write about Waugh and Firbank. But as Fred Hoffman had noticed, I have always been easily distracted, and when an acquisitions editor from Prentice-Hall came to my office to ask if I had any ideas for textbooks, I remembered the work on novel theory I had used in my dissertation and proposed that. In those boom days, publishers were eager to cash in on the increasing number of humanities majors—now if it can't reach the mass freshman market, they aren't interested—and after some weeks passed he returned with a contract for me to sign over lunch. Of course, gathering the material and then commenting on it was not as easy as I expected, but the process did force me to think through some of the issues I had only touched on in the dissertation, and it brought me into contact with Maynard Mack, Stirling Professor of English at Yale. I was impressed to be working with a major scholar whose work on Pope I had used as a graduate student. At the 1969 MLA convention, pleasant for me, disastrous for the profession at large, I was invited to Prentice-Hall's cocktail party because it had published my anthology on theory of the novel. Mack, that year's president of the MLA, was general editor of the series in which my book appeared and of Twentieth Century Views, which consisted of collections of essays on the works of major authors. The series did not include Waugh and, because Mack thought him insufficiently prominent, never did. So I shifted to another Catholic author, Graham Greene, who at the time was taken more seriously because he seemed to take himself very seriously indeed. Mack said that he would think about it. A month or so later, I received a letter from him asking me to do the TCV volume on John Steinbeck and assuring me that no editor in the series had suffered financially from participation. I realized that Mack was a very, very intelligent man—his reputation was based on much more than his work on Pope—but I wondered if he were suffering from a brief lapse or had followed the train of association from Steinbeck to Oklahoma to Davis. A better explanation, I realized later, was that he had commissioned Samuel Hynes to do the Greene volume, that he didn't know anyone obvious to do the Steinbeck, and that, despite the lack of evidence that I knew or cared anything about Steinbeck, he thought that I could handle the assignment.

Except for leading discussions of *The Grapes of Wrath* for sections of Paul Wiley's course at Wisconsin and reading a few other novels, I didn't know anything about Steinbeck and would never have thought of him. I had a brief struggle with my conscience in terms that my Jesuit ethics professor would have approved. Was it just for me to work on an author of whom I knew almost nothing? Was it prudent for me to take time away from the real lines of my research? On the other hand, my bibliography course, my experience with Hoffman, and my work on the novel anthology had given me the skills necessary for the job: how to find the material and evaluate it. On a practical level, did I want to refuse an offer from Maynard Mack, especially for a book in a series in which two very senior former colleagues at Santa Barbara were represented.

So, using the ethical principle of double effect, which in vulgar terms anticipated the theory that everything is always compared to what, I took the advance. At first, it looked as though God was punishing me, because with it I bought a used car which turned out to be a disaster. But in reading Steinbeck straight through, I recognized some of the settings, including the Dust Bowl, in which my family had lived, and some of values and strengths that had enabled them to endure. This was the first time I had made any connection between my personal past and my professional training, a connection that was to be important more than a decade later.

Later, an attempt to discover for a course what had been written about Donald Barthelme led me to others working in the field, diverting me from the Waugh archive. When I'd mined that for a catalogue, a bibliography, and a study of Waugh's habits of composition, I began to look for something or someone else to write about. Drawing upon a course in popular narrative forms and on a request for a contribution to *Acta Litteraria Academicae Scientiarum Hungaricae*, a ponderous venue for my very informal approach, I began to write about the literature and later the culture and history of the American West (more about that another time and place), as well as to draw directly upon my past experience and direct observation to write what is now called creative nonfiction, first in a comparison of the Danube and Missouri rivers.

The Western book was for a while more like a retirement fantasy than a serious project, at least until I had to use it as a pretext for a sabbatical leave in 1983. Faced with actually writing the book, I realized that I was less interested in what the novelists said or meant than in what their books meant to someone who had grown up watching two B-minus movies every Saturday at the Casino Theater in Boonville, Missouri. Seven years later, when I finished the book, especially the introduction, conclusion, and transitions, I had been forced to think even more seriously about who I was and why I was that way.

But in 1983, with the sabbatical and U. S. Information Service lectures in France, Yugoslavia, and Germany, I merely went to Paris to write another chapter of the book—perfectly reasonable, since that is where James Fenimore Cooper wrote *The Prairie*, which I had ducked as an undergraduate but finally had to read in order to lecture at the University of Paris. At the same time, I was trying to sort out my reactions to Paris and write about leaving my home town for the big city in wider and wider swings. But I couldn't settle on a voice that didn't sound smug or smartass.

By the late 1980s, I had a fairly satisfactory draft of the *Playing Cowboys: Low Culture and High Art in the Western,* but I had only a couple of essays, apparently unrelated, for the more personal book. Another semester in Hungary, this time in a provincial town which presented fewer distractions than Budapest, gave me the time and space to outline *Mid-Lands: A Family Album*, two-thirds of which I wrote in six weeks after I returned to Oklahoma.

In my early sixties I made a fourth trip to Europe and solidified some old friendships and made some new ones, leading to more and wider contacts and a desire to repay hospitality by doing what I could to make the region's writers better known to American readers. Those modest efforts incurred further obligations as conference organizers and editors issued invitations to participate, as scholar or creative writer, in Central and Southeastern Europe.

As a friend from graduate school said early in my career when I told him that I was giving a paper on Ronald Firbank at the Rocky Mountain Modern Language Association Meeting in Tucson, Arizona, "You'll go anywhere." (I didn't tell him that I'd already given a paper on Firbank and Aubrey Beardsley at Panhandle A & M College in Goodwell, Oklahoma, because that was a truth he couldn't have handled.) And since I had grown up in what one of my editors characterized as a world bounded by Kansas City, St. Louis, heaven, and hell, why not? Much later, my ex-wife perceptively summarized much of my career over the last two decades as "wandering around talking to people and coming home and writing about it." Along the way, I seemed to have metamorphosed from what a graduate school contemporary called my "very proper butler" stance into a simulacrum of Ernest Hemingway accurate enough to impress a very charming woman I met flying back from Europe. Even if I'd scorned Papa, which I didn't and don't, entirely, I have reason to be grateful to him.

Along the way, I was getting farther into my sixties, and while the university couldn't make me retire and I had no clear plans to do so, I could foresee, with increasing clarity, a time when I would stop teaching, and when I did, having observed that older colleagues who left town tended to live longer than those who stayed near the university, I was going to leave Oklahoma. When I did, I was not going to have my accustomed access to a comparable research library and would have to give up the heavily-footnoted mode of my early career. So I made a conscious decision to become a man of letters (sorry about the gender) and try to write for a broader audience, perhaps become a travel writer or work in other genres for general circulation magazines, writing in what the fat

Englishman Cyril Connolly called Vernacular as opposed to formal or Mandarin style and to become, in Philip Rahv's distinction, more Redskin than Paleface. Maybe even do movie scripts. (No.)

Those intentions were sometimes difficult to carry out because, like many wanderers in Western film and fiction, I found it hard to escape my past. Calls for conference papers and the desire to see old friends tempted me back to the academic circuit. The title or author of a scholarly book led me to request review copies, sometimes to the author's consternation. Even there, however, my approach became more personal, my style less formal. Of one such result, *Born-Again Skeptic & Other Valedictions*, my co-editor on our undergraduate newspaper remarked that I sounded much as I had in the 1950s, though I hope that the pretensions to knowledge are less obvious than they were almost sixty years ago.

But the lessons I more or less unconsciously absorbed then and later in graduate school have been valuable: work to deadline, accept editorial suggestions that make sense, know how much time and effort an assignment deserves, and avoid what Brother Antoninus/William Everson called "the fallacy of the perfect work." Or, as Kenny Rogers sings, "know when to fold em."

These guidelines have combined with the oral culture of my family and region to lead me to strive to follow at least one of fellow Missourian Mark Twain's rules governing romantic fiction, that "the talk shall sound like human talk, and be talk such as human beings would be likely to talk in the given circumstances, and have a discoverable meaning, also a discoverable purpose, and a show of relevancy, and remain in the neighborhood of the subject at hand, and be interesting to the reader, and help out the tale, and stop when the people cannot think of anything more to say." As my son said, no one who knows me expects that to happen.

Another Country

Looking back, I see a pattern of behavior that on an individual scale echoes Hemingway's view that people know when a country is used up and move on. That was the case in my leaving Kansas City for somewhere, the University of Kansas for Wisconsin, Loyola University for California, Oklahoma for Arizona and, one of the longest and most significant jumps, from the United States to Europe, which set off a series of personal and professional changes for me.

People who know about my thirty-year association with Budapest tend to ask obvious questions: why I keep going back and especially in the case of Hungarians what differences I see. While those deserve answers, they interest me less than the question of what differences, over three decades, I see in myself, especially those connected to my experiences in Hungary.

That's not too difficult to answer in general terms, but more specific-ally the response gets complicated by the interweaving of various themes and variations in my personal and professional life.

Another question is why I went to Hungary in the first place, and the simple answer is that by 1981 I needed to go somewhere. My marriage of two decades had collapsed, I had published the scholarly book about Evelyn Waugh I had been working on steadily for at least a decade and working towards for much longer. I thought it was good, but after enthusiastic readers' reports to an Ivy League press, the editorial board decided not to publish it and a lesser but respectable press hung onto it for months without making a decision. Finally a senior colleague who had founded a small press offered to publish it, and I decided to accept his offer and move on with my life. I had no idea what anyone else would think of it—the first reviews, in some of the best journals ever to mention me, didn't come out until the following year—and I had no clear idea of what I was going to do next. My relations with my colleagues of some fourteen years had stagnated at best, so that I was tired of talking every day to the same people about the same things, and the attractions, what they were, of Norman, Oklahoma, had worn thin. The most obvious out was a Fulbright fellowship, and after I examined the list of available jobs and countries and plugging in a few requirements, out came Eötvös Loránd University in Budapest, behind the Iron Curtain in Cold War days.

None of my family had been to Europe since my great-grandfather Herman Litschgi got off the boat from Germany in the 1870s, and I had only been outside US borders four times, in very brief cross-border visits to Tijuana and to Matamoros at opposite ends of the Mexican border and in two somewhat longer visits to Canada. In all of these, I could get by with English except at a fast-food chicken place in Montreal where they called out your order by number in Quebeçois French too fast for me.

I don't remember having lusted to go to Hungary or indeed anywhere in Central Europe. In fact, early in grade school, reading about the *Anschluss*, I wondered that the Germans were clever enough to drive tanks to Australia. Later, the 1956 revolution made me aware of where Hungary was and of what the broader geopolitical issues were, but that was the extent of my knowledge.

It's tempting to say, as Conrad did of his trip to the Congo, that before I went to Hungary "I was a mere animal." That would be too dramatic. I had a Ph.D., a tenured professorship, respectable curriculum vitae. I had more or less recovered from my divorce and had a steady relationship with a beautiful and interesting woman that might evolve into marriage.

By the time that relationship was burgeoning, I accepted a summer teaching job in Canada, gave up my apartment, stored my possessions, took off for the first of many cross country drives, and enjoyed every minute. The final arrangements for the Fulbright were made while I was in Canada, and I returned to Oklahoma only long enough to repack, add a romantic complication, say goodbye, and catch the first of four planes booked for me with more than usual bureaucratic inefficiency.

However, on every flight there were one or more people doing things very different from my colleagues: a woman troubleshooter for the Navy, a clinical psychologist who wanted to turn her dissertation into a book about fathers and daughters (a subject I was and still am interested in and a process I knew something about), a Nigerian architectural student, a striking woman dance instructor from the UK on her way to Brussels after a working vacation in the US. From London to Budapest on British Air, first class, I sat next to a youngish Brit technocrat who was full of general information about the business side of Budapest, centering on the Hilton, that was interesting but turned out not be very useful.

The first sign that I was behind the Iron Curtain hit me as the plane descended, for on a runway, a quarter mile from anyone and a half mile from anything else, stood a soldier on guard duty. When we walked down the ramp from the plane, we saw another soldier with a submachine gun slung butt upward over his shoulder. I had the feeling that Hungary was like the Hotel California in the Eagles' song: you could check out any time you liked, but you could never leave. A second sign, perhaps, was the failure of my luggage to show up at baggage claim, though this may have been due to the cargo limits of the plane or the inefficiency of Heathrow baggage handlers rather than the Communist desire to inspect my bags for contraband. By this time I had been awake for what seemed like days and was too tired to be indignant or paranoid.

The Embassy's press and cultural advisor and a driver met me at the airport and took me into the city. I began to realize that while many things might be different, some were not. The advisor pointed out some tall, sterile apartment buildings and called them Stalinesque. "In Chicago," I replied, "they're called projects." And I learned my first word of Hungarian, "virag," flower, because it is the name of Leopold Bloom's father in James Joyce's *Ulysses*. Of course, the banks of blossoms outside the store front were a good clue.

After that, things got more difficult. I was left at the apartment of Oliver Nagy on Tanács körút, a street name since tossed down the post-Communist memory hole. But I didn't have a decent dictionary, a map, or directions to the Embassy. Fortunately I met Nagy's father, who, I later learned in a three-way conversation with a South American student who spoke both English and Hungarian, had fought in World War II for the Germans against the Russians and then for the Russians against the

Germans, after being an Olympic-class pentathlete. That seemed to me authentically Central European. I was even more certain after he indicated slyly that I was free to have women guests, pretty much my lowest priority at that point. He gave me a map, and after the English department chairman phoned to invite me to dinner, I was able to call the Embassy and reconnect with what I still regarded as civilization.

Outside the apartment, things were even more complicated, since at that period no one except those who had a very good reason could speak English, and Hungarian, a member of the Finno-Ugric family, is emphatically not an Indo-European language. Even after thirty years and a dozen or so trips to the country, I find the conventions of transcribing sounds so difficult that I would have to learn the written and spoken languages separately because the supposedly logical pronunciation of Hungarian doesn't translate easily for Anglophones and the existence of several possible diacriticals over vowels indicates not stress but length. Hungarian has a few words cognate with English, and I formulated the theory that these words signified concepts that the Magyars didn't have when they came to the Carpathian basin in the tenth century. They had no "kolléga," so they had no "probléma." Probably I don't have the plurals right, and I've read that Hungarian has at least eighteen noun cases and perhaps twenty-one, but I'll never be competent to check that out. Also, Hungarian pronouns do not have genders, so speakers of what they call "Hunglish" will confuse "he" and "she." But Hungary does have genders, as I discovered early on when I didn't distinguish between "nök" and "férfiak" on my first visit to the university. "W.C.," pronounced something like "vaytsay," was one of my first words, good for getting general directions. The first Hungarian sentence I learned, which incorporates the only verb I ever learned, and I may have the ending wrong, was "Nem tudom Magyarul," which means "I don't understand (or speak) Hungarian."

Hungarians don't really expect anyone else to learn their language, and when I didn't understand Hungarian, they would try German. While I don't know any German except what I picked up from my Scots-American grandfather who married into a German-speaking family, it's possible for an English speaker to fake enough to get by in basic situations. . If I couldn't navigate that, I would say "angol" or "amerikai." There weren't many Americans in Hungary at that time, so that most people regarded me as a novelty. The manager of a clothing store in Óbuda, who had spent time in Canada, called his clerks over so that they could hear what a native speaker sounded like.

There was other evidence of Hungarian fascination with things western, dating back to the early twentieth century and the Nyugat or West movement, which tried to link the country to contemporary culture rather than to the Balkans and farther east. Sometimes attempts at imitation struck odd notes, like sweatshirts reading "Princeton Lions" and "California University."

But I didn't find out in those early days that I might be exotic and interesting. For the first week, I spent a fair amount of time being sorry for myself because I felt abandoned by the university (not the department) and the ministry of education. But the Embassy staff was more efficient than any other bureaucracy I encountered. I managed to get paid; I found a laundromat (not all that easy), I was given an office by a very nice senior professor who was going on leave, a linguist who looked like a well-fed Peter Lorre and who later died, I was told, while delivering a paper at a conference.

But the immediate problem was learning to meet basic needs. I was paid just over 7000 a month in forints, the local currency, about $169 at the artificially pegged rate of 42 to the dollar. The currency was and still is colorful and featured likenesses of artists like Bela Bartok or revolutionaries like Lajos Kossuth or both like Sándor Petöfi.

Forints couldn't be taken out of the country, as if, my Hungarian colleagues said, anyone would want them. The situation in Poland was so dire that Poles were coming to Budapest to try to acquire forints. Obvious foreigners were beset by touts chanting "Change money? Change money?" The Embassy staff emphasized strongly that this was forbidden and could lead to trouble for Americans, although one Hungarian had brought in a sheaf of photocopied dollars and complained of being cheated. The touts must have had their version of the bush telegraph, because one day in Ferenciek square I responded to the question with "Oh, yeah, buddy, I have a shit-load of forints I need to get rid of" and was never bothered again.

The sum doesn't sound like much, but I had no real financial worries, partly because I was also being paid in dollars. Besides, goods and services were cheap. I don't remember many prices, but a single ticket for the bus or subway was one forint, the same price as for use of a public toilet.

My housing was covered, and the apartment in which I had a room was in the center of downtown Pest on the inner ring, convenient to the university and the meeting place of the three subway lines. But I was unused to sharing living quarters, let alone a bathroom, with strangers, and after one of my colleagues expressed indignation that I wasn't being treated better, I was given an apartment in a project-like building in Óbuda, or Old Buda, on the other side of the Danube and three bridges farther north. It had a minimalist kitchen—one-butt, as a fellow Missourian later expressed it—and a washing machine with neither wringer nor dryer. But it was private, had a view of the Danube if I looked out, and, if I looked down, excavations revealing physical remains of many centuries of human occupation, Roman and perhaps before and a thousand years of Hungarian.

Food I mostly had to take care of myself. Fortunately, near the Tanács körút flat was a cafeteria, and by using the techniques nod and smile, point and grunt, I was able to get something to eat. In grocery stores, more like the family-owned neighborhood stores of my childhood than supermarkets, the clerks rang up items and pointed to the total. "Tonic," accented on the first syllable, meant any kind of soft drink. And coffee is coffee, though the intonation is different. Espresso was too thick for my taste, so I drank my first cappuccino in Budapest. I'd quit drinking alcohol (very confusing to the Hungarians and even more confusing when I didn't object to other people drinking), so I didn't have to learn the words for beer or wine. Street vendors of ice cream responded to the point and grunt method, though I learned that holding up an index finger got me two cones because Hungarians start counting with the thumb.

When I moved to Óbuda, the local ABC offered a little more variety than the Tanács körút store, and I could pick things like jars of Bulgarian cherries from the shelf. The meat or deli counter was more of a challenge, since it had more goods than I had words for, so that the words for cuts and weights of meat were beyond my competence. I did learn to say "fél kilo Trappista," which means a half kilo or pound of Trappist cheese (the Communists kept the name while deploring the order of its origin).

Fortunately, I was given commissary privileges at the Embassy, and that was useful, especially in providing guests with whiskey and American cigarettes. Even more of a novelty to Hungarians were the paper shopping bags. When I returned bottles to the ABC, the clerks would look at the bags in wonder. I'd say "amerikai," and they would nod and say "Ah!" This reaction was due, as a colleague told me, to the relative scarcity and poor quality of Hungarian paper products.

That included toilet paper, which was rather rough. But it was, mostly, available in stores, and toilet attendants would give customers about four squares after the fee was paid. When traveling by rail, it was wise to carry one's own supply because second class toilets rarely had toilet paper, and although first class had some at the beginning of a journey, it disappeared within fifteen or twenty minutes. Later things improved, but as I told a young American poet in Macedonia, it was a good idea to carry a stash anywhere east and south of Budapest.

My diet was supplemented by lunches at the faculty dining room, for which University employees, including Fulbrighters and visitors from other countries, were given chits. The menu featured pork and pasta and, in lieu of salads, beets, slaw, and other single-ingredient raw vegetables. (Hungarians have since figured out how to make what Americans think of as salads.) The food was not exciting, but on the whole it was at least as good as and often better than other institutional food I've eaten, and the companionship of various colleagues was a definite improvement over solitary meals, as silent as the original makers of the cheese.

Restaurants were problematic. What a colleague called the Communist capital restaurants—Berlin, Sofia, and so on—had extensive menus, sometimes in English, promising mouth-watering dishes of exotic meats and fish. But when one tried to order them, the response was a curt "Nincs" (roughly translatable as "fuggedaboutit"), at the time the default word at any shop for almost any kind of goods. But some restaurants served cold fruit soup, a marvelous way of getting dessert at the beginning of a meal as well as a torte at the end.

And Hungarian bread was a revelation. I'd read Henry Miller's "The Staff of Life," which does to American bread what Mark Twain did to *The Deerslayer* in "Fenimore Cooper's Literary Offences" (you can find both by Googling), but until now I had no way of confirming Miller's view that

European bread was far superior. Even the bread in the ABC was better than anything I'd found in an American supermarket, and one small shop at the Pest end of the Margaret Bridge sold marvelous darker loaves that were hard to get because old ladies lined up early in the morning to buy them. On a later visit, a Hungarian asked what kept bringing me back to Hungary. "The bread and the irony," I said, and like everything I say, that's more or less true. (More about the irony later.)

I'd brought two suitcases full of clothes, which was good because at that time Hungarian manufacturers seem to regard people my size as Gulliverian candidates for special projects. I didn't realize this until near the end of my stay, when I was trying to spend forints, as I'd go into one shoe store after another, see the clerk look at my feet, and say "Nincs." I did buy a sport coat that, when I returned to American half-gallons of ice cream, got a little tight, but it may be the jacket I wore while hosting a visiting Hungarian poet from which I pulled a plastic bag featuring words in Hungarian, thus winning his approval as an honorary countryman. I admired some of the leather coats on sale in the pricier shops, ranging from black ones reaching mid-calf that looked like something from a movie about the S.S. to a burgundy leather car coat. When I went into a shop on Lenin körút to buy that one, the clerk, as snooty as his counterpart in a Park Avenue haberdashery, said condescendingly, "That's eight thousand forints." "I know," I answered, mentally adding "you commie faggot," and started peeling off notes faster than the leather of the coat itself later peeled.

Once I learned elementary steps in taking care of myself, and as my social life began to pick up, the feeling of being abandoned began to wane. I was the only Fulbright lecturer in the country, and at that time Hungary was not a priority destination for congressional delegations, so that the American Embassy staff was pleased to see anyone new and was not only helpful but hospitable. The cultural attaché had an advanced degree in music history, more knowledge of the Hungarian language than most of his colleagues, and a quirky sense of humor that appealed to Hungarians. The office manager was friendly. I had long ago learned to be nice to people in that position, not only because my mother used to do that kind of work because they can really screw you, more by omission than direct action, if they don't like you. The press and cultural advisor and his very lively wife, underemployed by her standards, invited me to their home for official and unofficial parties, loaned me books, and in general made my life easier and more pleasant.

And there were other fortuitous connections. My Fulbright predecessor was marrying a Hungarian professor of physics, and I was invited to the wedding. (His predecessor, the first Fulbrighter in Hungary, had married a Hungarian before he came, and pointed comments were directed at me as a candidate for future nuptials, a prediction that failed.) There I met Professor László Orság, the revered founder of American Studies in Hungary and compiler of a Hungarian-English dictionary, who carried a cane and wore a cape and looked every inch a distinguished European scholar. We spoke briefly, but all I remember is his complaint about the amount of his pension.

But he was a very different kind of person than the kind I generally encountered in Oklahoma, and so was György Sándor, returned to Budapest to judge an international piano competition. The Embassy's cultural attaché invited me to join Sándor and a very Midwestern American and his wife on a trip to the Danube Bend. Sándor had played the premiere performance of Bartok's third piano concerto, and on the way we listened to a tape of that performance and to Sándor's commentary. I now know that he was even more distinguished than I had realized, but at the time he impressed me as the epitome of the European sophisticate: worldly, humorous, a bit cynical, a sharp contrast to the very Midwestern couple and me.

Some of the people I met at the home of the press and cultural advisor were perhaps less polished, but I felt more comfortable talking to them. At a screening of Neil Diamond's remake of *The Jazz Singer*, I sat next to Pál Safer, a scriptwriter and director. In an early scene, a young Black man is given a yarmulke as he enters a synagogue and perches it atop his extreme Afro. I leaned toward Safer and said, "That's funny, he doesn't look Jewish." Apparently the joke is universal, for he laughed, and for the rest of the film we traded snide jokes about the more obvious plot turns and sentimental situations and dialogue.

Later I met György Konrad, author of *The Case Worker* and co-author of *The Intellectuals on the Road to Class Power*, which drew uncomfortable parallels between the Communist apparat and the Tsarist regime and led Hungarian officials to suggest that he leave the country. He was delighted that I genuinely liked Budapest, spoke of some of the disadvantages of living under official disapproval, and invited me to meet him at a favorite restaurant. He didn't show up, and people to whom I mentioned his absence said that, since he was famous for not keeping appointments, it was obviously the same person. But it was worth meeting someone who had, in his writing and in his life, put something on the line.

A few times I was co-opted by the Embassy to show something of Budapest to visiting writers, most notably Robert Hass, good company, a lively mind, a similar Catholic background, and the kind of poet who helped me to realize that I might have something to say in that genre. As we crossed the Liberty Bridge, he said, "Imagine! Two country boys walking across the Danube!" Well, some are more country than others, but I was grateful for being put in his company.

But week to week, I depended on colleagues from the department. They were a varied lot, ranging from Feri Takács, a friend who seems still to embody the ironic spirit of central Europe, to quite serious scholars to a man who seemed more like a nineteenth-century German professor of philology than a Hungarian. Takács had the best geopolitical, mostly anti-Soviet jokes, and years later insisted that "a language is a dialect that has its own army." (Some versions add "and a navy," but that wouldn't occur to a late twentieth century Hungarian.) He and others helped me get membership at the Gorky Library (built for the YMCA and post-1989 called the National Foreign Language Library), which had some fairly current work in English, and also in the National Academy, which I never used.

My colleagues were less informative about the structure and goals of the higher education system. Later I compared it to traffic conventions in Paris: clearly there were some, but an outsider would probably never be able to figure them out. I did learn that students had to have two majors and carry about 24 hours of course work a term, and on the analogy of the Warsaw Pact joke that "they pretend to pay us, and we pretend to work," I decided that academically we pretended to teach the students and they pretended to study because the course load was as artificially inflated as the currency. This was particularly true of the fifth-year lecture course I taught once a week, though "taught" is an exaggeration. Many of the students were working, some practice teaching, and it was generally agreed that attendance was neither mandatory nor practicable. I gave one lecture, in quite a large hall with a good view of some Roman ruins and the Danube, to six people.

Since my topic was the American West, I undoubtedly got more out of the course than they did, since the Academy journal requested and published an article on Owen Wister's *The Virginian* which I wrote with what my colleagues thought alarming speed and which was another step towards a book that didn't appear until more than a decade later.

The other classes were better attended, and the students actually wrote and gave reports and, with some prodding, entered into discussions of the material and at least once even disagreed with me. A seminar in the American short story was one of the best groups I had in forty-five years of teaching, and two of those students are still friends.

Early in the term, some students asked if I would be willing to meet with them. Of course, I said, but there seemed to be little follow-up either because that was a pro forma request or because they expected me to take initiatives I didn't know how to take. But later the English club discovered me, and I conducted the Hungarian premiere of *Shane* for the fifth year people—that drew a crowd—and repeated it for the club. They liked the dog that lies on his master's grave. And, after some negotiation, I gave a lecture, with taped and *a capella* illustrations, on country and western music, drawing on music from the juke boxes of my youth in Missouri and on fourteen years of AM radio in Oklahoma. That was probably the most successful lecture I gave in Hungary. The women students particularly enjoyed the clueless patriarchal attitude in Shel Silverstein's "Put Another Log on the Fire."

Once in a while, students complained that I was talking too fast or in an unintelligible accent (students were familiar with BBC and New York English), and my colleagues kept urging me to slow down in general. I began to realize that, whatever their failings, American academics seemed to take their jobs a lot more seriously than my new colleagues, perhaps because we could actually live on our academic salaries and didn't have to take second or third jobs. At the time, I thought I was not only going slow but was in reverse and still losing most of the students in the rearview mirror. But when I cancelled a week of classes to extend fall break in order to take a triangular trip to Venice, Florence, and Vienna, my colleagues complimented me on finally adjusting to Hungarian pace. That was a pleasant interlude that, while it certainly expanded my range of cultural reference, had the odd effect of making me eager to return to my temporary home. In particular, my walks past the uniform architecture of the Ringstrasse made Budapest's eclecticism seem more attractive; the Viennese were clearly more prosperous than the Budapesters, but not as various; and seeing an Ibusz bus caused instant nostalgia.

It is clear, years later, that although I made friendships that have lasted for three decades, I had really fallen in love with a city. After fourteen years in Norman, Oklahoma, larger now but hardly more interesting than it was then and topographically challenged, I was hungry for something to look at besides strip malls and housing developments. In my undergraduate days, I had enjoyed Kansas City as far as the limits of public transportation and my pocket allowed. Chicago was even more exciting, but I was trying to finish a dissertation, begin a career, and start a family, so I had little time to enjoy it.

But in Budapest, I had no family in the vicinity and few personal ties, and I was free to roam the city in wider circles and longer tangents because Pest is laid out in a series of arcs looping from north to south and ending at the Danube. At first I walked through downtown Pest, charmed by vision of courtyards receding into the dusk, laughing at some of the more extravagant architectural touches like the building opposite Deák tér with at least five styles of decoration or the one south of the university that seemed like an ordinary, boring rectangular box on end until one looked up far enough to see the replica of a Greek temple on top.

Moving farther out was easy because, though locals complained about public transportation, and still do, the system covers a great deal of the city with great efficiency. Often I would get on a tram, ride to the end of the line, catch a bus or another tram and ride that. Outside the downtown area, scenery was sometimes industrial and often shabby, but I was learning that even the most beautiful buildings rest at some level on an infrastructure in which utility is more important than aesthetics.

Equally important was the fact that there was always someplace to go—not just the Castle or Heroes' Square with their museums and memorials to imperial aspirations, or gorgeous baroque churches, but more plebian attractions like the zoo. Early on, when I was least confident of my ability to function, I went to the zoo, perhaps with a buried memory of the line in Nathanael West's *Miss Lonelyhearts* about the man who might be steadied by looking at a buffalo. I didn't see any buffalo, but I did enjoy seeing a black panther cub stalking his mother, and overhearing a conversation between a large blond German father and a small blond daughter cheers me up every time I think about it. He was trying to interest her in an alligator, which was doing what alligators mostly do, lie still. "Das ist sleben," he insisted. The little girl looked skeptically at the gator and said, quite sensibly from her perspective, "Das ist nicht sleben. Das is tod!"

Interesting in a different way was the HungExpo, well outside the tourist area, which featured goods from places like Cuba and Albania where I was forbidden to travel. Judging from what I saw, I wasn't missing major shopping opportunities, but I regretted that the Russian part of the exhibit wasn't opened. The most surprising thing I saw was a large bank of monitors showing Tina Turner and her backup group. This was over thirty years ago, remember, when she could really shake a tailfeather. The crowd watching her, the largest at the expo, had never seen anything like it and stood in open-mouthed wonder.

I enjoyed the museums, especially an exhibit of small sculpture at the Hall of Art, where none of the pieces I liked won a prize, and the Museum of Fine Arts, which, along with the big names, including a marvelous small Rembrandt of a beef carcass, hung highly accomplished paintings by artists I had never heard of. The Hungarian National Gallery in the Castle had more dross, but also spectacular paintings by Tivadar Csontváry, whose work I have never seen outside Hungary, and other interesting artists whose work hasn't traveled well.

Some trips almost seemed like adventures. My guide book (now obsolete because many of the street names have reverted to their pre-Communist designations) described a castle museum in Nagytétény, as far southeast in Budapest as one could go, on the right bank of the Danube. Getting there by tram required at least two transfers to increasingly casual lines, and the one to the museum meandered through back ways, past small holdings and some larger ones, all with gardens, often out of sight of streets. At one point the tram ran on a single track, so that the driver had to stop and exchange keys with the driver coming from the opposite direction to give to the switchman.

In 1981, Nagytétény still seemed like a village remote from Budapest, to which it had been annexed in 1949. It was so small that it seemed to have only one Catholic church, and the houses and row houses seemed to have been left in their original state. The castle had been replaced in the 1740s by what Americans would call a mansion. It was difficult for a middle-class American to imagine how the inhabitants had used the space, except for a few of the state or ball rooms. Most of them contained furniture and decorative touches from the fifteenth to the nineteenth centuries, including a cabinet which opened into a miniature courtyard lined with ivory pillars.

My pleasure was later compounded by learning that no one at the Embassy had ever heard of the museum, let alone visited it. Now, I have learned, the tram line has given way to a bus; the easy walk to the Danube has been made more difficult by a new highway; and the satellite map reveals a number of apartment buildings—all signs of progress trumping picturesqueness.

A few times I managed to see something of the country outside Budapest. There was the excursion to the Danube Bend, repeated and augmented in a tour arranged for visiting professors that took us not only to the cathedral in Esztergom but the Ecclesiastical Museum, featuring, the guide told us, a painting traded by a parish priest for a new car. Certainly an interesting variation on the usual details about provenance. But I enjoyed even more a solitary trip to Szentendre, rather like the Taos of Hungary with museums devoted to the work of individual artists who had worked there. The old town, on the bank of the Danube, was even more picturesque than Nagytétény, if a little self-consciously so and a great deal more so thirty years later. Going by myself gave me time to wander through the streets at my own pace and to stop at museums and galleries to see the work of people I've never encountered elsewhere.

Twice I was invited to lecture at universities outside Budapest. In Szeged, described by Takács as something Hungarians keep to remind people from the Balkans that they were in Europe now, I was given a whirlwind tour of the major sights, including a large, beautiful synagogue whose members were rounded up, deported and probably killed during

World War II. More memorable was an overnight trip to Debrecen, known as "the Calvinist Rome," a status it was able to keep because it was shielded from the Counterreformation by the Turkish occupation. There I met Zoltán Abádi-Nagy, on his way to becoming the leading Americanist in Hungary, whose company I have enjoyed over three decades, and some of his colleagues. People in that part of Hungary may no longer be Calvinist any more than people in Budapest are formally Catholic or Jewish, but they definitely seem more serious that those in the capitol, though not less genial.

Of course, being too obviously religious was a handicap under the Kádár regime, and congregations were composed mostly of older people. And as György Konrad had told me, there were some inconveniences, minor to severe, for failure to follow official political doctrine. Sometimes colleagues asked me to get books for them from the Embassy library because it was unwise to be seen going into that or into the British Embassy. In Szeged, a man asked me if I were being followed, and I answered that I didn't know because I never looked and that I didn't know enough Hungarian to get into real trouble. I was, he assured me.

But I only encountered the police on three occasions: once each to register my different residences and once in a third and potentially more difficult situation. Coming out of a showing of the film "Blue Collar," in American with Hungarian subtitles that made me wonder what the translation for "motherfucker" was, I met a group of young Americans in Budapest to learn Hungarian. We stood on the sidewalk in the cold exchanging views about our experiences when two young policemen came up and demanded to see our papers. They spent the most time looking at the passport of the only woman in the group while we continued to talk among ourselves. I said to one of the young men that he was supposed to know Hungarian, so why didn't he explain the situation. One of the cops said, "Oh, we speak English," returned our passports, and told us to go home.

Some of my Hungarian friends had traveled to the West on fellowships; others had difficulty in getting beyond the borders of the Warsaw Pact countries and, if they did, had run afoul of currency restriction laws. None whom I knew of had been to jail. Undoubtedly there were some people put there for political crimes, but I didn't know of any, and no one told me about them. (American paranoia dictated questions back in Oklahoma about whether I had been debriefed by the CIA. No.).

In 1981, the twenty-fifth anniversary of the '56 Revolution was being noted if not celebrated. The official attitude seemed to be rather like that of the South African ecclesiastical authorities towards a nineteenth century interfaith communion, "Eminently pleasing to God but on no account to be repeated." Well, without God, but with the grudging admission that some corrections in policy had been necessary and that under Kádár they had been made. I decided that enforcement of political orthodoxy was rather like the enforcement of speed limits in the US. The cops can certainly arrest you for going a few miles over the speed limit, but unless they have a hidden agenda, they probably won't. That went for dissent. You had to ramp it up fairly strongly to get arrested unless someone at any level of authority decided that it was a good idea. After the collapse of communist regimes in 1989, some hard-line dissidents argued that if you hadn't at least been jailed, you were just a pet dissident.

But being any kind of dissident was apparently easier in Hungary than in some other Warsaw Pact states. For one thing, Hungary was relatively more prosperous than some of its neighbors, and I heard that some of the Fulbrighters in Romania were on very short rations and suffering from lack of heat and electricity. There wasn't a lot of variety in the shops, but they weren't empty, at least until the Christmas shopping season began. I guessed that while Hungarian foreign policy was at least 120% of what the Russians wanted—an anti-neutron bomb rally on the steps of the National Museum, where the 1848 Revolution had been proclaimed, featured go-go dancers who almost caused a traffic jam—domestic policy was more flexible. For example, a friend told me that his father had gone on a trip to America to learn something about our agricultural policies. The report said, in effect, to watch what the Russians were doing and then do the opposite. Naturally, the report was buried, but some recommendations were quietly put into practice, and that was the reason that Hungary had more food than its neighbors.

But there was a tight control on communications. Telephones were very hard to get, partly because the Russians had taken a lot of equipment as part of war reparations and partly, Hungarians supposed, because the regime didn't encourage people talking to one another, and anyway, one had to assume that there were at least three people on the line. At that time, of course, there was no internet, and photocopiers were kept away from people who probably would produce subversive work in samisdat.

Media was limited. There wasn't a lot of news available, but I didn't have a TV set or a radio and couldn't have understood the broadcasts anyway. There was a local four-page paper, half in German and half in English, that gave minimal news, but the only thing I remember was a protest by prostitutes who accepted forints that those who insisted on hard currency were given more respect and that this was contrary to socialist doctrine. I think that I learned of the assassination of Anwar Sadat only because my second landlord worked in the Egyptian section of the Hungarian foreign office. American newspapers got to the embassy a week late, so by the time I found out sports scores, most the sting had gone out of a mediocre OU football season. But I would have been better pleased to have more direct experience of the LA Dodgers' victory over the NY Yankees in the World Series.

There wasn't much more information in letters from friends and colleagues in America, but that wasn't unexpected, since, except in rare cases, most of the people I've written to over the years are very poor correspondents. That made it easier to detach myself from romantic entanglements, family complications, and professional confusions back home.

In any case, day to day it was easy for me to forget that I was living in a totalitarian state. When students asked me how it felt to be living under socialism, I said that it made little practical difference whether the person responsible for seeing that water and heat were provided and trash picked up was called a commissar or a councilman. Less publicly, I operated on the principle that I was not in a position to convert a whole country. Although no one at the Fulbright office or the Embassy ever said so, this seemed to be their unspoken policy.

My job, then, was to go around being American and presumably showing the Hungarians the virtues of an open society. I don't know how well I accomplished this, but I did read more American writing than I was accustomed to. The only exceptions were David Lodge's *Changing Places*, about the exchange of a California and a British professor, very apposite in my circumstances, and a few Hungarian books in translation.

My past, remote and immediate, began to appear in confused fashion in my dreams. My ex-wife, a college girlfriend, and a recent lover appeared in scenes along with high school classmates, a former student whose wedding was disrupted by the brother of a former lover declaring his love, and a mixture of colleagues from two different jobs, along with a composite of a high school classmate and a former colleague. All this in various settings like Enid, Oklahoma, Wisconsin, and Rome, the last a place I'd never been. A Freudian analyst could have worked on those for years. If anything, the dreams got even stranger and mixed more unlikely people during subsequent visits.

Perhaps my subconscious was trying to pull together parts of my past so that I could reach some kind of accommodation, if not resolution, and move on to the rest of my life. In immediate terms, that meant writing, including a feature article, my first in more than two decades, comparing the Danube and the Missouri River, which runs next to the town where I grew up, the critical piece on *The Virginian*, and a lecture on Henry James's *The Bostonians* to be delivered at the University of Paris through the auspices of a woman who was doing a dissertation on Evelyn Waugh.

Reading James's not especially sympathetic portrait of a provincial intellectual on the make who clashes with a New England bluestocking, I began, as I said in a journal entry near the end of my stay, for the first time, really, since I had finished (or so I thought) with Waugh "to get excited about that in the familiar way a germ of an idea knocking from inside my skull to be realized, with a dim sense of a total form into which it will expand and fit. One of the most private and intense pleasures I know. Calmer and more localized and expectant than in sex. In general felt very content with myself especially watching the fat snowflakes around the spire of the church. Not afraid to be alone though the lack of opportunity not to be might have something to do with this. I can accept the inevitable pretty well and not really too worried about the immediate future, though uncertain whether I can translate this pleasant and unaccustomed frame of mind back to the Norman environment."

Extracting myself emotionally from Budapest proved more difficult than I had anticipated, and the last glimpse of Castle Hill and the Danube caused unfamiliar pangs. But as I got on the plane to Paris I had plenty to look forward to. My lecture went well enough—no one threw anything, at any rate, and afterwards I ate snails for the first time and later had a quick tour through the Louvre. Then to London to stay with Aussie friends the Gallaghers—another Waugh connection—and have a sumptuous lunch with my Hollywood friend Sam Marx, whom I had encountered because he had attempted to film a Waugh novel. At the Gallaghers, we watched the final episode of the Granada production of *Brideshead Revisited*—I had to catch up with the rest the following year—sharing our intimate knowledge of the book and pointing out ways in which both dialogue and stage business were faithful to the novel.

Then to New York to chair a session on Waugh at the Modern Language Association, see academic friends from various points in my career, meet a woman who was to be the focus of my life, off and on, for seventeen years, and have breakfast with a beautiful blonde and encounter a teammate from Masters Swimming who was duly impressed but inaccurate in his belief in my romantic success.

And then back to Norman, the University, and, because housing was very tight, a rented trailer that made my Budapest accommodations look like the Ritz. So I was in a familiar setting, but changed in ways that perhaps only I could perceive.

A woman friend was warned that I wasn't domesticated, but in fact the experience in Hungary had in some ways had allowed me to go feral, releasing me into a freedom that, what with years of graduate school and then attempts to establish myself professionally, I had never experienced. As a result, when I landed in Oklahoma, I never really put both feet down. By spring break, I was involved in a long distance relationship that sporadically took me out of town to another university where I found a few people who were more interested in my work than anyone in Norman and with whom I didn't have to put up every day in committees and department meetings. And while I continued to serve on university committees and direct the graduate program, I began to define my professional relationships in much broader terms.

The trip abroad had given me a taste for more, and when I discovered that the State Department sponsored lecture tours, I applied to go on one and early in 1983 was sent to France, where between lectures I did further work on two areas I had dabbled in—Western American Literature and what is now called creative nonfiction—during my first

Robert Murray Davis

Hungarian trip. After that, the four Yugoslav republics I visited seemed exotic, especially since I couldn't decipher any street signs except in Slovenia, refreshingly Hapsburg-looking, and when, passing through Subotica on the train from Belgrade to Budapest, I saw signs in Hungarian, it almost felt as though I was going home. Certainly my Hungarian friends seemed more pleased to see me than my colleagues in Oklahoma.

In Budapest, the political situation had changed a little—a certain amount of private enterprise was being allowed and perhaps even encouraged. Colleagues and former students were felt able to talk more freely about their personal lives, including doubts, illnesses, and personal and professional discontents, and encouraged me to do the same.

They were also willing to discuss past and present political situations. One former student had been jailed for trying to escape to Austria during the 1956 Revolution (a term coming into use in private conversation if not public discourse until the end of the decade). A more significant indication of the regime's sensitivity to underlying unrest was the unannounced decision not to terminate twenty-five year leases on cemetery plots, clearly to avoid disturbing a large number of graves of those killed during the Revolution and the subsequent retaliation.

After spending six weeks in unfamiliar territory and anticipating another week or two more, it was a relief to be among people with whom I didn't have to be in constant visiting lecture mode and where I didn't have to ask directions. At the same time, I felt both the draw and strain of thinking about a totally different life, which only in fantasy would be simpler and more fulfilling than the one I lived in America. So I left to follow a rigorous schedule in Germany, thinking that I might never return to Budapest.

But I did maintain contact with friends in Hungary, and visited Zoltán during his Fulbright year at the University of Minnesota and help to arrange for him to spend two years at the University of Oklahoma, and before the second, with his encouragement, I was awarded a second Fulbright to his university in Debrecen for the fall of 1989.

Changes were obvious the moment I got off the plane at the new terminal at the Budapest airport, where I was met not by someone from my Embassy but by a bevy of handsome young women, recruited to greet

154

the more than two dozen Fulbrighters scheduled to arrive. And a Budget Rent-a-Car sign outside the terminal was the first clear indication that capitalism had gotten at least a toe-hold.

Later, at the hostel where I was temporarily housed, rules had relaxed so much that the staff didn't ask for documents to forward to the police. More important, the Hungarian government had opened the border to Austria, and the West German embassy had temporarily closed because the staff was overwhelmed by people seeking visas. The default location was the Italian Embassy, where a line stretched down the block. When I got to Debrecen, the crumbling of Communist power was even more evident. A young colleague casually pointed to a building that, he said, used to be the headquarters of the Young Communist League and had been empty for some time.

Then came the country-wide abolition of the university requirement that all students have a second major in Russian. (This was apparently true of other levels of education as well, having producing a nation of people who knew Russian but, except for Party members, refused to speak it.) As a result, administrators around the country had to deal with hundreds of Russian teachers wandering around bumping into each other, and completely unrealistic hopes were expressed that the incoming cadre of Peace Corps volunteers, the first in the country, could retrain them to teach English as a second language. I was invited to a meeting between the department's linguistics department and Peace Corps administrators, whose gratitude I earned when I pointed out that it was highly unlikely that any of the volunteers would be trained to teach the teaching of English as a second language.

This time my flat had a television set which received programs in three languages—Slovak, Romanian, and Hungarian—I couldn't understand but which I watched anyway. I figured out that one program was showing a meeting of the Communist Party but was puzzled that there seemed to be more hand-wringing than fist-pumping. When I got to the department on Monday, a colleague asked if I had seen what had happened. I saw it, I said, but I don't know what it meant. The Party had dissolved itself, he said. Later I saw an ad for *Playboy* followed by a Russian documentary on tractors—as stark a contrast between new and old as one could find.

155

Two weeks later, on October 23, the anniversary of the beginning of the 1956 Revolution, a large crowd demonstrated against the continued presence of Russian troops, though some Party faithful and even some of their opponents feared that if the Russians left there might be an invasion from Romania, whose border is about thirty miles to the east. But all over Hungary Red Stars were coming down, though the one over Parliament stood until the authorities figured out a way to get it down without smashing a large hole in the square beneath. It was easier to take direct action against the red star composed of flowers in the roundabout at the east end of the Chain Bridge in Budapest. For a while, drivers drove their cars straight over it, and there were calls to uproot the flowers. The gardeners came up with a simpler and typically Hungarian solution: fill in the gaps between points with more flowers in order to create an apolitical circle.

My daily life was much less exciting. Debrecen has been called, probably by people in Budapest, "the largest village in Europe." It was and is about a tenth the size of Budapest, and the Calvinist Great Church, where the 1848 Revolution was announced, is severe and massive; the baroque, created by and for the Counter-Reformation, was understandably not a style likely to be popular. Back home, asked about my experience there, I said that it was like being in Amarillo if you didn't speak Spanish or English. I did a lot of walking.

That's unfair. The university was more lively than Eötvös Loránd in Budapest because it wasn't a street-car college, where faculty and students disperse when the bell rings. Kossuth Lajos, which has dormitories and a real campus, brought me into closer contact with colleagues, though less with undergraduate students. But my colleagues were not only cordial but hospitable and as far as possible made up for the sense of being cut off not only from friends and family back home but from Budapest and friends there, especially the Embassy staff, who not only spoke the same language as I but spoke it in the same way.

This sense of being cut off led to remarks scattered throughout my journal like, "It is ok but it is not my life," "I am tired of doing things alone," "I'm tired of drifting," and, at the end of my stay, "I have to prepare to be old." More than two decades later, that sounds absurd even to me, but I was eight years older than during my first visit and suffering various minor ailments that limited my mobility. As it turned out, my plan to go to Prague ran afoul of the Velvet Revolution, and I wasn't prepared to negotiate another kind of revolution in still another unknown language.

So I was feeling sorry for myself. On the other hand, I had time on my hands to work towards two books which appeared three years later. And to write some poems, which I seem to do better the farther I am from home. And to read material, like a Royall Tyler play and *Walden*, which advocated simplicity in fifteen different ways.

I prepared to leave Hungary less reluctantly than I had the previous two times, but there were still some surprises. During the last week, Romanian television had gone off the air—not an aesthetic loss, since the programming was beyond parody—and on the train back to Budapest, in a compartment with young officers who had just finished a course in English and wanted to know about America, I asked what was going on. "Who knows?" one said. "There are tanks all along the border." Not until I got to Budapest did I learn of the overthrow of the Ceaucescus. (When I landed in New York, I asked for news of the revolution and was told about the conflict with Panama. One overthrow behind.) This time I headed home with no thoughts of returning.

But a couple of years later, I discovered that a Hungarian poet and translator was on a Fulbright in Georgia, and I arranged for her to be invited to my university. That led to a counter-invitation to a PEN conference in Budapest sandwiched between speaking engagements in Eger, Veszprem, and Debrecen, with side trips to Esztergom and Szentendre, the last now full of Japanese, German, and American tourists, unlike the rather sleepy village I had visited in 1981.

Traveling within the country was easier than in former years because there was a lot more English, sometimes spottily, sometimes creatively. In the fashionable and very expensive Ruszwurm Café, for example, the only English on the menu was "TIP NOT INCLUDED" and "Thank you." At least one provincial café, tried a little harder, offering dishes like "Beg of Chicken," "Crisp of Duck," and "Lard goose with steamed cabbage." And in the Ethnographic Museum in Budapest, a guard complimented me on my English. I'm not sure whether he thought I was a European speaking a second language or, like many of his countrymen, he found my Midwestern accent exotic. More and more Hungarians began to learn English, both at universities, where the facilities and faculties strained to accommodate them, and at private language schools.

I could tell friends made in previous visits who were curious about what changes I found on this trip, though big structural changes in government and in financial policy weren't always apparent to me. Still, there were far more beggars, not always Roma, and more homeless people, some living in what my parents would have called Hoovervilles, impromptu structures on the outskirts of town because the collapse of Hungarian industry led to wider unemployment and the collapse of the social safety net. Economic uncertainty led, as it almost always does, to scapegoating of Roma and Jews, a trend that has if anything increased. Graffiti, unknown in 1981, was shading over into tagging.

In practical economic terms, it was easy to see that restaurant menus were more varied and far less fanciful than they had been in 1981 and considerably more expensive. When I remarked to friends that many of the patrons of a Serb restaurant were speaking English, my friend said, rather sourly, that English speakers were the only one who could afford to eat out.

Besides restaurants with international cuisines, including fast-food chains, foreign influences were more widely spread, as large as a Suzuki assembly plant on the outskirts of Esztergom (in the cathedral of which Cardinal Mindszenty, a thorn in the side of the Communists, was now enshrined), as obvious as the availability of English-language films in the cinemas, and as minor as the appearance of a bottle of Jack Daniels on the shelf of a small shop. Two English language newspapers had appeared. Most striking was a military band in Moscow Square, a major transportation hub in Óbuda, playing "The Stars and Stripes Forever" to an appreciative crowd.

Several friends wanted to know when I'd be back, which, although I couldn't give them a precise answer, was gratifying, But I've learned over the years that one thing leads to another, and this seems especially true of the Central European literary community. The PEN conference led to a number of later trips, for I met a Slovak writer who invited me to his country and a Slovenian writer who invited me to his country, several times in both cases. In Slovenia I met a Romanian who invited me to lecture and read in her country and a Croat who invited me to a poetry festival in Zagreb and a Serb living in Holland who took me to the Frankfurt Book Fair where I saw people I knew from Central Europe and met a Hungarian living in Germany who asked me to review a book about Kosovo, and that review, very circuitously, got me invited to Macedonia. I had to turn down an invitation to Serbia and another to Romania because, even in retirement, my schedule had become too complicated. Some of these trips led to a book on Central European writing after the fall of Communism, more cultural journalism than scholarship but apparently providing welcome publicity to the writers mentioned. All because I'd applied for the original Fulbright.

Since then I've lost count of how often I've returned—perhaps a dozen in all, some passing through on trips to other countries, twice in one semester, so that a former colleague, encountering me the second time, said, "You didn't leave?"

In early September, 2001, I was in Bratislava when I got the news of 9/11. I had already arranged to take the train to Budapest the next day, and the prospect of returning to the city and to my friends there made more palatable the prospect of being stranded in Europe until airline flights resumed. If Budapest wasn't exactly home, it was then and over the years a very welcome refuge from complications in my life.

* * *

Apparently I had at some point promised my son John that I would show him Budapest. He has spent more time in France than I have, and a rail pass had taken him around much of Western Europe, but he had never been that far east. In 2011 he was ready to take me up on the offer with his wife's blessing on the theory that this would help us bond. It seemed to me that if we hadn't done so by my mid-seventies and his mid-forties, we weren't likely to, but I thought that we would both enjoy the trip, and I rented a flat in the center of Pest and got plane tickets for a trip a few weeks short of the thirtieth anniversary of my first visit.

This time I went to the airport in a far different frame of mind and from a different situation. Between mid-1981 and 2002, when I moved to Arizona, my mailing address had been my department office because I tended to move around even when I had a physical address of my own. By 2011 I had owned a house—my first since being turfed out in a divorce—for nine years, and for eight of those had been in a stable relationship.

Moreover, trans-Atlantic travel was no longer a novelty for me or for most of my family. I sat waiting to board my flight to Heathrow more in resignation than anticipation. The people I met didn't seem as interesting as in 1981, but probably it was I who was less interesting. Getting into the new Heathrow Terminal 5 wasn't easy, because only three passport officials were on duty to deal with two or more airliners full of passengers, and the one who examined me exhibited unusual interest in where I was from, where I was going for how long, and why. This, like the x-ray screening at the Phoenix airport, was no doubt a result of post-9/11 caution. Once I got into the terminal, it was less crowded, and better lighted than other Heathrow terminals had been, but I didn't see people ecstatic to be there as the actors had in the film *Love, Actually.*

However, I began to see clear symmetries between the two trips. Just as Evelyn Waugh had ushered me westward in 1981, he brought me eastward in 2011 to speak at a conference about *Brideshead Revisited,* which I'd worked toward for fifty years. It was a very pleasant experience, except for the institutional food, but that's another story.

I don't remember much about the flight from Heathrow to Budapest, except that it landed a bit late. But my luggage did arrive at the new terminal, much more welcoming than the gray, cavernous original, and a taxi-driver allied to my landlord met me and took me to the fashionable center of Pest. When John arrived, we worked out a routine: breakfast at home (Hungarians still don't do that well, except for buffets), a visit to a church or a museum, a meeting with some of my friends, a gelato at a favorite stand down the street from our flat, and sidewalk dinner at one of the restaurants on his favorite square, flanked by the university law school and its gorgeous baroque church, and traversed by well-dressed young women, gorgeous in their own way.

The Communist capital restaurants and the street vendors offering biscuit-sized hamburgers had long disappeared, replaced in part by American fast-food chains, including a McDonalds in the Art Nouveau restaurant at the Western railway station which seems less and less concerned to preserve the original décor. Hungarian food could be obtained, notably fruit soup and fish dishes, but there are also a number of ethnic restaurants like the Turkish cafeteria on Szent István körút and a Belgian restaurant nearby and a number of more broadly generic European restaurants and cafes. Brands of beer are more various; I can't speak for wines because none of my friends seemed much interested in them.

Pretty much across the board, things are somewhat to far more expensive than they were in 1981 or even 1996. The exchange rate was now about 185 forints to the dollar (under 200 for the first time in some years). The toilet fee was 100 forints, in unadjusted American currency more than twice what it had been in 1981, while a transit ticket was 290 forints, in exchange more than seven times the earlier price. Our first meal in Budapest ran to about $50; thirty years earlier that would have fed a squad, not just two people.

But transit service was still quite good, and riding was much preferable to trying to keep up with a man more than thirty years my junior who is determined to stay in good physical condition. He insisted on walking up and down six flights of stairs to our flat, and he managed the 121 steps to the top of the Museum of Art (not counting those down and up to the cloakroom) with discouraging alacrity. Several times, especially on even modest hills like those in Szentendre, I had to ask him to slow down, and I could hear echoes from generations of people laugh in triumph. What with stairs, record-breaking heat, and general decrepitude, I began to feel old. Actually, the first sign was on a British train when another passenger offered to help me put my bag into the overhead bin. Did I look that feeble? Obviously.

Some things hadn't changed since 1981, like the transit system and unrest in the Middle East, especially the early stages of the uprising against the regime of Gaddafi. That was far easier to follow than the assassination of Sadat, for we had access to CNN and BBC, internet connection, a local cell phone, and a phone which gave free calls to the United States. And the street hustlers had changed their pitch. On John's first night in Budapest, as we walked down Vaci Street, the Rodeo Drive of Pest, a man sidled up to us and said, not "Change money" but "Nuclear physics? Quantum mechanics? Naked women?" Something one would never have seen in the old days was a man sitting at the top of an underpass on Petöfi Street reading the Koran aloud. John and I were rather shocked, and I wonder if we would have, post 9/11, been equally unsettled if the man had been reading a Bible.

Another change was the absence in the National Museum of the shirt, washed and folded but still a bit bloody, worn before a firing squad by one of the revolutionaries of 1848, because that mixture of orderliness and national piety represented for me important aspects of the Hungarian character. In contrast, at St. Stephen's basilica, where in 1981 a sparse and elderly congregation was flanked by tourists circulating in the side aisles, after the Communist regime fell in 1989 the reliquary containing Stephen's right hand was brought out of hiding and placed in a place of honor in a room behind the main altar. It is accompanied by a printed legend presenting him, his wife, and his son Imre as the Holy Family. As I told John, who knows very little about Church history, sainthood in those days may have been analogous to contemporary nominations to ambassadorships, as much for what they gave as for what they did. Since Stephen had a rival blinded and molten lead poured into his ears, qualifications for sainthood have obviously changed over the years. His son Imre or Emeric, patron of Hungarian youth, was supposedly impervious to the charms of women, and from the way he is represented in statues and paintings, one could see why. John said that as prince he could have had all the women he wanted. Probably he did, I answered.

Much more cheerful was the street fair in the district where Feri Takács lives. Musicians performed on a stage blocking Poszony street, which grew more and more crowded as the afternoon went on. Feri and his wife Anna seemed to know almost everyone in the district, and even I encountered some people I had met on past visits. The artistic highlights were performances by opera singers from apartment balconies. I'd never seen anything like it, in Budapest or anywhere else, though it resembled scenes from 1930s films and even Sigmund Romberg operettas. Both John and I thought that this was finally echt Central Europe. Later, sitting in the Piccolo bar, we gave varying advice on romantic relationships to a lawyer much beset by bad choices. I think that John felt as worldly and experienced as I did, at least by comparison. The only continuity between the Communist era and the fair, a public gathering that had nothing to do with politics, was the street name, Pozsony—the Hungarian name for Bratislava as my 1981 map shows. Elsewhere, on more important streets, the process of replacing Communist-era names with more traditional ones had begun years before—Lenin körút became (Empress) Elizabeth körút, for example—had made the map obsolete. Although I welcomed the changes as a symptom of Hungarian independence, I did rather resent the change from Nepkotarsasag Avenue to the older Andrassy because I had put a lot of effort into learning how to pronounce the former. But I was perplexed by tram signs indicating a terminus at Széll Kalman Square until I learned that it was the recently restored name for Moscow Square, a major transit intersection in Óbuda. But most of the trams followed the same routes.

John was less aware of the past than I, but he was far more aware of and distressed by his inability to speak the language. He speaks French and was able to navigate in South America by analogy. I told him not to worry about it, but he was unconvinced. Once, when he could not find eggs in the local market and the clerks did not speak English, I reverted to old habits, made an oval shape with my thumb and fingers, and went "Cluck! Cluck!" He was very embarrassed, but as I said, we got the eggs, didn't we? He took care to learn the Hungarian word to avoid future reflected humiliation.

In tourist mode, I was more knowledgeable. I've been to Budapest often enough to be content not to revisit favorite museums and sights, and since the object was to make the visit pleasant for John, I offered him choices and stood back to see which ones he made. He was far less interested in examining churches or lingering in museums than I was, and he declined a visit inside the castle, but he enjoyed cobble-stone streets in some of the smaller towns we visited, and the recently excavated Roman ruins in my old neighborhood in Óbuda caught his interest. We took a short Danube cruise, my first because on previous visits I had not regarded myself as a tourist, and we agreed, as fathers, that a large family was paying far too little attention to the toddler who kept trying to climb the rail.

We enjoyed even more excursions with friends to Visegrad and to Zirc, Veszprem, and Lake Balaton because John was getting direct local information rather than reading it in guide books or hearing it from his father. For example, although he preferred the neoclassical architecture of St. Stephen's Cathedral to the baroque, he was fascinated by the beyond baroque abbey church in Zirc because he could wander at leisure, lie down on the floor to photograph the pulpit, and go into the confessional to have his picture taken, ironically. The most interesting thing about the visit to me was my friend's remark that the woman selling admissions thought that I was a priest. Perhaps I must give off an entirely misleading ecclesiastical aura. Anyway, that amused John.

In terms of change in Hungary, though, one of the most striking things to me about that excursion was the contrast between my friends' car in 1981 and 2011. Earlier, he and his wife had driven me to dinner in a Polski Fiat. It was less surprising that I was able to get into the back seat than I was to get out. Now he and his wife had a Suzuki assembled at the plant near the Slovak border which was by comparison quite spacious. And a good thing too, because I'm less flexible than I was in my mid-forties. (Cars in general were larger, and the two-cycle Trabants, made in East Germany with minimal materials and maximum environmental damage, were the object of protestors wanting cleaner air and were in any case, like the Russian Ladas and Czech Skodas, disappearing.)

A longer journey by rail—plenty of toilet paper in the restrooms— took us to Debrecen to meet my colleague Zoltán, who in the interim had been heavily involved in revising the structure of higher education, and a former student of mine, John's age, who is now head of the North American Studies department. He remembered coming to all of my classes in order to try to understand my accent on the theory that if he could do that, he could understand anything. It took him two and a half months.

The main street of the city, less sooty and glum than it had been in 1981, has been turned into a pedestrian mall. The English Department, once tucked into an upper corner up many flights of stairs, now occupies spacious quarters on the first floor, a result of a deal Zoltán made in exchange for becoming president of the university. That was made possible by the depopulation of the Russian Department. And at lunch I was complimented on my contribution to a collection of essays in honor of Zoltán's retirement and asked for another for a collection honoring an American acquaintance on his seventieth birthday. Apparently it was taken for granted that I would have something ready, which I did, but I don't know whether the request impressed John or not. His sister, told years earlier that it was impressive that her father wrote books, said "Some fathers write books. Some fathers lay brick." In effect, big deal.

My former student showed John the former offices—too many stairs for me—and he enjoyed that and meetings with other friends to whom he talked about business and politics earnestly and quite well. By now no one was telling anti-regime jokes because it had become obvious that not all of Hungary's woes could be blamed on Woodrow Wilson and Franklin D. Roosevelt and Josef Stalin but were to some degree self-generated. Independence had opened the way to irredentist complaints about the loss of territory in Slovakia, Romania, and Serbia after World War I, but since 1981 I had been to those countries and heard other sides of the story. Some people were so disgusted with the conservative government that they wanted to leave the country. The only barriers were economic, but since the end of the Cold War Hungarians could not count on a warmer welcome in the anti-Communist West than any citizens of the European Union.

Others, including non-Communist socialists, tended to shrug and hope for better times. And because of America's economic problems, about which John was very vocal, it was difficult to exhibit, let alone sustain, an air of superiority even if we'd wanted to. He didn't try, and my friends regarded him as an expert in the field. I suppose that I do too, since he's been my financial advisor for almost a decade. In literary matters, people listened to me. So perhaps the most significant result of the trip was that each of us got to see the other as an independent adult, not just in a family role, or at least as far as that is possible.

Like others before him, he wanted to know what kept bringing me back to Hungary. I took the question more seriously than usual as a chance to do something like bonding. Because it changed the direction of my life in several ways as a person and as a writer. Because it was nice to go back to someplace where people are glad to see you and value your qualities of mind and personality. Because many of the people find the same things funny that I do. Because it was there that I began still another stage in the journey towards growing up, and however Budapest has changed, changes in both of us are an indelible part of the process.

Over the years, Hungarian friends have asked if I'd consider moving to Hungary, and my answer has always been, a little regretfully, no. But relying on Pavel Vilikovsky's view that you don't have to be born in Central Europe to be Central European, I'm a lot more Hungarian now than I was in September 1981. At least I seemed so to a poet at a festival in Macedonia who asked, "Are you sure you're not Hungarian?"

But I know that for various reasons I couldn't live there permanently, however much I enjoy going back. And I'm not sure that my son quite understands my attraction to the country. At the end of our stay, he wondered if I'd return to Hungary and said that he thought not. As I told him, I'd thought as much many times before. But here I was again.

Usual Suspects

Trips in and out of Hungary over three decades didn't assuage my appetite for travel or to go somewhere besides Oklahoma. A long-distance relationship over fourteen years served that purpose when I couldn't catch a plane, but I took every chance I could to go abroad. Being a writer as well as a scholar gave me plenty of opportunity.

Scholarly conferences in the United States, at least in literary and cultural studies, are more like family reunions than feasts of reason. Of course, papers representing various degrees of learning or expertise are delivered, but only a few registrants beside those new to the profession attend them from a disinterested, or fairly disinterested, desire to learn. The speakers are less interested in enlightening than in triumphing, propounding a thesis which, like Aaron's rod, swallows the competition whole. But even those performances are not the real point of these meetings.

For the most part, the audience at any session can be divided into cliques and claques. The first are made up of people who support a particular theory or agenda, like political junkies attending a district party meeting. The latter consist of people who come to support friends made in graduate school, in previous jobs, or at previous conferences. Mostly, though, one meets friends in the lobby or at a bar to exchange gossip about, as my dissertation director said, who has gone mad in Pennsylvania or complaints, condolences, and who has published what or plans to publish.

These conferences are also hiring halls, where candidates shuffle from one hotel room to another to ask and answer the same battery of questions. You can learn a lot about the people on both sides of the questions and something about the climate of the institution, but intellectual discourse is beside the point.

All of this is very useful for people involved in the grittier parts of the profession, and as I said in the chapter on conventions in *Born-Again Skeptic & Other Valedictions*, I enjoyed and profited from most of the ones I attended and, if the location is convenient or attractive, preferably both, I have continued to go for the same reasons as ever although the attraction of the conference venue and its surroundings has become even more important than it was in my hungrier days.

But I didn't go to an international conference until I was in my early sixties, and they were interesting in a way entirely different from the national and regional one. The structure was familiar: numerous sessions on various topics, often at conflicting times. A few speakers—not many— have reputations glittering enough to be recognizable.

There is, however, a great difference in texture. For one thing, these conferences tend to be smaller than, for example, those of the Modern Language Association of America, where attendance reaches five figures, so that it is easier to choose what papers to hear. Moreover, it's unlikely that anyone at the conference will know anyone else, so that everyone is in the position of having to form temporary alliances based on immediate responses to personalities and sympathies. Without a shared past, there's less opportunity for really juicy gossip. And someone would have to have a huge international reputation to stand out in the crowd, so that in these meetings all of the animals start more or less equal, though the quality of the content and delivery of papers helps to establish that some are more equal than others.

For example, at a European Studies conference in England I hung out with a group of people of various nationalities and academic disciplines whose names, except for a Bulgarian woman who had been to my university, I had to look up in my journal, including a widely published and very pleasant writer whose work I had never encountered before nor have since but who was good company. We ate together in various combinations, heard some of each others' papers, and chatted about our work and our lives. We were amused by the sight of a clutch of Hungarian women being herded about by an alpha male. Though this was eight years after the fall of Communism, he looked a lot like a commissar trying to shield his charges from corruption by the capitalist West. I haven't kept in touch with any of the members of my temporary cadre, probably because we didn't have enough in common as scholars to be able to exchange notes in the future. Besides, since I didn't have much to gain professionally from the sessions, I felt free to wander around York, enjoy the historical monuments, discover that the local library had a few of my books, and realize that the major setting of Ronald Firbank's novel *Vainglory* was a slightly skewed version of the town.

A year earlier I had been invited to a PEN conference in Budapest. That was smaller and more focused than the one in York in that all of the speakers responded in some way to literature, though in terms of political, psychological, and stylistic values, in descending order, rather than in academic formulas. In fact, there is a kind of PEN-speak, earnest in a very different way and often more passionately rhetorical.

Part of this tone seems to be distinctly European. A group of gymnasium students in provincial Slovakia asked questions like "What gives you inspiration? What values do you try to involve in your work? What helps you fight against pessimism? What do you mean by friendship?" Given this experience, I was prepared for an invitation, a few years later, to speak on the question "Can literature save the world?" (Short answer: No. Sorry.) All of these questions are worth asking, though they aren't often raised in American classrooms or at poetry readings. Still, anyone who had a humanistic education (in my case Jesuit) in the early 1950s should be able to rise to the occasion without too much bad faith.

In fact, exposure to these questions, to the attitudes from which they arise, and to people who, as some Americans say, have had skin in the game in countries where, before the collapse of Communism in Central and Eastern Europe, let alone in countries which suffered and still suffer in various degrees of repression and various kinds of tyrannies—all of these can be useful correctives to American writers' greater or less detachment from questions of political and moral value. PEN is, after all, concerned with human rights and international understanding as well as with literature in all its forms. A sign of its earnestness was the naming of John Galsworthy as first president.

The general tone of the presentations is, therefore, usually quite serious, even solemn, but at their best they are addressed, unlike those of

American academic conference, to competitors, even co-conspirators, and deal with values rather than assertions. Of course, at the PEN conferences I attended in Hungary and Slovenia, many of the speakers had grown up under Communist rule and viewed the function of literature as an instrument of change, a position far more exalted than that of people to whom protest was a luxury taken for granted rather than, potentially, a physically dangerous activity which arose from deep necessity.

This makes PEN and affiliated conferences sound very serious, but they don't have to be. At my first conference, some of the older academics who were my peers tended to celebrate their new freedom while lamenting the bleak future of literature under capitalism. Younger members, many of them primarily writers, were a lively group. I was invited to join the Slovak writer Gustav Murín's Young Writers group. When I pointed out that I was sixty-two, I was assured that this was irrelevant because, apparently, I was young in spirit and worth recruiting as a colleague.

Even papers as dry as those delivered at American conferences can be somewhat mitigated by the fact that for the multi-lingual audience the speeches are filtered through a bank of translators, rather like the UN, so that there is an often welcome disconnect between what is being said and what is being heard. Or between what I was saying and the reaction, when in Budapest a translator in the booth gesticulated enthusiastically while presumably conveying the burden of my commonplace remarks about Steinbeck. I'd give a fair amount for a retranslation.

Sometimes printed copies of papers are distributed, so that a speaker often has to speak to the tops of the audiences' heads. Once, in Slovenia, having presented the top of my head a number of times, I vowed to make the audience establish eye contact and prefaced my speech with an announcement that I was going to depart from the prepared text. Heads popped up, perhaps in relief that the audience wouldn't have to read that nonsense.

Despite occasional shortcomings, the meetings show that the political nature of PEN and similar organizations gives both them and their members an advantage over most literary organizations, partly because the members form a network and support one other's work and have the power to issue invitations to still other festivals. Moreover, especially in European countries with which I am familiar, they are connected to governments which regard them as having significant cultural and even political influence. Therefore, politicians like Slovenia's Milan Kucan and university presidents like those in Tetovo, Macedonia, tend to show up, and in general try to show off the beauties and accomplishments of their countries.

Poetry festivals are more relaxed, perhaps because, although being a poet in Central and Eastern Europe is regarded as a calling, it is not considered a sign of abnormality. In the US, reactions by non-poets seem to cluster at one of two extremes. The delusional hyper-romantic end is represented by the graduate student who claimed that "It is dangerous to be a poet." No more dangerous than being a shoe salesman, I said and having been both, I can testify that writing poetry is a much saner gig. An alternative view was represented by a woman, apparently sympathetic to Baudelaire's view that the poet, like the albatross, can soar to great heights but stumbles on land, who wondered how I was able to write poems. Why? "A matter of sensitivity."

But to the average sensual American, being a poet or any kind of wit is suspect as a sign of unreliability at best or mental disease at worst. Early in a romantic relationship that seemed to have considerable potential, I was told, "Don't tell my family you're a poet." The only thing that survived from that fiasco was a sequence of poems and until this point an unpublished squib reading

> Don't tell my family you're a poet.
> That is something they don't need to know.
> If you are creative, please don't show it,
> Or I'm going to have to let you go.

My scholarly publications didn't seem to impress her either, but at least they didn't seem to be a social liability.

In European circles I've encountered, being a poet is not so much honored as expected of someone with a certain degree of cultivation and verbal facility. As a result, the people invited to poetry festivals tend to be more lively, regardless of the quality of their poems, which on the whole is quite good in translation. The quality of the conversation between sessions is even better. A young Croat poet, asked if she were going to come to the next day's sessions, said, regretfully, that she had to return to her job. And that was? "To hate the government." (I wondered, under the Bush W. administration, how to get a job like that but realized that there would have been too many applicants. Same for Obama, probably, though not as many poets would be in the pool of candidates.) The only Slovenian with Dadaist tendencies of whom I am aware. A rogue Turkish poet. Some charming Scandinavians, elderly but energetic. A talented Serb writer and translator living in Holland who offered me a refuge when I was briefly stranded in Bratislava by the 9/11 attack. A Romanian poet whose work I came to value and who introduced me to other writing from that country. All of these people and more give evidence that the spirit of PEN as fostering international cooperation.

Besides, were it not for that network, how else could a small-town boy from mid-Missouri get to read his poems in the courtyard of a medieval castle? Let alone a bouquet and kisses on both cheeks from the conference organizer.

Circling Back: Writers in the Family

For a quarter century I have been writing about my family and my background, but almost all of this material came either from direct observation or from listening to the many family stories which, as my older daughter recently said, get pinned up on an imaginary bulletin board the moment they happen. There was so much material that it never occurred to me to do research.

Fortunately, my paternal grandmother and two of her daughters were indefatigable DAR genealogists, and Cary Davis Blair amassed reams of material which I handed over to my sister Beth, who is now on the trail of our mother's family background. At last report, she had traced the Litschgis (Grandma Murray's family) as far back as 1700.

Relieved of that burden, I have been freed to play around in libraries and on the internet to see what information I can find about my ancestors and their collaterals. Quite a lot, it turns out, since we've got Carys and others as far back as the fifteenth century and counting, and besides the direct line there are a whole lot of collaterals. One of those may have been Henry Carey, musician, ghost-writer, playwright, and possible composer of "God Save the King." Since he and Alexander Pope were on the same side of literary and political battles, it is tempting, but wrong, to claim much of a relationship.

The same can be said of Henry Francis Cary, an Anglican divine, librarian at the British Museum, and best known as a translator of Dante. But there's less to regret than with the eighteenth century Henry Carey because Henry Francis sounds a good deal duller than his predecessor.

However, the writers among our ancestors whom we can claim are an interesting and varied lot, published and unpublished, however shallow the gene pool may have gotten over the years. We don't want to claim too much for a variety of reasons, since we have at least one eighteenth century counterfeiter who was arrested after his sister rolled on him and copped a plea. So what follows can be regarded as interesting rather than significant. Or at least it's interesting to my family, inveterate storytellers about themselves and each other.

My interest in deep genealogy took a while to develop, but my interest in language seems to have begun even before I learned to read. I was interested in what people can do with language, and when I learned that one can make a living by putting words together, I knew that was what I wanted to do. And since I turned twenty-one, that's what I have done. As I was growing up, no one in my family did that for a living, though various members of the older generation used language artfully in commenting on current events, telling stories about family members past and present, and fashioning lies for entertainment. But it wasn't until I was close to middle age that I realized that there was a family tradition of writing. Not as strong or as coherent as that of the Waugh family which has so far produced six writers over four generations and counting, plus some nineteenth century preachers. But interesting in very different ways.

The first writer I'm aware of is William Whitaker, D.D., Regius Professor of Divinity and master of St. John's College, Cambridge, who died in 1595. My father's older sister, Cary Davis Blair, discovered him on a trip to the Mormon's genealogical library in Salt Lake City. She seemed more interested in sibling counterfeiters in eighteenth century Connecticut. As I've said elsewhere, my family seems to think that it doesn't matter what you do as long as it makes a good story. (To help establish some family continuity, I reminded her that in the late 1930s her son had been investigated by the federal government for filing lead slugs into the size of nickels.)

I was more interested in an academic tradition interrupted for nearly four centuries, and the more I found, the more interesting the parallels and contrasts between our lives began to seem. I was a cradle Catholic; according to one rather suspect source Whitaker had been removed by a powerful uncle, who was "inadvertently the inventor of bottled beer," from the Romish influence of his parents. I had been educated at a Jesuit college and taught in another; he was famous for, among other things, his controversies with two Jesuit saints, Edmund Campion, martyred under Elizabeth (and subject of a biography by Evelyn Waugh, a lifelong scholarly interest of mine) and Robert Bellarmine, whom I regarded as my patron saint because, as a Jesuit professor once told me, many of his manuscripts remain unpublished because no one could read his handwriting. Bellarmine kept a portrait of Whitaker in his study, and when asked why, said, in one version, that "although he was a heretic, and his adversary, he was a learned adversary." (Technically speaking, I'm an apostate rather than a heretic.) In a spirit of generosity unusual in any age, especially in the sixteenth century, Whitaker wrote of Bellarmine in the dedicatory letter of *A Disputation on Holy Scripture against the Papists, Especially Bellarmine and Stapleton.* that he was "a man unquestionably learned, possessed of a happy genius, a penetrating judgment, and multifarious reading;—one, moreover, who was wont to deal more plainly and honestly than is the custom of other papists, to press his arguments more home, and to stick more closely to the question." On the other hand, a heretic is a heretic and a Jesuit a Jesuit.

The academic worlds in which Whitaker and I lived were equally contentious, though in the twentieth century the stakes weren't as high. One could be denigrated for not believing in Derrida, but no one literally lost a head over that. Whitaker was close enough to the Established Church not to risk martyrdom, but he was perceived as leaning toward the Puritan side, and he was made Master of St. John's College, Cambridge, as the Rev. William Fitzgerald put in the preface to *A Disputation,* "in the face of obstinate and powerful opposition." This wasn't just intellectual opposition. One account relates that, when he was conducted to the college to be installed, faculty and students barred the gates against him.

He was installed, apparently with the weight of Elizabeth I's displeasure behind him. On one occasion, the faculty voted to do one thing and Whitaker pulled rank and did the opposite. However, in what sounds more like panegyric than sober history, he was said to have won over his opponents by fair and just dealing and by increasing the size of both faculty and student body. One complaint lodged against him was that he was too often absent, and he was once accused of allowing a presbytery meeting, a crime that only specialists can fully appreciate, though in his absence. For whatever reason, he did not receive further preferment;

perhaps it was the mere fact of his remarriage after the death of his first wife.

Whitaker apparently worked long and hard in Biblical and other studies and was, in Benjamin Brooks' words in *The Lives of the Puritans*, "an invaluable collector of scarce and curious information." He left a "very choice and valuable" library which "the queen desired to obtain for herself," a desire that it seems safe to assume was fulfilled. I don't know that I've work that hard—certainly not on Latin and Greek and the Church Fathers. And books being more common now, it's probable that there's not going to be a tussle over my library, but it's pleasant to have that precedent in the family.

Brooks' hagiography attributes all sorts of virtues to him: "In the public exercises in the schools, his great learning and singular eloquence gained the admiration of all his auditors. When he read in rhetoric and philosophy, he seemed to be another Basil; when he catechised, another Origen; and when he preached his *Conceo ad Clerum*, it abounded with sanctity and all kinds of learning." Those sound like virtues one would want to claim, as would be "a solid judgment, a liberal mind, and an affable disposition; but that which added the greatest lustre to his character, was his great meekness and humility." This last characterization leads me to question his place in the family tree. Certainly the judgment that he was "the oracle of Cambridge, and the miracle of the world" is unlikely to be echoed by any of my former colleagues. On the other hand, it is heartening to discover his judgment of another writer: "I pray God I live not, if ever I saw anything more loosely and almost more childishly written. It is true that for words, he hath great store, and those both fine and new: but for matter, as far as I can judge, he is altogether barren."

It was said of Whitaker that he gave the world a child and a book every year. Of the books, I borrow Dr. Johnson's line that I would rather praise them than read them, since the one I have acquired in English translation, *A Disputation* and so on, runs to just over seven hundred pages, many of them containing line by line refutations, often through competing authorities or interpretations of them, of Bellarmine and other papists. But the book can still disquiet Catholic controversialists like Dave Armstrong, who in the on-line *Biblical Evidence for Catholicism* sets out to refute Whitaker point by point in eighteen lengthy replies further extended by responses from and to his readers.

Fitzgerald, Whitaker's translator, admits that "there is a prolixity in Whitaker's style which contrasts unfavourably with the compactness of his great antagonist, Bellarmine," a not-unharsh judgment given Victorian standards of economy. Whitaker's sermon *The Mediator of the Covenant Described in His Person, Nature, and Offices* is considerably shorter, though not short by modern standards. It is organized in a way that would delight a high school English teacher of the late 1940s, for it has heads like Doctrines, Objections, Reasons, and Uses, followed by subheads with roman numerals, letters, and arabic numerals, heavily dotted with citations from scripture.

Whitaker takes the view, not uncommon in his time, that

> God cannot now look upon men out of a Mediator but as rebels, traitors, as fit objects for his vindictive wrath; nor can men now look up to God but as a provoked Majesty, an angry Judge, a consuming fire. And therefore were it not for a Mediator, (that is, a middle person interposing between God and us, who are at variance, to procure reconciliation and friendship) we could not but so dread the presence of this God, that, like our first parents, (in that dark interval betwixt their sinning, and the succour of that promise, Gen. 3:15) we should have endeavoured to hide ourselves what we could "from the presence of the Lord" (Gen. 3:8).

The mediator, of course, is Jesus Christ, both of whose names are glossed, and He can be the mediator only if He has a dual nature, both God and man. Like many theological arguments, this can seem to the outsider a circular one. Christ has to be both in order for Whitaker's theory to work; He is both because Scripture says so; Scripture is true because it is the Word of God; it's the word of God because his sources say so. My paraphrase is not an argument that would have been safe to advance in Elizabethan England or in many other times and places, including certain parts of the United States in the twenty-first century. Whitaker concludes by offering Uses for his doctrine. First, "This may inform us of the unspeakable folly and misery of all such as despise this Mediator." Second, "Be persuaded then to make use of Christ in all his offices, in whom you have an universal antidote against all discouragements."

These arguments may not be exactly circular, but they describe a lot of loops. Still, given the major premise about the Bible's infallibility and seen in historical and in some current Protestant contexts, the position can be seen as convincing if not exactly valid. And being remembered enough to be preserved archivally, both in print and pixels, for more than four hundred years is an achievement. Even more impressive is the continuing ability to annoy people enough that they try to refute your arguments.

Whitaker's other legacy to the world was the seven children he begat. The last, my ancestor Jabez, was born posthumously to his second wife, the widow of Dudley Fenner, a well-known reformist who spent part of his life in voluntary exile from Elizabeth's church. Fenner left two children, More Fruit Fenner and No Fear Fenner, the names a clear sign that their father had been an extremist. The withholding of further official preferment from Whitaker may have been due not just to the fact that he had remarried but the marks on the widow Fenner's husband's reputation.

Like the majority of Whitaker's biological children, the younger Fenners seem to have escaped the reach of Google, but two Whitaker sons turn up. Jabez emigrated to Virginia about 1618 and, as a Lieutenant and then Captain, supervised the building of the first hospital and the first rail fence, or fence of any kind, in America. He died at the age of thirty-one, having begat one son from whom a whole string of Protestant ministers named William Whitaker or some variant may have descended, though Whitaker's Puritan credentials may have led other lines to honor him. The name survives in my branch into the twentieth century as the middle name of my uncle, Gough Whitaker Davis, very much not in the Presbyterian tradition, and of his son Michael Whitaker, raised, ironically, as a Catholic.

As far as I can discover, Jabez never published anything, but his older half-brother Alexander did after he left a comfortable parish in the north of England in 1611 to do missionary work in the Virginia colony, settling in Henrico, near what is now Richmond, on the James River, where he drowned in 1617—a bad year for the family, since his older brother Samuel died the same year.

Before his death, Alexander performed two memorable feats: he baptized Pocahontas (who also died in 1617), though probably not in the style depicted in John Gadsby Chapman's painting since Alexander and his father had doubts about using surplices; and he wrote what at least one source claims to be the first book written in America—though a short one—*Good News from Virginia.*

The book, which stretches to forty-four pages with the help of a dedicatory epistle by William Crashaw (father of the poet Robert), is about half sermon and half recruiting poster. The text is Ecclesiastes 11:1—*Cast thy bread upon the waters: for after many daies thou shalt find it.* The argument—do not value riches overmuch; give freely but prudently; expect no immediate or even earthly return—is larded with numerous scriptural texts and divided into five points, including an explication of what bread and water mean and who should give and receive, and spending at least as much time on those who don't give, including "those that have wealth either abuse them to the satisfying of their prodigall lusts, in Whoring, Dicing, or Drinking, till all or the most be spent; or else (as others) use them only to looke upon them, or that it might be said they have them: few or none there be that use them aright to the glory of God and reliefe of his children." And on those whose needs are not satisfied.

Not until he has laid the theological groundwork for his argument does Alexander mention Virginia about a third of the way through the sermon, urging his readers in England "to behold the waters of *Virginia*, where you may behold a fit subject for the exercise of your *Liberalitie*, persons enough on whom you may cast away your *Bread*, and yet not without hope after many daies to find it. Yea, I will not feare to affirme unto you, that those men whom God hath made able any way to be helpfull to this Plantation, and made knowne unto them the necessities of our wants, are bound in conscience by vertue of this precept, to lay their helping hands to it, either with their purse, persons, or prayers, so farre forth as God hath made them fit for it." Give, in short, because "Are not these miserable people heere better than hawks, hounds, whores, and the like?"

Virginia is in special need of help because

> the Divell is a capitall enemy against it, and continually seeketh which way to hinder the prosperitie and good proceedings of it; yea hath heretofore so farre prevailed, by his Instruments, the covetous hearts of many back-sliding Adventurers at home, and

also by his servants here: some striving for superioritie, others by murmurings, mutinies, & plaine treasons, & others by fornication, prophanenes, idlenes, and such monstrous sinnes; that he had almost thrust us out of this kingdome, and had indeed quitted this Land of us, if God had not then (as one awaked out of sleepe) stood up and sent us meanes of great helpe, when we needed most, and expected least reliefe.

The Indians are in even worse shape as "naked slaves of the divell" for "they esteeme it a vertue to lie, deceive, and steale as their master the divell teacheth them." On the other hand, Alexander says admiringly, "they are of body lustie, strong, and very nimble: they are a very understanding generation, quicke of apprehension, suddaine in their dispatches, subtile in their dealings, exquisite in their inventions, and industrious in their labor. I suppose the world hath no better marke-men with their bow and arrowes than they be; they will kill birds flying, fishes swimming, and beasts running: they shoote also with marvellous strength."

Their priests, however, are probably witches. They live apart from common men and are sustained by them rather like a rector, one could say if in a mischievous mood. Alexander does admit that the priests care for their charges and that

there is a civill governement amongst them which they strictly observe, and show thereby that the law of Nature dwelleth in them: for they have a rude kinde of Common-wealth and rough governement, wherein they both honour and obey their Kings, Parents, and Governours; both greater and lesse, they observe the limits of their owne possessions, and incroach not upon their neighbors dwellings. Murther is a capitall crime scarce heard of among them: adultery is most severely punished, and so are their other offences. These unnurtured grounds of reason in them, may serve to incourage us: to instruct them in the knowledge of the true God, the rewarder of all righteousnesse, not doubting but that he that was powerfull to save us by His word, when we were nothing, wil be merciful also to these sonnes of Adam in his appointed time, in whom there bee remaining so many footsteps of Gods image."

To a modern reader, it sounds as though the Indians are doing pretty well by themselves, but theology overcomes Alexander's better impulses.

After calling on a few, or, better, a lot more Englishmen to come to Virginia to help conquer the land and convert the natives, Alexander begins an inventory of what bread might be returned a hundred-fold to those who invest in the colony. Virginia is another Land of Canaan. The geography, climate, mineral wealth, flora and fauna—the "female Possown" and "flying Squirrell" particularly interest him—sound almost Edenic.

"Wherefore," he says, "since God hath filled the elements of the earth, aire, and waters with his creatures, good for our food and nourishment, let not the feare of starving hereafter, or of any great want, dishearten your valiant minds from comming to a place of so great plentie: If the Countrey were ours, and meanes for the taking of them (which shortly I hope shall bee brought to passe) then all these should be ours: we have them now, but we are fain to fight for them, then should we have them without that trouble. Feare not then to want food, but onely provide meanes to get it here." [People in Jamestown did starve in 1609, and evidence of cannibalism has recently been discovered. My forebears didn't get there before 1611, so we didn't do it.]

Clearly, William and Alexander come from another age with very different premises—at least admitted premises—from most of us. And the genre in which they wrote can seem offputting except to listeners to the Christian Broadcast Network, whose website reproduces Alexander's sermon. But the scholarship of the former, however partisan, sets an example that is as lofty as it is laudable, worthy of emulation in any field. Alexander embodied the modern family's willingness to strike out in new directions, cover new ground, and make a different kind of life for himself. What their writing reveals between the lines about their character seems more important than what the lines themselves say.

The third writer I have been able to discover in my family, Eli J. Wamsley, my great-great-grandfather in the maternal line, was a brick mason from Indiana whose life span exceeded both of the Whitakers' combined. Although he lacked their education and religious indoctrination—he first memorized the Lord's Prayer when he was in his mid-thirties—he led a far more eventful life as a Union soldier in the Civil War, serving as a private in Company E, 65th Regiment of Indiana Infantry between 1862 and 1865. He fought in battles in Kentucky and Tennessee before he was taken prisoner by Confederate forces in December 1863 and was held until December 1864, first, probably, at the notorious Andersonville prison camp and the last few months at Florence Stockade in South Carolina. Since it was not closed until February 1865, it is not clear why he was released. He refers to his experience only once in a diary entry: "received a long letter from my soldier friend and fellow prisoner and sufferer at Florence S.C. Albert Mill."

He returned to active duty before April 1, 1865, when he was sent by a very circuitous route to rejoin his company in North Carolina. While in very leisurely transit, he learned of Lee's surrender and the assassination of President Lincoln, got to see General Sherman passing in the street, and do guard duty while waiting impatiently to be mustered out. On the way home, he traveled on the James River more safely than Alexander Whitaker had.

The only writing by Eli that survives deals with the Civil War, and until the latter part of the twentieth century, he would not have been considered a writer at all, for his works seem to be limited to two letters, only one published in his lifetime, and a pocket diary with entries between April 1 and July 5, 1865, when he had been mustered out but not sent home. But this kind of material is now valued because of its contribution to the historical record and for its quality as vernacular history, a term borrowed from architecture.

Eli's writing is very different from that of the Whitakers. They, especially William, wrote as if time, ink, and paper were irrelevant considerations. Eli's pocket diary allowed only ten lines per day on a 5.5 x 3" page, and he never used more than the available space. He began every entry by noting weather conditions, and most of the entries deal with everyday matters like food, duties, letters he has sent and received, making camp more comfortable, and fashioning things like a cane or a ring for his little daughter Rose Ann (my great-grandmother, as my sister's research into that branch reveals). Judging from parallels in the World War I diary written by my daughter-in-law's grandfather, it is not untypical of any soldier's brief record of service.

Unlike the Whitakers, Eli was very little concerned to display his learning, though several entries show that he was eager to acquire it through what books he could locate, like Bayard Taylor's travels (from which he copied two poems), "the Biography of John Jacob Astor of N.Y. the great millionaire," and the New Testament. But he was also eager to acquire knowledge by talking to people, including Confederate citizens who had lost everything in the war but were recovering enough spirit to start a garden. Once he combined reading with oral history: "I was reading the early History of North Carolina By Dr. Caldwell this evening & had a talk with an old Black man gained some useful knowledge."

The diary contains very little interpretation, except about very pleasant or unpleasant geographical features or, except for the mention of the fellow prisoner and other friends and comrades, reference to any past events. Occasional clichés describe patriotic or aesthetic sensations, but for the most part the style is direct and economical, qualities probably enforced by the physical format.

His two letters deal more fully with emotions. The first, apparently an excerpt, a letter of condolence written to Dr. Ansell White, shifts from a factual account of the death of his son, written as precisely as he would have laid brick to an eloquent tribute in the conventional style of the period.

> George W. White was killed in action 22 day of September 1863, in a severe fight at Blountsville, Tennessee, the regiment lost fifteen killed and wounded of Company E.

> George was a Noble youth a brave boy a good Soldier and a generous Messmate. His last act toward me was an act of generosity as i have already stated in a letter to Mr. Jacab Potter we had stopped for dinner and George went out in search of something good for his sick comrade (George Hartell) to eat. Some good lady gave him a warm wheat cate a roll of butter and some apple butter. He called me to share it with him and while we were eating we first heard the booming of the opening canon we instantly quit our eating and mounted our horses and rode to the scene of action heard officers of other Companies remark how

cheerful George dismounted and shouldered his musket and marched to the bloody conflict in the defense of our Country's right witch he seemed to fully understand and appreciate he fell at my side the first rally that was fired at us they were concealed in the bushes on the top of a Mountain and we were ordered to drive them from that position and we were advancing on them with Captain Baker ten steps in advance and George and some of us following. Thus fell a noble youth, by the hand of as mean a set of slave drivers as ever crossed Gods footstool. Captain Baker detailed Sergeant Julian Rees young John Barnett, Charles Barnett, James Hale, Presley Hall and Thomas Chambers to see that George was decently buried. He was buried at Blountville, Tennessee in Sullivan County. North east corner of the Burial Grounds. They cut his name on a board to mark his grave.
Yours Truly,
Eli J. Wamsley

The second letter, written to the *National Tribune*, devoted to the interests of Union veterans of the Civil War, draws upon the diary, and a comparison illustrates the difference between Eli's private style and that intended for an audience.

Monday June 5 1865
Weather clear and warm. Went to the US Christian Commission Rooms and received A comfort bag from one of the Sunday School Girls of Ware Mass. The bag contained Dried Apples Needles thread Buttons pins jam soap and candy and a Religious Tract.

The letter to the editor has the same details but more sentiment:

THAT LITTLE COMFORT BAG
    215 Bland Ave.
    Evansville, In
    February 3, 1884
To the Editor National Tribune
    I have before me a little blue comfort bag that I find, in looking

over my pocket diary of June 5, 1865, I received at Greensborough, N.C., from a little Christian Commission girl of Ware, Mass. I find that the bag contained needles, thread, buttons, pins, yarn, soap, candy and apples and a religious tract with the fair donor's name. But the sweetest thing the bag contained I failed to record, and that was her dear name. How could I be so thoughtless as to neglect the name of one who thought of us then? I recollect that I wrote her a little letter, giving her my name, regiment and company, as follows: Eli J. Wamsley, company E, 65th Indiana volunteer infantry. [Note: This and part of next line blurred and illegible]

How my old heart [several words illegible] joy if her eyes should recognize [several words illegible] and write me a letter after these long years have fled. The Lord bless the ladies and little girls of old Massachusetts. I still hold my little comfort bag dear, and we have it folded away in the bottom drawer. These little silken ties help to bind us together in one mighty Nation.

Eli J. Wamsley
Co. E, 65 Ind. Vol. Inf.

The diary does not conclude; it just stops after the mention of Eli's receiving a letter from a B. Waller. If he experienced any post-traumatic stress syndrome, there is no record of it. The remaining entries of the diary, dated from January through May 1869, practical to the point of being pedestrian, are a "Cash Account for the year." Receipts include fifty cents from his twelve year old daughter; business and household expenses.

It's easier for me to identify with Eli than with the Whitakers, and not just because his world seems closer to mine. In the first place, his writing gives the impression of an actual living man who ate and drank and suffered cold, toothache, and boredom which he tried to assuage by talking with and working for others. In the second, he was apparently to my grandfather Murray what grandpa Murray was to me, a mentor and example, so that I can triangulate from one relationship to another.

But it's also clear that, in my writing, life has borrowed from both traditions, the textual thoroughness of the Whitakers and the vernacular fashion of dealing with everyday experience of Eli, walking around and talking to people.

From a practical point of view, William Whitaker did have one advantage over Eli Wamsley. When I visited Cambridge, I went to St. John's College and was politely confronted by a woman taking admission —95 pence.

"I'm sure it's worth it," I said.

Although I have annoyed many women in very different ways, I had never been sniffed at before. This was a Lady Bracknell class sniff.

"Of course it's worth it," she said. "It's a lovely college."

I was quick to try to repair the damage. "I have no doubt of that," I said in my most conciliatory tone. "But I'm interested because my ancestor William Whitaker was Master here in the late sixteenth century."

"Oh," she said, and pushed my 95 pence back to me.

Even if I could find a place where Eli Wamsley had lived, I doubt that his name would carry that kind of weight.

Robert James Murray had a more public career than his grandfather Eli, serving, as a Republican, in Cowley County, Kansas, offices and as state legislator in Kansas and later in Missouri before returning to his native Indiana in World War II to work in a defense plant helping to built P-47 Thunderbolt fighter planes, which for the rest of his life he claimed were superior to P-51s. (The debate continues, inconclusively, on-line.)

Almost none of his writing survives. I remember seeing a newspaper clipping of a letter written from Kansas to a friend in Indiana extolling a climate so healthy that the undertakers had to sell furniture to stay solvent. Alexander Whitaker had praised the healthy climate of Virginia and dared "boldly affirme it that sicknesse doth more rage in England quarterly, than heere yearely. I doubt that hereafter when our Hospitall or Guest-house is built up, you heare of many more cut off by the sword of Justice (unless the better people be sent over) than perished by the diseases of the Countrey." But he was serious, in his family's tradition.

One set of Grandpa Murray's notes, apparently made in preparation for a Congressional campaign which he never pursued, deals with the unoriginality of Franklin Delano Roosevelt's Social Security measure and with the folly and indeed illegality of FDR's pre-Pearl Harbor isolationism, especially the embargo on the sale of arms to the Republican government of Spain. (In *For Whom the Bell Tolls*, Robert Jordan impresses the guerrilla band by saying that his grandfather had been a life-long Republican.) The notes are as full of citations of legal precedent and of quotations from authorities like Tom Paine as anything the Whitakers wrote.

Grandpa Murray clearly could write, but his most memorable discourse was oral. He was a marvelous teller of tall tales and disputer (as distinct from debater, who at least recognizes that there is another side). One story, which he told about someone else, illustrated his taste. A man was passing a store-front with a gallery of loafers, one of whom said, "Stop and tell us a lie."

"I can't," he said, "Joe Jones just fell of his roof and broke his leg, and I'm going for a doctor."

Five minutes later, Joe Jones walked by.

Unfortunately, as with many oral performers, his legacy has been lost. That's a little less true of his daughter, my mother, and some of her relatives by marriage, for Aunt Cary preserved some of the correspondence.

The juvenilia of my father and his older brother can be charitably dismissed, though my father's as an early teenager could be contrasted with one of mine about the same age: he was wanting, I was getting. But some letters by their mother and sisters as well as my mother might have met Evelyn Waugh's exacting standards for correspondence. He reproached his wife for the dullness of her letters, advising her that "A letter should be a form of conversation; write as though you were talking to me."

Some of my female relatives' correspondence sounds, if not like yelling, like bitching and moaning about each other. Grandmother Davis's daughter from her first marriage, Nanelou Sweeney, wrote to her half-sister Cary complaining about their mother:

> Harry Fry is sick, has strained the ligaments in his legs & this a.m. she started. She didn't care what the doctor said, she knew, he had the 'sylifis' or however you spell it, she harped & she harped & then She got off on Pug [my uncle Gough] & [his older brother Johnny] & then the door slammed. Oh gosh, I was mad. I've listened to her run down Pug & Johnny till I could die & now Mrs. Barton is here and she's cussing Johnny out. Damn! I'd love to hear her say

something nice about someone just once. She's told everyone in this town, with her voice pitched up to high X, that "my daughter's husband has a government appointment & they're in Washington City now." In other words I got up out of the wrong side of the bed this morning. I'm so damned tired of seeing her prance around the house & neighborhood with absolutely nothing on but an apron, not even shoes and stockings, the apron an unstarched and unbleached one. All she needs is a snuff stick.

Grandma Davis was no mean complainer herself, especially about her second youngest son, whom she characterized at some length as a fool and a possible degenerate. She tells with obvious relish of the rivalry between her two youngest sons (Bubs is my father) Her spelling is as idiosyncratic as Alexander Whitaker's.

One night about mid night Bubs came in told Pug to move over in Bubs bed— or get up and get in his own Bed— Pug got up to give Bubs to understand who he was talking to, that he slept where he wanted to, and if Bubs didn't like it was "just too bad"— They went at it tooth and nail—for ½ hour—with me reffereeing—at last Bubs slung him out of the door—Kicked him down the steps and slammed his clothes after him and told him to stay out of his room. Well he stayed out that night. Next morning they were up on time It was Sunday too, after breakfast Pug took his things and hung them in the closet —Bubs went up Behind him and told him to take his traps out of that closet—which Pug said he would be blankete blanked blank he wouldn't do—So Bubs went at it again —and they fought and fit—and fought and fit. Bubs wrasled—and Pug Boxed— Bubs got a cisors holt on Pugs leg and arm—and made old Pug— holler—and squall—that he was being murdered—killed—ruined —anyway—when Bubs let him up he got up and begun to cuss—and swear and Bubs took him around [?] again and when he let him loose from another cisors hold he kicked him down stairs—his clothes on top of him and Pug stayed down and out—He began on me after the first time up and I think it was that that started it all over again for the final down and out. Bubs told him to keep a civil tongue in his mouth for ever more— just let him hear him cussing me again what he would get would be a good and plenty—That was four weeks ago last Sunday and it has been the first four weeks for years that we have lived like people when he was home.

My mother complained less, but she had a sense of character and drama. Thanking Nanelou for presents she had sent the three children, she created a scene: "They each opened their packages when they came home at noon and Bob showed his books around and Beth showed her ribbons and little bear around and Johnny just put his in his lap and said nothing. I thought it was kind of funny because I knew you knew what kids like and I felt that maybe you had sent him something that he just did not like at all. Finally, he called me in the other room and showed me what it was and offered me a piece. He was not about to open that box of candy in front of all those ravenous wolves. He is not crazy."

He and my sister are by no means crazy, but Beth seems to write only e-mail and Johnny even less until at the age of sixty-five he founded a funeral home in our home town in central Missouri and began to write obituaries. Reading those, one can tell how well he knew the deceased and the level of the family's tolerance. For example, one obituary lists as survivors the man's ex-wife and his male life partner, and gay couples are consistently recognized. Other touches are lighter. One man "was an avid St. Louis Cardinal fan and he enjoyed bragging about his oversized tomatoes." Another enjoyed evading the game warden; another took off for the Missouri River whenever he had a chance. John says that his wife used to proofread his drafts and object to these touches but finally gave up when none of the survivors complained. I've told him that he's like the undertaker in *Adventures of Huckleberry Finn* because "A little thing like that don't cost nothing, and it's just the little things that makes a man to be looked up to and liked. There warn't no more popular man in town than what that undertaker was."

Both he and my sister fit very well into the family's oral tradition, and one grandson seems to enjoy my stories about his forbears, though his mother would prefer stories with fewer firearms and general rowdiness. My children do some writing in their business lives, but their jobs as family therapist and financial advisor require more talking than writing.

More in the line of Eli Wamsley's factual account is the extensive record produced by my brother-in-law, Bert McClary. In his fifties and beyond, Bert has begun to write reminiscences of his life. Not, like me, with the hope of reaching a larger audience and commenting directly on social patterns, or like my cousin Hibbard, with the hope of bringing his fellow-citizens to some understanding of and appreciation for democratic institutions and behavior, but of recording details about his life so that his grandsons will have some idea of what it was like to be him, at that time and in that place.

Take, for example, Bert's account of his job at a pharmacy in downtown Boonville, Missouri. He talks about what he did, when, and in what order, stopping to explain things that kids born after the turn of this century wouldn't otherwise know about. For example, after mentioning that the drug store had a soda fountain, he goes on to define the term:

Not what we often call "soda" today, the fizzy flavored drinks we buy in cans or big plastic bottles. That's what we called "soda pop," "sody pop" or mostly just "pop" back then (even though some people did call it just "sody"). It came in 8, 10 or 12 ounce glass bottles, in a six-pack called a carton, which was open, made of cardboard, and had a cardboard handle on top. Most of the time as kids we would just buy a single bottle of pop from a "pop machine" that was one of three types. Most of them were just chest-type refrigerated coolers with a lid on top, and some had about six inches of cold water in the bottom. The bottles of pop were lined up on the bottom. You would open the cooler lid and pick out the kind you wanted by the name on the bottle cap, the color of the pop in the bottle and the shape and size of the bottle. I usually had orange or grape, but sometimes strawberry or Pepsi-Cola. 7-Up was OK, but I rarely bought it because I liked the others a whole lot better. Now that I think about it, I don't think I ever bought a 7-Up. I didn't like Coca-Cola (Coke) or root beer or Dr. Pepper. I never saw a bottle of sarsaparilla. And for several years I didn't like Pepsi because Mom used to put my "red medicine" (Benadryl liquid) for my asthma in it. I didn't know that I just thought that's what Pepsi tasted like. Anyway, you would pull out the one you wanted and open it with an opener that was fixed onto the side of the cooler and sometimes had a receptacle built in that caught the lid as it dropped. On some there was no receptacle, so you had to catch the lid and throw it in a trash can, or just let it fall on the floor if you didn't care. Then you would go to the cash register and pay the cashier a nickel.

There's more detail about other kinds of pop coolers before going back to how to make his kind of sodas and a history of the soda fountain.

Much of Bert's writing is similarly detailed: names of friends from fifty years ago, with descriptions of their appearance and habits; more than 40,000 words on motorcycles he's ridden over fifty years, where he rode them, and what he wore; how far apart the railroad ties were on the Missouri, Kansas, and Texas Railroad bridge over the Missouri River, how to elude the bridge tender, and how to get a motorcycle across it.

His writing isn't dramatic, as my female relatives' was, and it doesn't have the obvious links to significant historical events that Eli Wamsley's or even Alexander Whitaker's does. But historians of the future might find the details in his writing far more useful as a help to understanding what it was like to live in a small town in the second half of the twentieth century.

Or useful in a different way. When I published my first book of creative non-fiction, *Mid-Lands: A Family Album*, someone said that she wouldn't dare write a similar book because her siblings would complain that things didn't happen that way. The only response I could think of was to tell them to write their own books and let the reader decide. In fact, there's room for every story, and it doesn't make any difference what it's about or how it's put as long as it's interesting. But first you have to set it down.

More in the Renaissance family tradition was my cousin Hibbard Davis, son of my father's older brother Gough, one of the most prolific if seldom published family members in modern times. And as moralist and controversialist, he resembles William Whitaker more than any of his other descendants.

The bulk of Hibbard's works, written over more than fifty years, from the mid-Sixties until a month before his death in November, 2011, may not only be uncollected but undiscovered. At the beginning of that period, working at a blue-collar job, he began to write every day, "filling a lot of notebooks with a lot of words, wishes, speculations, criticisms, rants and woeful laments, as well as descriptions of both pleasurable and sad moments." A little later, working in Civil Service in St. Louis, he wanted to be a writer like "the larger than life figures" from the heroic days of exile and adventure in the Twenties, but he had no idea of how to offer his writing for publication, and his writing turned into a sprawling diary observing, like Samuel Pepys, "the mundane and not so mundane life around me."

Although Hibbard's interests changed and developed as he grew more involved with politics, where his writing became polemical and sometimes satiric, this passage accurately describes the style of his personal and general observations. He would draw upon what seems to have been wide and diverse reading for analogies, mostly historical, and only occasionally upon his training in English and American literature for references. His writing, focused mostly on everyday experiences familiar to most people, is mostly plain and direct and accords with his distaste for pretension and authoritarianism. He was only able to appreciate high visual art, he said, after realizing that "under the roof of an art museum is contained not merely a worn and aged collection of art [intended for an elite audience], but a display of the singular, patient, lifetime efforts of many individuals to make something that would outlast their unknown and unsung selves far into the future."

But that was in the last decade of his life. In the 1960s, after Hibbard became disillusioned with the pointless work of doing security checks for the government, he returned to Wichita, where he had grown up and graduated from college, and enrolled in the Masters program in English at Wichita University. None of his writing, including a draft of a thesis on Faulkner, seems to have survived, and he dropped out—not surprising, since he disliked analyzing the work of writers, learning about Renaissance verse conventions, and the notion that he had to approach literature a certain way because "I could never quite get a grip on such an institutionalized way of doing things." So he qualified to teach secondary school and began a side-line and then full-time career selling Fuller Brushes, which he pursued for the rest of his life.

At some point, he seems to have abandoned the idea of becoming a published writer in the usual sense, but he was far from being a "mute inglorious Milton," partly because he seemed never to have sought glory and partly because, what with letters to the editor and the internet, he produced a steady stream of opinions and reminiscences.

Some of these he collected in a self-published thirty-eight page pamphlet, "2000: The Debacle of Democracy," dealing with his quixotic campaign for the state senate in a district so red it was and still is practically crimson. As a Democrat, he was challenged by pro-lifers, anti-taxers, and closet racists and ignored by local media. And soundly defeated by a far-right opponent who raised and spent far more than he did to win re-election. It would be comforting to say that a dozen years have made a difference, but Hibbard's pamphlet reads like a blueprint for rightwing control of any number of states. Unfortunately, the pamphlet mostly sits in storage in the house where his widow still lives. The only consolation is that while Hibbard was defeated in the 2000 election, as he had been in others, he never gave up.

Those who aren't fortunate enough to get a copy of "The Debacle" can find material from the last decade of his life, which ended in November, 2011, in letters to the Wichita *Eagle*, which is so conservative that it is a wonder not that they published only a few but that they published any, and, from 2003 to 2005, to F5, a more receptive alternative paper which gave him space not only over his own name but over that of Buster Deducere, supposedly a Cajun displaced by Hurricane Katrina. Those contributions amount to more than 60,000 words. Most of these attack the policies and practices of the Republican Party from the crown to the grass roots, calling for reason and justice and logic in the wilderness of Red-State Kansas.

Hibbard was even more prolific in emails, most of them from 2007-2011, amounting to more than 150,000 words. Some messages duplicate or express sentiments similar to those of letters to the editor; some deal with mundane considerations of friends and family. However, the longest and most significant amount to a serial autobiography and social history focusing not only on him but on his large and extensive family.

Like many writers, Hibbard sometimes struggled against the

difficulties of writing precisely and gracefully. And like many of them, he was able to write about the struggle, about the slipperiness of language, and about the possibilities that his writing would survive. But he seems never to have had serious doubts about the purpose of writing: "to articulate our perceptions and feelings about the world we find ourselves in."

That world, for Hibbard, was often difficult and emotionally confusing. Again and again he refers to the example of his father, self-described as an "'independent oil operator.' It sounded so, well, independent. He didn't have much oil production, and lost all that he had, but was independent. I liked that about him." Like a Dickens character, Hibbard grew up with the illusion of great expectations: a large house in a fashionable part of Wichita, well-furnished, servants, the family Lincoln, matriculation at Dartmouth College. From that point, he had to get used to being a member of what George Bernard Shaw called a "downstart" family. One dry hole after another, an increasing number of children, the last pregnancy confirmed the day his father got bad news about his heart condition, a series of dead-end jobs for the older children whose income helped to support the family, his father's death and his mother's retreat into depression. One sister apparently felt that they were too many, but rather than killing her siblings and herself, like the character in Thomas Hardy's *Jude the Obscure,* merely disappeared. Unlike a Dickens plot, there was no rich benefactor or, as Henry James said of the typical Victorian novel, "a distribution of prizes, pensions, husband, wives, babies, and appended cheerful remarks."

Hibbard was aware that his younger siblings had lives in some ways more difficult than his. Drawing an analogy with the institution of slavery, he wrote that "The master in our large family's case, was our dad, and I being the oldest son, could at least savor the bit of responsibility and authority of being the chief servant. I felt a duty call. Work hard at home, and in school, to attain some respectability and sense of purpose."

In reaction, perhaps, against his father's dreams of wealth, Hibbard seems to have rejected similar aspirations. Late in life, he wrote: "I wonder what ever happened to Ambition. I must have missed Ambition somehow. Did it pass me by in the middle of the night? Did it wear a scarf over its face to make it incognito? Or a terrorist mask?

It left somewhere in middle age. Now ambition is little more than a dim memory. It had, I'm sure, something to do with testosterone. If there is still testosterone flowing in my system, something in the medications I take must mask its presence."

But according to Hibbard's fragmentary autobiography, he never had ambition in the conventional American sense. He gave up the highest paying job he ever had, in Civil Service, for graduate school and then various service jobs. School-teaching put him for a while on the lower rungs of the middle class, but he left that in order to sell brushes door to door. But his experience with his family as well as his Democratic politics gave him a lifelong connection to the less fortunate because "it was easy enough for me to see all of us as underdogs.'"

Inevitably, at least in the minds of English majors, Thomas Gray's "Elegy written in a Country Churchyard" comes to mind:

> Let not Ambition mock their useful toil,
> Their homely joys, and destiny obscure;
> Nor Grandeur hear with a disdainful smile
> The short and simple annals of the poor.

Hibbard was fiercely opposed to a number of injustices, but he seemed to take few of them personally. But mocking useful toil set him off. Remembering a doctor from his hospital orderly days, he was disturbed because

> He referred to someone or somebody as "nothing but a shopkeeper." Like that person was little better than a gnat or a worm, only interested in filling its belly.

> .

> He moved away to take a residency at Duke University hospitals and became a highly regarded child psychiatrist and married a rather wellknown American novelist [Anne Tyler].
> I became, essentially, a door to door peddler. A walking, talking shopkeeper but without even a shop.

Much later, Hibbard visited

a friend in the California desert who is a capable and talented and successful artist. He is very alone and admitted being depressed due to a big personal loss.

   While visiting, we drove into the little town nearby. It was a Friday morning and the well manicured and green roundabout was setting up for a farm & art fair. Venders had shielded their goods from the sun. They were selling produce and there was a table with a lady selling some handmade jewelry.

   It all looked so good and tempting and friendly.

   I suggested he could bring some of his work down and set up a spot to sell his works.

   My idea offended and enraged him. He was no "shopkeeper." His work was not to be haggled over for $50 or $100.

   It would just be a way to get to know some of the folks around him, I suggested, but I found it best to let the matter pass.

   Once again I had a friend with contempt for shopkeepers.

   Little people, worms, like me.

Oddly as it may sound after reading this, Hibbard seemed to have little class as opposed to cultural and financial resentment. He was appalled and angry at growing disparities of income, at ignoring the poor, including those part-time contract workers like one of his sisters, and at the seemingly inexorable destruction of the middle class, whom he compared to the Disappeared in Argentina, nationally by ludicrous tax measures and locally by the decline of Boeing Aircraft, but he did not seem to envy or wish to emulate people who were simply rich and famous.

   What he valued most was independence. Thinking of himself as a shopkeeper, he wrote that he "enjoyed just being free from being under the thumb of a boss, school administrator, or manager who could control my pay, my time, my future, my life." Turning over the maxim "Knowledge is Power," he insisted that "Power is Power" and should be resisted until it was shared.

   As the remark about thumbs shows, a central tenet of Hibbard's writing and life was a resistance to authority in whatever form. And the more concentrated power was, the more resistance. He wrote fiercely about the separation of church and state, and he was pretty unhappy about churches all by themselves. After some years of being fallen away from the Catholic Church, he returned, married a devout woman, continued to go to church, and was buried from one. This seems out of character, but his approach to Catholicism was as idiosyncratic as everything else about him. He would listen to sermons, but he would find modern and political interpretations of the texts on which they were based. When a priest, drawing from the verses in Second Book of Maccabees in which one of seven brothers dies under torture, chooses to talk about the woman who had seven husbands, Hibbard wrote:

> I hoped the priest would seize the moment and arouse his flock to a spiritual awareness of torture as the wrong and evil action that it is.
>
> Instead, he dwelled on something from the gospel, which also had Jesus discussing the eternal implications of a woman who had seven husbands. Not exactly a big issue these days, like torture.
>
> The Church on Sunday didn't choose to adopt a position, even though the fourth son in Maccabees gave them one. It could have.

Nor was he an uncritical fan of Mother Teresa:

> It's not easy to see the newly-beatified Mother as anything but a saint, who was able to draw on the guilt of the wealthy to support her projects, but never, as far as I can see, said a word in protest to the conditions of utter destitution the state would not lift a finger to alter.
>
> It would be preferable to have a political leadership that refused to accept such desperate conditions instead of allowing the poor to die in the streets or in charity wards funded by the churches. Mother Teresa's work, in short, fits the politically correct viewpoint of the present conservative oligarchy in America, which preaches the gospel according to Limbaugh, Pat Robertson, J. Falwell, and Dubya let the masses die or do whatever they want, free the wage slaves from their jobs, send the sons of the poor who can't afford college to go off to free the world from terrorism or die trying.

197

On the other hand, he rejected an atheist friend's contention that since Mother Teresa's diaries apparently revealed that she could not believe in God, she could not be considered a saint.

> I said I didn't know that Atheists could not be Saints. Why should a Saint be prohibited from being a Saint just because of their beliefs? Their works must qualify them for sainthood.
>
> What is all this talk about faith anyhow? Some folks talk about having faith, like it is some valuable piece of mortgage-free real estate or fancy Cadillac. Something they have acquired that makes them special, born again, or what have you. Just yesterday I read Jerry Falwell put his money on his life with huge life insurance policies designated to pay off the debts of his Liberty University and his own church of the everlasting almighty dollar. His faith appears more practical than most men of the cloth. He wasn't one of those shiny-eyed types who prayed for the Lord to provide. He bought nearly 60 million of life insurance, if I read the article right. 54 Mil for Liberty Univ. and 5 mil for his church.
>
> I said Mother Teresa sounds like someone who had the most honest form of faith--the kind that is never assured, that must be wrestled with in one's conscience, constantly reexamined and held up to the light of truth. And if their struggle for faith leads them to believe there is no God, what of it?
>
> Atheists and Believers, just as debtors, loan officers, the uninsured and the well-insured, all of us, find a common resting place in the earth.
>
> Even Jesus had his doubts when he called out on the cross, Father, why hast thou forsaken me?
>
> Good question. Folks have been trying to answer it ever since.

Hibbard had a healthy skepticism about spectacular miracles used as bona fides for sanctity, preferring everyday miracles at the church Christmas tree lot he helped staff, "Like the gentle, tired looking older man inviting his 25-year-old autistic son to get out of their old car. Then getting the wheelchair out of the car trunk for his wife and loading her into the wheelchair and rolling her through the lot, telling her about the prices and qualities of each different type of tree." By their works you shall know them was an unspoken thesis in much of what he wrote.

He refused to shrink from talking about politics and religion because, he wrote,

> everything we are involved with in life is concerned with politics and religion!
> A small example. I sell brooms and the company whose brooms I sell has had trouble providing good quality wood handles. Have you noticed how brooms and mop handles are so often plastic or metal these days.
> Ever wonder why? The wood for those handles is generally ramen wood, and it comes from Indonesia. Years before the tsunami clobbered Indonesia, there was civil war, and it forced the one company that supplied the world with the best wood for handles to go bankrupt, thus cutting off the supply.
> Never thought how what you swept your floors with was much affected by political and religious clashes on the other side of the earth!

For Hibbard, perhaps more than for most people, the political was inextricable from the personal. Weeding his garden reminded him of the need to get Republicans out of office. He opposed Right-to-Lifers not just because one had murdered Dr. Tiller in his own church but because he had had experience with botched illegal abortions in his family and in his experience as a hospital orderly. He opposed the Do Not Call list because it put people, including one of his sons, out of work. He supported Hugo Chavez because the rich and powerful were against him and Mao's Cultural Revolution because it put powerful people to work in factories and fields, citing a man he read about who was glad to serve his country in that way. Apparently he never met an actual person who had done so, and for once his resistance to authority was tempered by what he regarded as legitimate ends.

Hibbard refreshed the cliché "walk the walk," running time and again for political office as a Democrat in the scarletest part of a very red state, with money and demographics against him, using his door to door skills and sometimes riding a bicycle from one neighborhood to the next. Like his father, he had a Quixotic streak, and as a good Kansan he knew how large and daunting windmills could be.

A customer asked him if he were running for or from something. His answer?

"'I'm running for awhile. Trying to get my fellow citizens to care enough to get out and vote to free this state from the lies and minimum wage bondage they are held in!' But is that For or From? I still don't know the answer to his question!"

Given Hibbard's resistance to every kind of authority, it may seem odd that he was such a fervent supporter of the Democratic Party. Two explanations are possible: one, it supported the ideals he believed in; second, and more cynical, Democrats never had much power or authority in Kansas.

But Hibbard was more than, in Gray's lines,

> Some village Hampden that with dauntless breast
> The little tyrant of his fields withstood.

For one thing, he found real pleasure in peddling. "Oddly," he wrote, "I rather enjoyed bothering people at their doors, getting to know all sorts of my fellow citizenry who would give me the time of day, often in order to talk about themselves, their infirmities and losses, and place an order."

He enjoyed talking to the people he encountered, like the East Indian owner of the motel in Chanute, Kansas, and sharing her sorrow at the death of her daughter as well as the good news of the family's increasing prosperity, and the transients at the motel named after the Dalton gang in Meade, Kansas. Just being on the road was an intermittent adventure as he observed shrines to accident victims and dinosaur skeletons and armored vehicles in small towns along his route. But he also found interesting the people he encountered at his health club and at the weekly breakfast of the Westside Democratic Club with fellow windmill-tilters.

Hibbard also enjoyed gardening, the process as much as the results, even when fighting off weeds and the depredations of his dog. As his health deteriorated, he became philosophical about weeding as a form of denial, but he also tuned in to the cycle of the seasons.

Periodically, he would return to the history of his family, going over the names and their sources of his father, mother, and siblings, less from a sense of piety than in an attempt, as he says of writing in general, "to make the inchoate world coherent." It's not clear that he ever came fully to grips with his father's failure and the burdens it cast on the rest of the family, but he managed to survive all that, to be a prop for those who needed it most, and to outlive the confusions and passions of his young manhood.

Hubbard's writing will probably be preserved, if at all, in electronic form copied from various sources. It serves as a testimony to a man who saw and embodied various complexities and who was passionate about a number of the right things.

Ambrose Bierce, who resembled Hibbard in a number of ways, took off from Gray's "Elegy" in "A Mute Inglorious Milton'":

> O, I'm the Unaverage Man,
> But you never have heard of me,
> For my brother, the Average Man, outran
> My fame with rapiditee

As is usual with Bierce, it's difficult to tell which way the irony cuts. But it's clear that, despite his proclaimed lack of ambition, that Hibbard was defiantly and refreshingly Unaverage.

It's not clear if the next two generations in my extended family will produce writers to carry on the spotty family tradition. Neither my children nor my nieces and nephews seem inclined to write, though my son-in-law probably would do more if he had the time. But in the generation after that, a couple of grand-nephews show signs of being avid readers and precocious in expressing themselves verbally, and one my grandsons reads far beyond his grade level and has enough interest in his forbears to ask me what my father looked like. I was pleased to be able to show him several pictures of his great-grandfather in one of my books about the family, so perhaps that will give him a nudge. If not, the family history shows that we can afford to skip any number of generations.

Epilogue: Professional

In the winter the MLA convention is always there, but I do not go to it. Glancing through the program of the 1996 meeting, perhaps the last one I looked at, I see that once again I am typical of my generation, for none of my friends are delivering papers or chairing sessions. I do not know their motives, but they are probably much like mine. I am not in the market or, at my age, really marketable for another job. Speeches delivered at the sessions, though not any duller than the ones I increasingly avoided when I did go to MLA, tend to be delivered in a jargon I find harsh and incomprehensible. It used to be amusing to find out who had gone picturesquely mad in Pennsylvania, but it is less pleasant to hear news about the people who have gone really mad or, as is more and more often the case, died in Pennsylvania, California, Illinois, Michigan. Worst of all, the sight of hordes of desperate job seekers causes depression and guilt.

I remember these people circulating hopelessly through the halls when a bright student looks at my office—furnished comfortably, if shabbily, with a recliner, garage sale stereo and piles of cassettes, separate desks for writing and computing, three file cabinets, and eight thousand books—and says, "I want a job like yours." They are taken aback when I tell them that there aren't any more jobs like mine.

That isn't universally true—as my Wisconsin contemporary said, the top four or five people in each year's Ph.D. crop don't have trouble finding good jobs—but it's the kind of truth that most people need to hear.

Not because, as another Wisconsin contemporary said of the graduate students we were teaching, "They're not as good as we were." Many were probably, even certainly, not, but some very bright people still begin graduate degree programs either not knowing what they will face or thinking that the worst will happen to other people. This explains wars and

203

unwanted pregnancies as well as graduate students in the humanities.

The difference between us and them is not in talent but in circumstances: economic, demographic, social. My father used to say, more to console himself for having an eldest son who seemed to be a perpetual student, "Well, an education is something they can never take away from you." That was true until 1969. Now, in social and economic terms, at least, it seems that they can.

As the preceding chapters have tried to make clear, my career—like that of the people from Oklahoma who got jobs at Wisconsin, Washington, Wellesley, and so on—was more the result of luck than design.

Today, students every bit as good as we were would probably not find tenure-track jobs. The last time I served on a search committee to fill a position in our department, twenty-nine years after I entered the job market, more than four hundred people applied for it. The committee selected eight for interview at the Modern Language Association convention. All had published books. Several had tenure-track or even tenured jobs but were looking to move up from positions that were beneath their talents but that they had taken because they could do no better. Not only were they lucky to find jobs at all; they were even luckier to find jobs that gave them time to publish to write their way out. Or to hang on to the jobs they had. Gone are the days when someone could be tenured with one short book review; now, anyone without a book is on the bubble for tenure, and in a recent case, a candidate with more articles in print than many of the full professors in place when I joined the department got a heavily, and justifiably, negative vote.

These changes are directly traceable to the collapse, precipitous and continued, of the job market. What my generation of scholars and those who followed assumed as normal was, in fact, an aberration. Older and stuffier members of the profession knew better. A colleague who got his Ph.D. from Princeton tells of a senior professor who, in the early 1960s, exclaimed indignantly about the rumor that some new assistant professors were actually trying to live on their salaries. He assumed that it was a gentleman's calling—and that in turn assumed private means.

Not all members of his generation thought this way. As I have said, Don Cameron Allen's predictions of the mid-1960s were disastrously wrong, primarily because he assumed that an infinite number of assistant professors would be able to live increasingly well on larger and larger salaries resulting from a seller's market. He ignored the demographic evidence that produced the slump in enrollment in the early 1970s and led to widespread breast-beating about what departments had done to drive students away. Nothing, as it happened. There were fewer students, and those that remained turned away, as the Vietnam War wound down, from activism and humanities to programs that could promise more lucrative jobs.

By the late 1970s, prognostications of the academic marketplace were taking account of demographics. In the early 1990s, analysts said, a new wave of students, children of the first Baby Boomers, would be arriving on campus. Moreover, faculty hired early in the fat days would be retiring in large numbers. Therefore....

What the prophets could not foresee was shift of public priorities away from higher education, so that English and all other departments have had to do more with less. By the 1970s, it was widely held—and by one dean stated—that replacements would be authorized only for positions opened by tenure denial. Not resignation, not death, not retirement. If not official policy, it was certainly the practice, so that, despite the increase in the university's enrollment from just under 19,000 in 1967 to more than 27,000 in 2013, size of the tenure-track faculty is about the same, while the teaching load per year has been reduced from six to four courses, and in a number of cases to two. How is this possible? Adjuncts.

Prophecies about the job market are now grim enough for a naturalist novel. Cary Nelson, who found a job as the market was collapsing, predicts that "Over the next decade we are likely to see a gradual increase in the percentage of part-time and fixed-term college teachers, a decrease in the percentage of tenured and tenure-track employees, increased teaching loads, and a notable drop in salaries for beginning faculty in some markets." ["Lessons from the Job Wars: Late Capitalism Arrives on Campus," *Social Text*, 13 (Fall/Winter 1995), 119.] Why are administrators moving in this direction? Because they can and, given dwindling resources, because it is the easiest solution to very real problems.

Current conditions are bad enough to justify Nelson's tone. Yet, even though everyone in the profession should be aware of these conditions, too many graduate programs retain admission policies suited to the fat days.

One graduate director exulted that his program was getting more applications to the Ph.D. program from better and better students. He seemed puzzled when I pointed out that, because responsible programs like Stanford and Kansas were restricting admissions, he was seeing a box-car effect of students being bumped farther and farther down the line. How, I asked, are these students going to be able to compete on the job market if they can't even compete for admission? Not to speak of the increasing number of applicants to his program who are not even considered for teaching assistantships, the only financial support available. Recently I reiterated my point that admitting large numbers of students to our graduate program was irresponsible. "But," he said, "we won't be able to fill our seminars otherwise." (This from a former member of Students for a Democratic Society.)

Nor would the University of Oklahoma or any large state university be able to staff over a hundred sections of freshman English. Cary Nelson estimates that it would cost his department an additional $4.6 million a year to replace teaching assistants with full-time faculty. That money is not and will not be available.

It would be bad enough, as Nelson argues, if at the end of the graduate program the apprentice teacher were denied the chance to become a journeyman. I add "simply" because, financially, the student is often worse off than when she or he entered graduate school. Even colleagues fifteen years younger came out of graduate school, as I did, debt-free. But this was before the days of the guaranteed student loans that many students now carry. Those take a long time to pay on an academic salary. If one is driving a taxi, the financial as well as psychological burdens must be intolerable.

In any regulated profession, the solution would be to limit enroll-ments—the federal government is paying some medical schools not to train doctors—or to toughen standards, or both. Graduate programs in humanities haven't figured this out.

For one thing, some of these programs are admitting students who lack basic writing and reading skills. A friend who runs a writing center—where students come to improve their writing skills—told me of a graduate student in English who didn't know basic rules of punctuation, a situation that is unfortunate but not rare. That's the fault of the educational system to that point.

But some of the fault lies with graduate programs. Current general examinations seem pathetically easy by the standards of my time, when prelims were designed to produce generalists; specialization was for the dissertation. The concept is as dated as the old-fashioned literary history we were taught in most courses. Today, Ph.D. candidates in my department take individually designed examinations in two fields, one of which must be a literary period, and each candidate negotiates reading lists, a minimum of thirty works, with his or her committee. This presumably enables the student to move more quickly into and through the dissertation stage. The rationale is that literature has expanded in so many directions that the old model of coverage would require a lifetime of preparation and is in any case outdated.

However, current students don't seem to move through the process any faster than they did under the old system. Perhaps in recognition of this fact, my department periodically talked about revising the structure of the Ph.D. general examinations. Some of my colleagues proposed, and passed, a regulation that students, instead of taking two four-hour examinations, be given take-home examinations because the faculty tends to excuse bad performances because of the pressure of time. In any case, some thought, the current format tested quickness and ingenuity, qualities which would never be demanded in a professorial career. (Their lectures must be incredibly well-prepared and must fill fifty minutes so tightly that there is no time for inconvenient questions.) That way, committees could distinguish between good and bad performances and possibly even fail the worst. Even then, one colleague said, "But if we already know they're good...."

These discussions are like rearranging the deck chairs on the Titanic. Louis Menand, who teaches at the Graduate Center of the City University of New York, is more radical or more retrogressive. Like the Don Cameron Allen commission in the 1960s, he wants to shorten Ph.D. programs to three years, eliminating both teaching and the dissertation and making it more like a law degree. Graduates who did not find teaching jobs—the majority, he admits—could then get on with their lives in other fields and perhaps bridge the current gulf between academia and the wider culture.

None of these issues has an inherent connection to the so-called "culture wars" in humanities departments. There are generational and ideological splits, but these have existed for at least fifty years, and though the current hegemony seems more rigid than those in earlier scholarly generations, different kinds of splits will probably occur.

Of course, scholars of my generation sometimes feel as though programs in which "cultural studies" has triumphed devalue or ignore entirely traditional methods of scholarship like bibliography, textual study, and even prosody, all of which help to answer important questions that sooner or later arise, or should, in the serious study of literature. But the materials and examples of the methods can still be found in libraries, and perhaps the current call for diversity can be expanded to include neglected fields as well as gender and ethnic issues.

The current crisis, which has now endured for four decades, is, in short, is at least as much economic as ideological. More cultural studies specialists are being hired than bibliographers, but there are not enough jobs to go round for people in any field, no matter how fashionable.

This does not mean that graduate departments should post the sign, "Abandon hope, all ye who enter here." If the candidate thinks that the material is worth studying for its own sake and that the skills—especially and increasingly computer skills, which are at least transferable to the outside world—are worth acquiring, then the time, money, and effort will be worth it. But the candidate should know in advance about the vows of obedience, or discipline, chastity (or at least deferring a family), and poverty implied in a commitment to the profession. And it will be a very different kind of commitment from the one I made in innocence or ignorance more than a half-century ago. And a very different profession.

Epilogue: Personal

"The rest is only personal"
Jay Gatsby

When the local TV announcer referred to an elderly man by his age, I was indignant because I was three years older and not at all willing to regard myself as elderly

I've had something like the same response to editors' suggestions for revising my work. Mostly, though—except for the editor who introduced grammatical errors not only into my prose but into that of Evelyn Waugh—I have backed off, taken a second look, and decided that the suggestions had some or often a great deal of merit in terms of style, coherence, and logic. So when I got up the morning after the insulting broadcast and felt familiar pangs of generalized osteoarthritis and a degenerated disc or two, I was better prepared to consider my status as an elder.

For years I had been able to sustain the illusion of relative youth by virtue of good genetic inheritance and of a reputation as an athlete gained among my colleagues through a decade of Masters Swimming. When separate joint surgeries made further competition unwise, I could blame honorable injuries rather than age for physical deterioration. Something of the same could be said of the onset of glaucoma, which may but not necessarily be connected to age. And discovering that I had osteoarthritis was a relief because one aunt similarly afflicted had managed to stay active into her nineties and because it wasn't rheumatoid arthritis, which had crippled her half-sister. Lower back problems afflict people much younger than I am.

Robert Murray Davis

As a result of luck and conditioning, then, people, including physicians, often said that I didn't look my age often enough that I began to believe it. A blond, fresh-faced Utah state trooper stopped me, quite rightly, for speeding, looked at my driver's license, and said, "You can't be that old!" I replied that I had told him, truthfully, that I was going fifteen miles over the speed limit, so why would I lie about that? For once, truth worked, and he gave me a warning rather than a ticket.

The illusion of relative youthfulness survived my move to what is called "an active adult community." But even then it seemed clear that most of the other denizens looked older than I did and often were. Many of my fellow retirees seem to have ossified mentally and concentrate on golf, bridge, and right-wing political positions. Once, at an outdoor luau, being serenaded by a steel band (all those colored island people look alike, apparently), my companion looked around and said, "You're the best-looking man here." "Christ, I hope so!" was my honest but socially inappropriate response.

But that was seven or eight years ago. Now when people say that I don't look that old, I say that they should see me getting up in the morning. Or taking my before- and after-meal pills. Or stopping, after rising from a chair, to dispel momentary dizziness. Or, more recently, trailing my son around Budapest, laboriously climbing long flights of stairs—121 plus at the National Art Museum—or resting my joints and back far oftener than I used to. Or taking the elevator while he climbed up and down six flights of stairs to our apartment. Or—and a number of people from my past and present will think of karma—asking him to slow down so I could keep up with him.

It seems to me that there are two ways to deal with physical deterioration. One is to accept the inevitable. Some twenty years ago a woman friend said that I should consider getting hair plugs—that part of my genetic inheritance was not that fortunate. I could say, truthfully, that there was so much structural wrong with me that I couldn't waste time on cosmetic issues. Besides, I have more hair than my younger brother, and considering my maternal grandfather's early baldness, any day I have hair is a good hair day. As for physical activities, like running or competitive swimming or bicycling, I sometimes regret, mildly, not being able to do them anymore, but I've learned to let them go.

More surprising is the betrayal of body parts one usually doesn't think about. For example, a French woman poet asked if I were descended, at least in part, from Chinese Muslims in the west of that country. Why would she think so, I wondered. Well, she said, the upper lids of my eyes drooped like theirs. When I got to a mirror, I could see the droop, but I could tell her that it was caused not by genetics but by gravity.

More distressing was the discovery that my ability to whistle had seriously diminished. I used to have some facility as a whistler—never quite to the standards of the man featured in Ted Weems's "Heartaches" or early Bing Crosby, but quite passable for an amateur. Now the muscles in my lips have slackened and produce more air than sound.

And previous physical benchmarks now seem unreliable. Recently I have managed to lose about fifteen pounds and looked forward to being able to wear some pants in my hope closet (in the sense that I hoped that they would fit) because the weight loss should have made my waist a size or two smaller. Unhappily, not so. Apparently it's true that body weight is subject to gravity.

These discoveries are surprising but not fatal, and I have tried to mitigate as far as possible some other effects of age. I've been doing back exercises for years, and though I'm not sure they do me any good, they've become part of a ritual to fill the time prescribed for my eye drops. Soon after I moved to my active adult community, I bought a folding cane in case I need it. So far I've only used it to lean on to ease my back, though it did cause some excitement at Frankfurt security when the staff seemed to think it might possibly be a disassembled rifle. And I carry various back braces and knee supports in case of emergency.

And pills, of course. But some have side-effects, like the naproxen sodium which mitigated my back and arthritis pangs until my gastroenterologist discovered that I had an ulcer. The good news, he said, is that we know what caused it. Perhaps, he said, I might be able, once the ulcer cleared up, to use it on an as-need basis. But I need it every day, so that's one less pill to take for the rest of my life.

Also, I can try to follow the advice of various doctors. Raise the good cholesterol by exercising more. (The triglycerides are responding to medication.) My g.p. says that my occasional dizziness could be caused by dehydration, sitting too long, or standing up too fast. Drinking more fluids isn't difficult, and I have learned to set a timer so I can get up and move around every thirty minutes—not ideal for a writer or professional reader, but bearable. But getting up slowly, as my friends and family recognize even more clearly than I do, is going to challenge my life-long habit of moving at 6,000 rpm. I haven't been the fastest physically or mentally, on the baseball field or at the desk, but I've gotten by on quickness and endurance.

Physical quickness isn't possible any more, but while I may not be as agile mentally as I was in my forties, I'm still publishing my work, more, in fact, than in the decade before my retirement, as well as giving the occasional lecture and poetry reading in Europe, attending professional meetings, and doing a little consulting. A high school contemporary asked when I was going to retire and to my claim of having done so responded, "I mean, really retire."

The answer to that is, I hope, never. As I said to my oldest friend from college, the only place I never feel old is at the keyboard of my computer or sitting with a pen in my hand. My memory has faded, but if I can't remember a fact or, increasingly, a common noun like "Styrofoam," there's always Google. Most of the time, though, it's a struggle not to find a word but the right word, and that's something that writers of all ages deal with.

Still, even at the desk there are signs of physical deterioration. My back occasionally bothers me, though mostly I've learned to ignore minor pangs. And the joint connecting my left thumb to the hand acts up for reasons I can't fathom, since it's not involved in typing. However, I can live with that, since the only time I consciously use that thumb is to start a coffee grinder or to punch numbers into my cell phone. And a little rest and some acetaminophen can take care of the worst of that.

Some people who operate at a slower rate may be lucky. Recently I encountered a friend and collaborator of four decades who's at least four years older than I and keeps going at the same steady pace as he did in his forties. I envy him because he has learned, effortlessly as far as I can tell, how to be old. After all, I'm not going to be seventy-nine forever .

Clearly I'm going to have to learn that, though I was somewhat cheered by the remarks of two former students. One, told that I was beginning to feel old, said, "You'll never be old." Perhaps, as comedians and t-shirts have said, "You might not be able to stay young, but you can always stay immature."

The other replied to my remark that I can't believe that I'm as old as I am, in a laconic Oklahoma accent, "That's what happens when you don't die." As consolations go, it sets a fairly low bar, but one I'm glad to clear.

It helps to think about what I have done rather than what I can no longer do. In C. S. Lewis's *Out of the Silent Planet*, a Martian says about love that "it takes his whole life." The earthling responds

> "But the pleasure he must be content only to remember?"
> "That is like saying, 'My food I must be content only to eat". A pleasure is full grown only when it is remembered. You are speaking, Human, as if the pleasure were one thing and the memory another. It is all one thing."

If you expand "love" to other forms of commitment, the remark seems a lot wiser than it did when I first read the novel a half-century ago, and a great deal more consoling than any version of "It beats the alternative."

How are you?
Plundered.

CPSIA information can be obtained
at www.ICGtesting.com
Printed in the USA
FFOW02n0803080514
5258FF